Understanding Juan Benet

**Understanding Modern European
and Latin American Literature**

James Hardin, Series Editor

volumes on

Ingeborg Bachmann
Samuel Beckett
Juan Benet
Thomas Bernhard
Johannes Bobrowski
Heinrich Böll
Italo Calvino
Albert Camus
Elias Canetti
Camilo José Cela
Céline
Julio Cortázar
Isak Dinesen
José Donoso
Friedrich Dürrenmatt
Rainer Werner Fassbinder
Max Frisch
Federico García Lorca
Gabriel García Márquez
Juan Goytisolo
Günter Grass
Gerhart Hauptmann

Christoph Hein
Hermann Hesse
Eugène Ionesco
Uwe Johnson
Milan Kundera
Primo Levi
John McGahern
Robert Musil
Boris Pasternak
Octavio Paz
Luigi Pirandello
Graciliano Ramos
Erich Maria Remarque
Alain Robbe-Grillet
Joseph Roth
Jean-Paul Sartre
W. G. Sebald
Claude Simon
Mario Vargas Llosa
Peter Weiss
Franz Werfel
Christa Wolf

UNDERSTANDING

Juan Benet

New Perspectives

Benjamin Fraser

Foreword by Malcolm Alan Compitello

The University of South Carolina Press

© 2013 University of South Carolina

Published by the University of South Carolina Press
Columbia, South Carolina 29208

www.sc.edu/uscpress

Manufactured in the United States of America

22 21 20 19 18 17 16 15 14 13   10 9 8 7 6 5 4 3 2 1

Library of Congress Cataloging-in-Publication Data

Fraser, Benjamin.
   Understanding Juan Benet : new perspectives / Benjamin Fraser.
      pages cm. — (Understanding modern European and Latin American literature)
   Includes bibliographical references and index.
   ISBN 978-1-61117-152-5 (hardbound : alk. paper) 1. Benet, Juan—Criticism and interpretation. I. Title.
   PQ6652.E5Z65 2013
   863'.64—dc23

                                   2012039469

This book was printed on a recycled paper with
30 percent postconsumer waste content.

for Abby

Contents

Foreword

"Es cierto, el viajero que saliendo de Región pretende llegar a su sierra siguiendo el antiguo camino real—porque el moderno dejó de serlo—se ve obligado a atravesar un pequeño y elevado desierto que parece interminable." This sentence, the first of Juan Benet's landmark novel *Volverás a Región* (Destino, 1967), changed the course of my intellectual trajectory and my life. That paradoxical phrasing about a place of Juan Benet's invention launched me into a dense literary labyrinth from which I really only emerged decades later and to which I still return on occasion.

Understanding Juan Benet: New Perspectives offers readers such as another opportunity to return to Región and to the work of one of a great tradition of Spanish polymaths whose professional work and literary production transformed Spain for the better. Professor Fraser's volume delivers on both counts mentioned in its title. It contributes richly to our understanding of Juan Benet's work and his place in Spain's evolution, and offers a fresh perspective that takes our thinking about Benet in new directions. This is true for those who, like myself, have spent a great deal of our professional lives enjoying Juan Benet's artful prose and the strongly held positions embedded in his narratives and essayistic forays into a number of areas, from the nature of literature to politics. It is equally so for those whose first engagement with Juan Benet is filtered through Ben Fraser's compelling contextualization of the author.

What Fraser's book is able to do is to take several key elements, all of which revolve around space and all of which connect Benet's real-life passions with his literary avocation, and weave them into an analytical framework that offers brilliant insights into the relationship between life and literature for Juan Benet. In so doing it suggests new avenues for addressing this body of work.

Spatial issues are not the only defining elements out of which Fraser crafts his reassessment. He is attentive to the author's texts and their critical tradition and offers a comprehensive contextualization of Benet's relationship to history, especially the Spanish Civil War. The latter is fitting since history and historiography were longstanding interests of the Spanish writer. Moreover, his essay *¿Qué fue la guerra civil?*, as Fraser underscores, is one of the best interpretive essays on the conflict and is fundamental to understanding the writer's fictional and other essayistic work. This said, Fraser sees space as central to a fresh understanding of Juan Benet, and this is his work's major contribution. Few are in a better position to understand the interconnectedness of space and culture than is Professor Fraser. He has written extensively on the subject from an interdisciplinary perspective, including works dealing with Lefebvre and Bergson and their influence on Spanish cultural production.

Three elements intersect to form *Understanding Juan Benet*'s frame of reference. The first is a thorough analysis of Benet's career as a civil engineer and his writing about engineering issues, especially hydrology. Fraser provides a long-overdue reading of Benet's professional career and his contributions to his field of expertise in relation to his avocation as a writer of fiction and commentator on contemporary Spain. All of this helps to situate Benet's imagined spaces against the backdrop of the author's involvement with the sometimes problematic real spaces he inhabited. The second element is a reappraisal of Benet's Bergsonism, a reading that is both philosophical and spatial since Fraser, who has written widely on the influence of Bergson in Spain, locates in the French philosopher, whom Benet greatly admired, the initial impetus for the work of later spatial theorists from Lefebvre to Deleuze. The third element is an examination of Benet's work through the lens of critical geography as it develops out of the work of Henri Lefebvre and David Harvey. Critical geography offers a compelling frame of reference to elucidate how spatial concerns are inscribed in Benet's imaginary.

Understanding Juan Benet suggests a roadmap which will allow the reader to interpret Benet, his work, and its significance in exciting new ways. It is a powerful tool and one that should excite those who have spent a considerable amount of time engaging Juan Benet's world as well scholars who share a passion for some of the areas Fraser believes are crucial to understanding the author, his works, and his context. It will, I am sure, make the journey to and through Región much more comprehensible, rewarding, and, most of all, intellectually exciting.

MALCOLM ALAN COMPITELLO
The University of Arizona

Series Editor's Preface

Understanding Modern European and Latin American Literature has been planned as a series of guides for undergraduate and graduate students and nonacademic readers. Like the volumes in its companion series *Understanding Contemporary American Literature,* these books provide introductions to the lives and writings of prominent modern authors and explicate their most important works.

Modern literature makes special demands, and this is particularly true of foreign literature, in which the reader must contend not only with unfamiliar, often arcane artistic conventions and philosophical concepts, but also with the handicap of reading the literature in translation. It is a truism that the nuances of one language can be rendered in another only imperfectly (and this problem is especially acute in fiction), but the fact that the works of European and Latin American writers are situated in a historical and cultural setting quite different from our own can be as great a hindrance to the understanding of these works as the linguistic barrier. For this reason the *UMELL* series emphasizes the sociological and historical background of the writers treated. The philosophical and cultural traditions peculiar to a given culture may be particularly important for an understanding of certain authors, and these are taken up in the introductory chapter and also in the discussion of those works to which this information is relevant. Beyond this, the books treat the specifically literary aspects of the author under discussion and attempt to explain the complexities of contemporary literature lucidly. The books are conceived as introductions to the authors covered, not as comprehensive analyses. They do not provide detailed summaries of plot because they are meant to be used in conjunction with the books they treat, not as a substitute for study of the original works. The purpose of the books is to provide information and judicious literary assessment of the major works in the most compact, readable form. It is our hope that the *UMELL* series will help increase knowledge and understanding of European and Latin American cultures and will serve to make the literature of those cultures more accessible.

J. H.

Acknowledgments

The idea for *Understanding Juan Benet: New Perspectives* first occurred to me while I was in the early stages of putting together the edited volume titled *Capital Inscriptions: Essays on Hispanic Literature, Film and Urban Space in Honor of Malcolm Alan Compitello* (Juan de la Cuesta, 2012). Dr. Malcolm Alan Compitello—in addition to being the adviser of my doctoral dissertation at the University of Arizona and the director of an independent study I took on Benet and Luis Goytisolo—was also one of a handful of scholars in the late 1970s who saw in Juan Benet's complex fiction and essays not only a sharp break from the traditionally realist narrative that thrived under the dictatorship of Spain's Francisco Franco (1939–1975) but also reason enough for attempting to reimagine the very contours of the field of Hispanic studies as it then existed. Along with others (such as María Elena Bravo, Vicente Cabrera, Ricardo Gullón, David K. Herzberger, Jo Labanyi, Roberto Manteiga, John Margenot, Esther W. Nelson, Nelson Orringer, Janet Pérez, Randolph Pope, Gonzalo Sobejano, Robert Spires, Stephen Summerhill, Mary Vásquez, Kathleen Vernon, Julia Lupinacci Wescott, and many more), Compitello not only helped to put Benetian studies on the map, he also effectively started a conversation about the scope, method, and purpose of literary scholarship. I hope that this book stands as a further tribute to both Juan Benet and Malcolm Compitello—committed intellectuals who shared a respect for both materialist historiography and also the necessarily enigmatic nature of literary production.

In addition this book is an extension of research into Benet's work I have published in the *Journal of Spanish Cultural Studies* (the essay "The Art of Engineering: The Bridge as Object and Method in Juan Benet's Fiction," 2010) and in my book *Encounters with Bergson(ism) in Spain: Philosophy, Literature, Film and Urban Space* (2010), specifically chapter 3, "Juan Benet: Recalibrating Time and Space in Región." While those publications are of a different character and scope, selected ideas and materials discussed therein are quite relevant and have unavoidably found their way into this work—albeit in recontextualized form.

I would like to thank James Hardin, editor of the Understanding Modern European and Latin American Literature (UMELL) series at the University of South Carolina for believing in the somewhat nontraditional method with which I approach Juan Benet's work. I truly believe—of course—that the "new" directions taken in each of its chapters are fundamental if we are to understand Juan Benet. Thanks go also to my friends and colleagues in the Department of Hispanic Studies at the College of Charleston. Special thanks are due to Chair Mark P. Del Mastro, former Chair Joseph Weyers, and LCWA Dean David Cohen; and to Sarah Owens and Raúl Carrillo Arciniega, who consistently encouraged me in this undertaking.

Readers should be aware that—consistent with the approach of the UMELL series—while this book seeks to understand Juan Benet, it attempts neither to address each of his works individually nor to provide concise summaries of those works. Summaries of selected works published by Benet (through 1978) are available in Vicente Cabrera's 1983 book *Juan Benet*. Although it dialogues with many of the most characteristically Benetian themes, more thorough explorations of those themes can be found, undoubtedly, in the critical studies cited in the bibliography included at the end of this book (although it is not comprehensive, I have relied on bibliographies by Compitello, Margenot and Labanyi). This limitation is a necessary consequence of my intention to rejuvenate the field of Benetian studies with new approaches. Nonetheless, the present book does address a great many of Benet's most recognized (and underrecognized) works in depth—including the novels *Volverás a Región*, *Una meditación*, and *Herrumbrosas lanzas*; the book-length essays *La inspiración y el estilo*, *El ángel del señor abandona a Tobías*, and *¿Qué fue la guerra civil?*; and selected other texts, each within the context of its chapters' major themes.

On Citations, Translations, and Notes

Page numbers are included in the notes for all references to works by Juan Benet. When possible, these numbers refer to the available English translations of *Volverás a Región* and *Una meditación* (both by Gregory Rabassa). Unless otherwise noted, all other translations to English from Spanish sources—whether Benet's oeuvre or critical scholarship—are my own. When they are first mentioned, Benet's titles appear in both Spanish and English (italics if translated/unitalicized if not).

While I wrote this book with a general reader in mind, I have provided an extensive dialogue with the critical scholarship on Benet's work in the form of notes written for more advanced readers. My intention has been that these more advanced discussions and references not distract from the beginner's desire to *Understand Juan Benet*. Nevertheless, many of these notes, in fact, pursue further those connections with Benet's texts under discussion in a given chapter.

Interested readers should consult the bibliography for information regarding work by or about Juan Benet.

Chronology

1927—Born in Madrid 7 October.

1936—Outbreak of Spanish Civil War 18 July.

    Juan Benet's father, Tomás, is killed by a firing squad, victim of the conflict.

1939—The Spanish Civil War ends, 1 April.

    The Dictatorship of Francisco Franco officially begins.

    Final defeat of Republican Government by Nationalist/Francoist forces.

    Moves back to Madrid with his mother, Teresa, his brother Francisco, and his sister Marisol.

1948—Begins study at the Escuela Superior de Caminos, Canales y Puertos.

1953—First play, *Max,* published in *Revista Española.*

1954—Receives diploma in civil engineering.

1955—Marries Nuria Jordana (four children—Ramón 1956, Nicolás 1960, Juana 1961, Eugenio 1962).

1956—Joins the Compañía de Ferrocarriles de Medina de Campo a Zamora y de Orense a Vigo (MZOV, later Cubiertas y MZOV)

1958—Play, *Anastas, o el origen de la constitución*/Anastas, Or the Origin of the Constitution.

1961—First short-story volume, *Nunca llegarás a nada*/You'll Never Get Anywhere.

1966—First book of essays, *La inspiración y el estilo*/Inspiration and Style.

    Juan Benet's brother Francisco is killed in a car accident abroad.

    Play, *Agonía confutans*/Agonia Confutans.

1967—First novel, *Volverás a Región*/Return to Región (delayed publication in 1968).

    Play, *Un caso de conciencia*/A Case of Conscience.

1970—Novel, *Una meditación*/A Meditation (Biblioteca Breve Prize, 1969).

Essays, *Puerta de tierra*/Door of Dust.

Dramatic works, *Teatro*/Theater.

1971—Short-story volume, *Una tumba*/A Tomb.

1972—Novel, *Un viaje de invierno*/A Winter's Journey.

Short-story volume, *Cinco narraciones y dos fábulas*/Five Narrations and Two Tales.

1973—Short-story volume, *Sub rosa*/Sub Rosa.

Novel, *La otra casa de Mazón*/The Other House of Mazón.

1974—Nuria Jordana dies.

1975—Francisco Franco dies on 20 November.

End of the dictatorship. Transition toward Spanish democracy.

1976—Essays, *¿Qué fue la guerra civil?*/What Was the Civil War?

Essays, *En ciernes*/In Bloom.

Essays, *El ángel del señor abandona a Tobías*/The Lord's Angel Abandons Tobias.

Essay, "Ingeniería e intimidad"/Engineering and Intimacy.

1977—Novel, *En el estado*/In the State.

Short-story volume, *Cuentos completos I*/Complete Stories I.

1978—Novel, *Del pozo y del Numa*/Of the Well and of Numa.

1980—Novel, *Saúl ante Samuel*/Saul before Samuel.

Novel, *El aire de un crimen*/The Air of a Crime (finalist, Planeta prize).

1981—Essays, *La moviola de Eurípides*/Euripides' Editing Projector.

Short-story volume, *Trece fábulas y media*/Thirteen-and-a-half Fables.

Short-story volume, *Cuentos completos II*/Complete Stories II.

1982—Essays, *Sobre la incertidumbre*/On Uncertainty.

1983—Novel, *Herrumbrosas lanzas*/Rusty Lances, vol. 1 (Premio de la Crítica, 1984).

Essays, *Artículos I*/Essays I.

Edited book, *Ingeniería en la época romántica: Las obras públicas en España alrededor de 1860*/Engineering during the Romantic Era: Public Works in Spain around 1860.

1985—Marries the poet Blanca Andreu.

Novel, *Herrumbrosas lanzas*/Rusty Lances, vol. 2.

1986—Novel, *Herrumbrosas lanzas*/Rusty Lances, vol. 3.

Book, *El agua en España*/Water in Spain.

1987—Forms own engineering firm, la Compañía Hidrocinética Regional.
  Essays, *Otoño en Madrid hacia 1950*/Fall in Madrid around
      1950.
1989—Novel, *En la penumbra*/In the Half-light.
  History/travel book, *Londres victoriano*/Victorian London.
1990—Essays, *La construcción de la torre de Babel*/The Construction of
      the Tower of Babel.
1991—Novel, *El caballero de Sajonia*/The Gentleman from Saxony.
1993—Juan Benet dies 5 January.
1994—The Porma Dam—on which Benet worked over many years in the
      1960—is renamed in his honor (as the "Embalse Juan Benet").

Introduction

Juan Benet and the Limits of Existing Criticism

In the increasingly interdisciplinary landscape of twentieth-century literary and cultural studies, understanding the work of Spain's Juan Benet Goitia (1927–1993) remains a difficult but nonetheless important task. Benet's novelistic prose is labyrinthine, his essays are dense and formidable, his themes are deceptively simple, and the philosophical basis of his thought is complex and deliberately enigmatic.[1] The intrepid contemporary reader faces the additional challenge of having to reconcile two aspects of his seemingly unexhausted creative activity that have seldom been intertwined in previous literary studies: Benet-the-author and Benet-the-civil engineer. His intellectual range spanned not only the world of novels, plays, short stories, and essays but also the realm of dams, bridges, canals, and other public works. Approaching Benet's work in the twenty-first century means integrating these two apparently discrete areas of his practice into a coherent whole. Understanding Juan Benet requires that we acknowledge the connection between the author and the engineer as a way of articulating a Benetian worldview in which history, fiction, philosophy, engineering, and aesthetics all interact.

Although Juan Benet has been the subject of a modicum of scholarly attention since he published his first novel in 1967—*Volverás a Región*, translated into English as *Return to Región* by Gregory Rabassa in 1985—he remains an underappreciated genius of twentieth-century Spanish letters.[2] What is more, the canonical work on Benet published in the 1970s, 1980s, and 1990s—although significant—has left several aspects of his work under- or even un-explored. *Understanding Juan Benet: New Perspectives* thus has two interrelated goals: (1) to continue to explore a still underappreciated figure of Spanish literature and, more important, (2) to employ an interdisciplinary perspective as a way of highlighting the relationships between

Benet's literary production and a wide range of contemporary discourses. While chapter 1 grounds the reader in the fundamental importance of the Spanish Civil War for understanding his work, subsequent chapters offer new perspectives on Juan Benet's literary and essayistic production. Chapter 2 suggests that we (re)read Benet's worldview through the lens of his first chosen profession as a civil engineer, exploring lesser-known engineering texts and essays in relation to his creative and literary vision. Chapter 3 applies a newly revitalized (and interdisciplinary) critical interest in the thought of French philosopher Henri Bergson (1859–1941)—who was cited by Benet himself as an influence—to selected novels, short stories, and essays in the Spanish writer's oeuvre. Chapter 4 harnesses the development of cultural geography and spatial theory over the course of the twentieth century to explain the role of space and place in his novels—highlighting in particular the elaborate spatial dimensions of his own invented cartography of the fictitious, novelistic place he called "Región." Finally, the epilogue takes on the core attribute of Benet's thought, underscoring his persistent interest in the more enigmatic aspects of literature, Spanish society, and even thought itself.

Appropriately, the first section of this introduction offers a concise biography of Juan Benet's life and work—with particular attention given to the balance between his literary and engineering work. And yet, if the reader is to understand Juan Benet, a mere biographical summary will not suffice. It would be a mistake not to also review existing Benetian scholarship as a matter of course. That said, much previous criticism on Benet's work—quite valuable in its own right—gives us only a partial or sporadic understanding of his major influences (civil engineering, Bergson). Moreover, such previous work is ill equipped to explain why Benet's work continues to fascinate us in the twenty-first century, particularly given the interdisciplinarity that has come to characterize the contemporary scholarly landscape (the collision of literature with philosophy and geography, for example). As a consequence, the subsequent sections of this introduction seek both to ground the reader in the broader context of Spanish literature and also account for the strengths and limitations of existing Benetian criticism. They address, in turn, the state of Spanish literature under the dictatorship that followed Spain's Civil War—the time in which Benet penned many of his major and early texts—and also the nature of various critical approaches to his work that have been employed since the 1970s. In this way—fusing literature and engineering work in a concise biography, putting Benet's work in its proper historical context, and characterizing previous approaches to his literary production—the reader will be better prepared for new perspectives on Benet's work.

It bears emphasizing that the intent of this book is neither to repeat what has been written on Benet in previous criticism nor merely—as the book *Juan Benet* by Vicente Cabrera (1983) accomplished, in part, some decades ago—to yield helpful, if somewhat descriptive, accounts of his major works per se.[3] Instead, it is precisely by working through a series of new perspectives that we arrive at a greater understanding of the essential qualities of Juan Benet's work as a whole. Of course, many aspects of the new perspectives do indeed follow logically from insights signaled in previous Benetian criticism—connections that are highlighted for the reader when appropriate.

Juan Benet's Life in Context (1927–1993)

On 7 October 1927, Juan Benet was born in Madrid to Teresa Goitia and Tomás Benet amidst the tensions governing the first third of Spain's twentieth century. To understand the context into which he was born, we must briefly go back to the previous events that had shaped Spain's contemporary social landscape.[4] During the nineteenth century, the struggle between what have been called "The Two Spains" had been left largely unresolved.[5] This phrase signals the distance between one Spain that was progressive, modernizing, secular, and republican and another that was rigidly conservative, Catholic, monarchist, and intransigent. Benet himself once characterized Spain's turbulent modern history by writing that "we have been forced to pay for every five years of liberalism and democracy with a half century of absolutism or dictatorship."[6] It is possible, for our purposes, to trace this tension from 1868 to the Spanish Civil War that began in 1936 and beyond. Following a revolution known as "La Gloriosa/The Glorious [Revolution]," Queen Isabel II fled the country in 1868, and after a few passing governments the first Spanish Republic was finally declared in 1873. A mere fourteen months later, however, the Republic "dissolved in chaos" and the monarchy was reestablished in 1874 under King Alfonso XII's rule.[7] After 1898, the loss of Spain's remaining colonies (in Cuba, Puerto Rico, the Philippines, and Guam) only exacerbated the schism between the various traditional and progressive bands of Spanish society. In 1923, King Alfonso XIII finally accepted General Primo de Rivera as a military dictator of the country, perhaps swayed by the potential (if, in retrospect, illusory) opportunity to resolve the myriad conflicts that continued to dog twentieth-century Spain.

The Primo de Rivera dictatorship (1923–30) was deemed necessary—in the eyes of the Spanish king at least—on account of the turbulent sociopolitical circumstances that Spain had experienced over the first two decades of the twentieth century. The seemingly perennial, historical conflict between "The Two Spains" had continued to manifest itself in a number of ways—not only in the growing distance between the working class and the bourgeoisie wrought by the continuing and uneven development of Spanish industrialization, but also through a series of general strikes in which worker syndicates such as the socialist UGT (Unión General de Trabajadores [General Workers' Union]) and the anarchist CNT (Confederación Nacional de Trabajo [National Workers' Confederation]) played powerful roles. This turbulent period in Spanish history was also shaped by a wave of convent burning in Barcelona during 1909 motivated by anticlerical sentiment (known as "La Semana Trágica" [The Tragic Week]), and of course the pan-European tensions of the first World War (1914–18), in which Spain had declared itself neutral.[8] The country's first of two long-term twentieth-century dictators saw himself as a reformer of sorts, and the Spain into which Juan Benet was born in 1927 was one plagued by calls for national "regeneration."[9] Imposing a state of autarky as a way of improving Spain's economy, Primo de Rivera's dictatorship also invested heavily in public works such as roads and dams and "rationalized" the Duero and Ebro river systems through state-supported engineering projects.[10] As his popularity waned, however, Primo's government lost its legitimacy, and ultimately he was forced to "resign" in January of 1930. In the end, even the reputation of the Spanish monarchy as a whole had been sullied by its previous support for the dictator. Consequently, in 1931 the monarchy was once again overthrown and Spain's Second Republic was declared, this time lasting for some five years. Supported by a diverse coalition of republicans, socialists, and other leftist intellectuals, the Second Republic (1931–36) underwent a series of drastic shifts, internal conflicts, erupting tragedies, and changes in leadership, ultimately devolving into the civil war that rocked the country in 1936.[11]

Just as the Spanish Civil War (1936–39) and the dictatorship that followed it (1939–75) cannot be understood without recourse to the characteristic sociopolitical tensions of modern Spanish society, neither can one attempt to make sense of Benet's difficult narratives without assigning the war and its aftermath a privileged role.[12] Although the Spanish Civil War has rightly been the recipient of numerous complex treatments over the years—not least of which is Benet's own 1976 essay *Qué fue la guerra civil?* (What Was the Civil War?)—its central conflict can be portrayed in stark terms as one between two sides, both of which continue to reflect the distance between the "Two Spains." On the right were heterogeneous groups of nationalist, traditionalist, conservative, Catholic, monarchist, and even Falangist and fascist Spaniards; and on the left were an eclectic formation of democratic, secular, socialist, communist, anarchist, and republican interests.[13] The Nationalist forces, led by General Francisco Franco, rose up in Morocco on 17 July 1936 (18 July on the Spanish Peninsula), and finally declared victory over Republican Spain on 1 April 1939, plunging the country into a dictatorship spanning some four decades.[14] In the end, the Franco dictatorship that began in 1939—although at first conceived as a way of transitioning the country back toward a traditional Spanish monarchy—eventually led Spain into a transition toward democracy following Franco's death in 1975 and even to the formulation of a new democratic constitution of 1978—a change that Benet lived to experience firsthand.

Juan Benet has remarked that the Civil War was the most influential event of his youth—and rightly so, as he was only nine in 1936 when his father was killed during the conflict.[15] As he has related quite candidly about his father's death: "one day, they took him from the house and led him to a ditch and shot him. My mother covered it up; when we found out more or less officially, three years had already gone by and the emotional effect was practically nil."[16] Elsewhere, Benet elaborates on the circumstances surrounding this event, which occurred in Madrid where the family was living at the time: "my father was a lawyer and he worked for businessmen from the North, he was shot by the Republicans. The reason was unclear, probably a vengeance bereft of any grand political meaning."[17] Although the precise nature of Benet's political sympathies has been both debated and overlooked by critics, this is a matter that requires much less attention than his complex novelistic prose.[18] Taking into account that he distances himself from assigning blame to the republicans for his father's death, that he once professed to have anarchist sympathies, and that—after Franco finally died on 20 November 1975—he celebrated by drinking a bottle of wine from the year 1936, all signs point to the fact that Benet's allegiances throughout were clearly never aligned with the Nationalists.[19] One prominent critic rightly points out succinctly that "Benet, on a number of occasions, has been ringing in his condemnation of the Francoist regime."[20]

After the Spanish Civil War began in 1936, Juan's mother moved with the three children to the city of San Sebastián in the Northern Basque Region of Spain, where she had relatives, moving back to Madrid only upon the conclusion of the war in 1939. It was there in Spain's capital city that Benet finished his high-school degree (*el bachillerato*). While pursuing his *bachillerato* in Madrid, the young Juan Benet had an insight regarding the two kinds of maps (physical and political) that were routinely used for high-school study at the time.[21] Although the physical or topographical map "showed what Nature had granted man before his arrival," the political or annotated map "showed what man had done with what Nature had prepared for him."[22] The memory of these maps of his early years stayed with him until at least 1982, when he was able to make a prescient remark:

> This is the reality: that the Political map represents that which is most important and closest and the Physical map that which is farthest away and all but unachievable. But moreover, since the latter silences all the data of interest to the former, it will be observed with that suspicion aroused by any prohibitive law and it will be judged with that school-aged mixture of distrust and disdain reserved also for official doctrine and in this way, just as the Physical map gradually comes to be the instrument of the teacher's repression, the Political map becomes the refuge of the rebellious student. Until years have gone by and that disobedient student begins to lose interest in things which are the order of the day or around every corner; and one fine day, weary of everyday matters, he once again turns his gaze toward that unalterable and poorly colored Physical map in order to dream, defiantly, in an instant, of everything prior to the voices that come from the outside and talk about a present in a perpetual transformation toward a more welcoming future, as he searches for a spot left unspoiled by the crude chromatic spectrum of the box-shaped Hispania.[23]

Benet's reflection on the maps of his youth forms an important point of reference for reasons both concrete and abstract. Considered on its surface, it is clear that, just as he had loved writing ever since he was young, he had also been fascinated by maps from an early age.[24] Moreover, his love for landscape and topography was to play a role not only in his civil-engineering work as a designer of dams and other public works but also in his fiction. For example, his first novel (*Volverás a Región*) places a heavy emphasis on the spatial and topographical qualities of the fictitious area of Spain he called Región.[25] Benet's comment must be read also in light of the fact that he composed his own elaborate topographical map of Región—the characteristic setting for the majority of his novels, not just his first—a map that was in fact included with the 1983 publication of the first installment of his extensive multivolume project titled *Herrumbrosas lanzas* (Rusty Lances).

At a more abstract level, Benet's revealing comment regarding maps also points to his appreciation of the distance between competing and overlapping understandings of space (for example, physical space and political space).[26] Present also in his direct juxtaposition of the political and the physical is a strong critique of authoritarian power—specifically, that power exercised by the governing structures of Franco's dictatorship. In the above quotation, Benet's reference to the "instrument of the teacher's repression" recalls the overtly ideological nature of instruction under the Francoist state—which he directly experienced—while the value he assigns to the unfettered exercise of creative forces, here those of the young student, is easily traced throughout his essays on the nature of literary production as well as his novels themselves.[27] In a sense, the invented novelistic place he called "Región," which he developed through prose and even maps (both mental and physical), may in fact well be that very "spot left unspoiled" which he describes in the above quotation.

Having received his high-school degree in 1944, Benet began preparation for admission to the prestigious Escuela de Ingenieros de Caminos (School of Civil Engineers), where he would begin classes in 1948, also in Madrid. This was an intellectually fruitful time in his life, as he frequented the *tertulia* (literary circle) of noted Spanish author Pío Baroja (and those in Café Gijón and the Gambrinus restaurant) and read assiduously.[28] It was during this period, while taking preparatory math classes, that he discovered the work of Franz Kafka, Thomas Mann, Friedrich Nietzsche, William Faulkner, and many others.[29] Even then he was effectively showcasing his trademark ability to straddle the worlds of both literature and science. In the essay "Barojiana," originally published in 1972, Benet reflects on this period, in which he came to meet Baroja in 1946 by way of his brother Francisco.[30] Between 1948 and 1954 he studied civil engineering in Madrid, making journeys to Paris to visit his brother in exile (1949, 1953), to Toledo for a period of mandated military service (1951), and even to Helsinki, Finland, for Engineering work (1953).[31] In 1955, he married Nuria Jordana, with whom he would have four children: Ramón (b. 1956), Nicolás (b. 1960), Juana (b. 1961), and Eugenio (b. 1962), and by 1956 he had signed on with the firm MZOV (Compañía de Ferrocarriles de Medina de Campo a Zamora y de Orense a Vigo, which later became merely Cubiertas y MZOV). Between 1954 and 1964, after receiving his engineering degree, Benet lived outside of Madrid—working on noted public projects such as canals in Ponferrada, roads near Oviedo, and the Porma dam.[32]

Even as a professional engineer Benet was able to devote substantial time to his literary production. He has remarked that "the truth is that I have always written, ever since my student days"—and while it is true that he had already published his play *Max* in the *Revista Española* in 1953, it is during his first decade of work as a professional civil engineer that his writing really took off.[33] His first published prose work was a book of stories, *Nunca llegarás a nada* (*You'll Never Get Anywhere*, 1961), although it was all but ignored by the literary critics of the time. When he was not working, he was able to work on a book of essays, *La inspiración y el estilo* (Inspiration and Style, 1966), and even what would later become his first novel, *Volverás a Región* (1967, written between 1962 and 1964). In addition, his second (prize-winning) novel *Una meditación* (1969; Biblioteca Breve Prize, 1969) was begun as early as 1965, testifying to the intense nature of his creative literary activity during his first decade of professional work as a civil engineer.[34] Perhaps more than any other, this period testifies to the competition between literary production and engineering work in his life.

Having returned to Madrid in 1966, Benet continued to write and publish an astounding number of impressive literary works over many years: books of essays (*Puerta de tierra* [Door of Dust], *¿Qué fue la guerra civil?*, *En ciernes* [In Bloom], *El ángel del señor abandona a Tobías* [The Lord's Angel Abandons Tobias], *La moviola de Eurípides* [Euripides' Editing Projector]; short stories (*5 narraciones y 2 fábulas* [5 Narrations and 2 Tales], *Sub Rosa* [Sub Rosa], *Trece fábulas y media* [Thirteen-and-a-Half Tales]); and novels (*Un viaje de invierno* [A Winter's Journey], *La otra casa de Mazón* [The Other House of Mazón], *Del Pozo y de Numa* [Of the Well and Of Numa], *En el estado* [In the State], *El aire de un crimen* [The Air of a Crime]), and *Saúl ante Samuel* [Saul before Samuel]—continuing to develop his fictional novelistic world of Región.

Tragically (also in 1966), Benet's brother Paco died in a car accident in Iran—and, fittingly, one of his essays from *Puerta de tierra,* titled "Un extempore" [An Extemporalization], is composed in the second person as a tribute of sorts and a meditation on death and temporality, in the form of a letter written directly to Paco. Another tragedy in his personal life occurred eight years later in 1974 when his wife Nuria died, and he would not wed again until 1985, when he married poet Blanca Andreu. During all these years, although Madrid had once again definitively become his home, he still traveled: to China in 1976 and to various conferences in the United States from 1978 to 1980.[35] The latter conferences, in fact, speak to what was a particularly important part of Benet's development and critical reception. At the beginning of his literary career, Benet in fact received much more critical attention in English publications than he did in Spanish ones.[36] American Hispanists in particular—such as David K. Herzberger and Malcolm Alan Compitello, who both befriended Benet during the 1970s—were critical in stimulating interest in his work, both in the United States and, in turn, among Spanish literary scholars.

In 1982 Juan Benet began what is undoubtedly—along with the *Antagonía* tetralogy published over the previous decade and written by his contemporary, Spanish author Luis Goytisolo—one of the most ambitious literary projects of the postwar period and perhaps also of Spain's twentieth century. The first installment of *Herrumbrosas lanzas*—a series that spans three volumes (vol. 1, 1983; vol. 2, 1985; vol. 3, 1986)—narrates a military campaign launched by the Republicans against the Nationalists during the Civil War that would ultimately end in failure.[37] As Benet himself has remarked, he wanted to write a fictionalized historiography of the Civil War in Región.[38] This extensive multivolume work showcases both the compelling novelistic treatment of the ruins of war he had presented in his earlier works as well as the deep knowledge of military strategy and history he had displayed in his essay *¿Qué fue la guerra civil?* (1976). As such it presents a curious fusion of history and fiction—in his own words, "what I didn't want to do was represent a concrete event, like the siege of Madrid or the battle of the Ebro [River]. . . . For me it was the entirety of the Civil War or nothing at all. And . . . I said to myself: I'll create a civil war in context, I'll invent the capitals, the campaigns, the battles, the offensives, using the Spanish Civil War as a model."[39]

Following the continued literary success brought on by this monumental work, Benet kept writing, publishing a number of other works: essays (*Otoño en Madrid hacia 1950* [Fall in Madrid around 1950], *La construcción de la torre de Babel* [The Construction of the Tower of Babel]); a dense travel guide, *Londres victoriano* (Victorian London), for a series titled "Ciudades en la Historia" (Cities in History); and another pair of novels (*En la penumbra* [In the Half-Light] and *El caballero de Sajonia* [The Gentleman from Saxony]).[40] And yet, as he also continued to practice as a civil engineer, Benet authored (or contributed to) a number of publications of relevance to his first chosen profession: for example, an edited book from 1983 featuring Spanish public works projects (*Ingeniería en la época romántica: Las obras públicas en España alrededor de 1860* [Engineering during the Romantic Era: Public Works in Spain around 1860]), a treatise on the construction of tunnels published by the Civil Engineering School in Madrid (also from 1983) and the book *El agua en España* (Water in Spain) in 1986, as well as many other engineering essays.[41] As a crowning achievement to a career in public engineering works, Benet decided to form his own civil engineering firm in 1987, giving it a revealing title that referred to the fictional world of Región he had created—the "Compañía Hidrocinética Regional."

On 5 January 1993, Benet died in Madrid.[42] Significantly, he received many posthumous honors, including being remembered with both a special issue of the prestigious Spanish literary magazine *Ínsula* in mid-1993 and a complementary homage in the *Revista de Obras Públicas* (Journal of Public Works) in 1994.[43] To top it all off, however, in 1994 the Porma dam on which he had worked as a young civil engineer in the early 1960s was renamed the "Embalse Juan Benet" in his memory.[44]

Benet's Place in Spain's Dictatorial Literary Landscape (1939–1975)

Because Juan Benet's first, major works—the short stories in *Nunca lle-garás a nada* (1961) and well as the novels *Volverás a Región* (1967) and *Una meditación* (1969)—were conceived, written, and published under the Franco dictatorship, it is important to understand how his work fits into the general development of Spanish literature during that period. The Spanish Civil War and the dictatorship that followed were to have a disastrous effect on Spain's literary landscape. While some notable authors died during the Civil War conflicts—Federico García Lorca and Miguel de Unamuno among them—others were imprisoned by the dictatorship or fled into exile abroad, mostly in France, the United States, Latin America, or some combination of these.[45] Since the great majority of Spanish intellectuals were aligned with the democratic ideals of the Republican forces, those who remained in Spain after the Civil War faced strict government censorship of their works in 1939 when the dictatorship officially began.[46] Although Spanish censorship eventually waned in the latter part of the dictatorship—and although it was possible, in many cases, to pass veiled critiques by the government censors (who tended to be relatively unfamiliar with the subtleties of literary discourse)—Juan Benet was still able to remark in 1969 that "in Spain, one just can't write about any old theme, there are still many topics that writers are prohibited from exploring."[47] In addition to censoring authors writing from inside Spain, the dictatorship upheld a strict censorship of works originating outside the country.[48] Nonetheless, many Spaniards living abroad still smuggled prohibited works into the country, using various means and routes—many prohibited books entered the country via the Spanish-French border, for example.[49] While it is perhaps unfair to say, as did one critic in 1967, that "inside Spain, since the end of the war, few works of merit have been published," overall, the quality and quantity of works published by writers in exile on the topic of the war and its effects far surpassed those published within the country that were able to deal directly and critically with those themes.[50] In general terms it is safe to say that postwar writers confronted a literary landscape that lay in material, political, and moral devastation.[51]

The narrative strategies used by Spanish novelists shifted considerably over the course of the dictatorship.[52] What is in many respects the definitive characterization of Spain's postwar prose literature has come from scholar Gonzalo Sobejano, who identifies three strains of the novel during the period 1940–74. In his book *Novela española de nuestro tiempo* (The Spanish Novel of Our Time), he discusses what he terms the "existential," the "social," and the "structural" novels. Sobejano's categories are not intended as a chronological model of self-enclosed periods of literary production, but rather as various "directions" that the novel took during that time. It is still possible, however, to speak of a general tendency of Spanish literature to move from realist modes at the beginning of the dictatorship toward more experimental structures at its close. While Juan Benet's literary production falls into the latter category, working briefly through the characteristics of the existential and social novels—directions of the Spanish novel that existed prior to his own literary career—can help us to understand how the structural novel in general and his work in particular constituted a shift from and even a rejection of these previous narrative strategies.

After the war, remarks Sobejano, "the great majority and the best of novelists [pursued] what we may call realism, understanding realism as a fundamental attention given to a present and concrete reality, to the real circumstances of lived time and place. To be realist is to take that reality as the end goal of the work of art, and not as a means of achieving it: to feel it, comprehend it, interpret it with precision."[53] The two most important novels of the early dictatorship were *La familia de Pascual Duarte* (The Family of Pascual Duarte), published in 1942 by Camilo José Cela (who would later win the Nobel Prize for Literature in 1989), and *Nada* (Nothing), published in 1945 by Carmen Laforet (one year after the book had won the coveted Nadal Prize). Sobejano takes both of these works to be examples of the "new realism" that became synonymous with the postwar period, but he also points to their existential aspects, as they highlight "extreme situations that put the human condition to the test." Juan Goytisolo's *Juegos de manos* (Sleights of Hands) (1954) and Ana María Matute's *Primera memoria* (First Memory) (1960, Nadal Prize of 1959), then, become examples of the social novel, which portrays "the life of a community in states and conflicts that reveal the presence of a crisis and the urgency of a solution"; while Luis Martín-Santos's *Tiempo de silencio* (Time of Silence) (1962) and Juan Benet's *Volverás a Región* (1967) fall under the rubric of the structural novel, as they stress "knowledge of a person through the exploration of his conscience and through the structure of his social context."[54]

These last two "structural" novels were both published in a 1960s Spanish society that differed in many significant respects from the circumstances governing the immediate postwar years. Commonly known as the *años de desarrollo* (years of development), the end of the dictatorship (1960–75) saw measurable internal economic growth, increased tourism, and a progressive opening to external markets.[55] In effect, as the authoritarian and closed character of the dictatorship began to wane, Spanish novelists became less realist and more experimental in their narrative strategies. Literary critics soon identified a group of authors who were given credit for creating the "New Novel" in Spain—a list that usually included Martín-Santos as this novelistic form's initiator, and privileged Benet as one of the form's most complex practitioners.[56] In fact, the authors had been friends—Juan first met Luis in Madrid in 1948.[57] Although there are certainly stylistic and thematic differences between the two, it is fair to say that both of them succeeded in breaking with the earlier forms of literary realism engendered by the dictatorship, each in his own way.[58] Moreover, while the "structural novel" presented a challenge also to what Sobejano has called the "social novel," readers should keep in mind that social criticism did not disappear from novels published in the last decade of the dictatorship—instead such criticism merely became more subtle.[59]

Benet's narrative rupture with the somewhat straightforward realist prose of the earlier social novel is—like that of Martín-Santos and Juan Goytisolo's novel *Señas de identidad* (*Marks of Identity*), similarly published in the 1960s—total and even excessive.[60] In its presentation of the effects of the Spanish Civil War, the plot of Benet's first novel *Volverás a Región* has been described as "painstakingly complex and powerful."[61] Part of the book's complexity lies in the fact that the book is almost bereft of dialogue, something that potential publishers found to be off-putting. In Benet's own words, *Volverás* "enjoyed one peculiarity; it was a matter of continuous discourse, with very little dialogue, and with only a few—not many—periods."[62] The work is complex not merely for its lack of dialogue but due to Benet's implicit assessment of the value of matters of language and style to literary discourse. One critic has concisely summed up the complexity of Benet's work in general by listing a series of hallmark techniques harnessed en route to the creation of what seems to be a deliberately confusing text: "an excessively elaborate, almost Germanic syntax, page-long sentences, the complete absence of paragraph and chapter divisions . . . , a highly technical vocabulary, character-narrators who border on lunacy, the fusion of various narrative voices, and of course the contradictions in plot."[63] The plot of *Volverás* itself is so confusing that critics have attempted to chart it out for the reader using intriguing schematics and visual representations.[64] Nonetheless it may be said that "the novel takes place in the semi-fictional area of Spain named Región that has been ravaged by the Civil War, and that it is loosely centered on the arrival of Marré Gamallo to the house of Doctor Daniel Sebastián in a small war-torn village. In a sense, however, it is the Civil War that is the real protagonist of the novel."[65] Placing Juan Benet's work in context means understanding that, although the writer's own use of complex narrative techniques and devices certainly reflected his specific thoughts on literary style, such strategies were in fact commonly found in work by writers of the later, more experimental period in Spanish literature under the dictatorship.

Benet's second and prize-winning novel *Una meditación* (1970), however, presented a much greater challenge to earlier social-realist narrative practices. The novel was originally composed using one continuous roll of paper and, in fact, in published form it consisted of one single uninterrupted novel-length paragraph.[66] In the English translation of 1982 (by Gregory Rabassa, who also translated *Volverás a Región*), this paragraph runs to some 366 pages without a break, likely frustrating many potential readers merely through its length. Moreover, the narrative voice here is "indifferent to the chronological succession [of time]," and floats seemingly without direction—in the manner of the "meditation" signaled by the novel's title—among diverse memories: of childhood events in the North of Región, of the Civil War, and of various friends, relatives, and acquaintances.[67] Just as in Benet's first novel, the reader must grapple with the fact that, as even literary critics have been forced to recognize, "It is difficult to speak of a story line in *Una meditación.*"[68] In Benet's prose, what tends to trump storyline in importance is the notion of style—something he praises in the work of one of his undeniable and self-professed influences, Nobel Prize–winning novelist William Faulkner. This name may perhaps be the best point of entry for English-language readers who seek to understand Juan Benet. There are numerous essays in which Benet cites Faulkner's novels and the effect they had on him—a connection that has proved fruitful for many critics.[69] In one early essay, penned in 1951, Benet writes of his admiration for the American author: "Faulkner's form and his language are what distinguishes him. He has created a style . . . but Faulkner's style is inextricably linked to his Idea; and thus, in my opinion, in order to make sense of him we must go beyond interminable analyses of his paragraph [structure] and his [use of] metaphor."[70] Quite understandably, this characterization might just as equally apply to Benet's own novels.

Juan Benet's interest in the question of style, of course, is one to which he devoted much attention throughout his career, not only through his fiction but also through his essays, as can be seen in his early publication of *La inspiración y el estilo* (1966). According to Benet, style is something about which "it has never been possible . . . to speak with precision," but that nonetheless comes to be synonymous with the concept of what we might call, for lack of a better term, "good literature."[71] In that book, Benet disparages the realist strategies of Spanish literature prior to the twentieth century, just as he disparages much of the realism that came to typify the Spanish literature produced under the early-to-mid-dictatorship, instead harkening back to what he calls the *grand style* (employing the term in the original

English)—a model of literary production he much prefers over the realistic, didactic style that begins to predominate in Spain in the early modern period.[72] Taken together, Benet's definitive break with the social realism that characterized the postwar literary landscape of Spain and the priority he assigned stylistic concerns both contributed to the reputation for difficult prose that has been attached to his work ever since.

The "Discovery" of Juan Benet by Literary Critics

When Juan Benet was "discovered" by Anglophone literary critics in the 1970s, the expectations for scholarly criticism were in many ways different from what they are today.[73] Reformulated formalist and structuralist theories were gaining ground in the study and critique of Hispanic literature, and, as might have been expected, innovative studies of Benet in particular largely harnessed many formalist and even structuralist interpretive approaches to emphasize his works' "literariness"—that is, the challenges it presented to "realist" modes of narration that had thrived under the repressive dictatorship of Francisco Franco (1939–75) as well as their unique presentation of the historical themes of the Spanish Civil War (1936–39). It is undeniable that a number of edited volumes and foundational critical texts as well as other articles and book chapters (going back to the journal *The American Hispanist* in the late 1970s) have been enormously helpful in revealing the narrative strategies and formal or structural qualities employed in his works.[74] Existing scholarship has also charted out the connections and dissonances between Benet and other novelists of his time (such as Juan Goytisolo, Luis Martín-Santos) and those of other times and places also (Benito Pérez Galdós, William Faulkner), just as it has successfully analyzed the major themes of his novels and stories—themes such as memory, the ruin of war, self-invention, prohibition and transgression, the unknown, and more still.

Although the interdisciplinary character of today's literary criticism requires that we update our understanding of Juan Benet's works, it is fitting to outline briefly the trends of previous Benetian criticism. Pursued with vigor during previous decades, these trends are far from obsolete, and in fact readers may come to see where combinations of old approaches and new approaches may be of interest to future Benetian scholarship. Ultimately, understanding previous research into Benet's themes and complex narrative techniques is, in fact, a prerequisite for making a claim to a more interdisciplinary perspective on his literary production. In the brief characterizations of the four major trends of Benetian scholarship that follow, the implication is not that each is mutually exclusive to the others. In fact, in many cases there is much overlap, with some critics pursuing multiple trends of analysis—for example: narrative structure, myth, history and fiction, and time and memory—all within the same publication. In addition, this list is not intended to be exhaustive; it is merely meant to serve interested readers as a rough, initial sketch of what has been done up until this point. There may certainly be approaches that have been left out, and there are clearly numerous potential directions for Benetian scholarship that have not yet begun to be explored by critics.[75]

Narrative and Structure

Many early studies of Benet's work focused on the unique narrative structure employed in his novels.[76] The most complex of these harnessed an impressive range of Russian Formalist and French Structuralist approaches to analyze Benet's novels, relying on a technical "narratological" vocabulary that consisted of concepts such as *discours, histoire, ordre, durée, fréquence, mode* and *voix*; or following up on this latter concept (*voix*), narrators that might be classified by terms such as *extradiegetique, intradiegetique, and homodiegetique.*[77] This in itself was unusual, since many Hispanic studies scholars during the late 1970s and early 1980s saw literary criticism as an activity far removed from theoretical concerns.[78] Other critics took less theoretical and more traditionally "literary" paths toward similar conclusions: exploring the qualities of Benet's narrations, asserting their similarity to interior monologues, and making pertinent observations regarding their complexity (for example "The narrator also acts as a center of consciousness for other characters").[79] One scholar has rightly seen Benet's narrative strategy as shaping a discourse that stresses its nature as a literary creation through "the principles of uncertainty, irrationality and stylistic density"—in opposition to the discourses of science, reason and rationality, for example.[80] This idea was in fact something professed by Benet himself in his own essays and noted also by critics who saw in the latter the basis for a Benetian theory of literary production.[81]

Myth and Epic Studies

The relevance of myth to Benet's oeuvre begins with the fictional character of Numa and the legend that surrounds him. Numa is a "mysterious and ubiquitous guard" who watches over the forest of Mantua in Benet's invented land of Región throughout numerous works, such as *Volverás a Región, Una meditación,* and *Del Pozo y del Numa.*[82] This figure has been analyzed at length by some Benetian critics, who have signaled a connection with the King of the Wood in *The Golden Bough* (1890) the classic study of myths by anthropologist Sir James Frazer.[83] According to his own account, Benet was clearly aware of this connection, and its exploitation by the novelist led to a heightened appreciation by critics of the mythic, symbolic dimensions of his fiction in general.[84] In Benet's texts, the legend surrounding Numa's origin is vague, and descriptions are contradictory, owing to the fact that he has seldom, if ever, been seen. Numa nonetheless has an important role to play as "regulator of life in the area of Región": "Rather than being responsible for the cyclical regeneration or revival of the area, el Numa is there to maintain the status quo," one scholar has written.[85] A study from 1989 elaborated on this critical view through an extended discussion linking myth with the fascist ideologies of the Spanish dictatorship under which Benet lived and wrote.[86] Ultimately, for Benet, "Mythical thought is shown to be a failed attempt to impose ordered structures onto an unstable history."[87]

History and Fiction

Benet's complex response to the official ideology of the Franco dictatorship has also been highlighted by critics analyzing the curious interplay of history and fiction in his novels. After Franco's death, Benet was able to more openly criticize the regime's essentialist view of history, but as critics had already asserted, this critique was implicit in the essays and fiction he had published under the dictatorship.[88] As part of its strategy for silencing the oppositional voices within Spanish society—and parallel to its practice of literary censorship—the Franco government promoted and enforced an official view of past events.[89] Through the characteristic reliance of his complex narratives on enigma, uncertainty, contradiction, ambiguity, and multiple perspectives, for example, Benet's novels rejected the idea of one single, official interpretation of the past, and in this way presented a challenge to Francoism's "master discourse" of history.[90] The blending of history and fiction became most pronounced in the three-volume (and incomplete) *Herrumbrosas lanzas* project, where Benet's "historical" exploration of military strategy and Región's topography (accompanied by excessive footnotes) vie for the reader's attention in a highly literary discourse where different genres intermingle: as one scholar reflects, the narrative voice effectively "turns into any other imaginable voice, that of history, myth, legend, and literary art."[91]

Time and Memory

By far the most important theme of Benet's novels—owing in part but not solely to his literary influences of Faulkner and Proust—is the nature of time.[92] Critics have explored the significance of subjective temporality and the role of memory in Benet's novels, both of which stand in contrast to the rigid notion of an objective or calendar time.[93] Benet himself has remarked that "modern narrative has come to shatter . . . the chronological, linear succession [of time]," and his preference for run-on sentences (and paragraphs) might be described by reference to the stream-of-consciousness novel.[94] Whether through seemingly omniscient third-person or subjective first-person subjective narration, Benet tends to depict the interior lives of his characters, the contrast between instinctual time and intellectual time, and the relationship of past moments to the present.[95] In the end, Benet's notion of temporality is fluid and multiple, and although chronological objective time is largely done away with, "memory remains, but it is either distant, or else . . . it is marred [by time], rendering remembrance dormant, only functional once it is forgotten."[96]

These necessarily brief snapshots of previous approaches have left out a variety of other intriguing ways of reading Benet's work, among them: the self, desire and sexuality, biblical references, politics, modernism and postmodernism, and countless other binaries prominent in his work.[97] The reason both for these omissions and for the brevity of the above accounts is that the focus of this work is on new perspectives that allow us to gain a greater appreciation of the themes and qualities most central to Benet's work as a whole. These include the importance of Benet's civil engineering work, the formative influence of the philosophy of Henri Bergson, the relevance of recent developments in cultural geography, and the significance of the notion of enigma for understanding his literary production.

Chapter 1

The Spanish Civil War and Beyond

The Spatial Question

> The Civil War of 1936 to 1939 was, without a doubt, contemporary
> Spain's most important historical event and perhaps even the most decisive
> in its history. . . . Exactly forty years and a fortnight after the first day of
> the conflict, a royal pardon has been necessary to do away with, partially
> and legally, the open wounds and deep schisms, which—continuing to
> divide the country, ever since that remote date, into different camps that
> may only be reconciled with difficulty—have been preserved in a state of
> latent, if not open, bellicosity.
>
> Juan Benet, *¿Qué fue la guerra civil?*

One cannot begin to understand Juan Benet's novels, essays, and worldview without understanding the Spanish Civil War (1936–39) and the
Franco dictatorship (1939–75) that followed it.[1] In turn, the war itself
cannot be understood without reference to the long-standing tensions that
had shaped Spanish society throughout the nineteenth century and into the
twentieth.[2] While the phrase "The Two Spains" is a concise substitute for
a complex exploration of the social and political dynamics involved, it is
necessary to elaborate further on their nature if the reader is to understand
Benet's work as a particular kind of response to those tensions. The complexity of Spain's civil war goes far beyond the scope of a book focused on
Benet's literary and engineering work, and it is neither possible nor relevant
here to attempt an exhaustive treatment of the conflict, which of course has
been so extensively documented elsewhere.[3] Instead, I seek to balance two
necessities: (1) the obligation of emphasizing the social context that shaped
Benet's life and informed his literary production, and (2) the importance of
advancing a "new perspective" on his work.

First, the discussion that follows relies heavily on Juan Benet's own
account of the Spanish Civil War, *¿Qué fue la guerra civil?* published in

1976—after the death of dictator Francisco Franco on 20 November 1975 and during Spain's transition toward democracy. If the scholarly record is any indication, this significant and relevant essay lamentably remains of only peripheral interest to Benetian studies, and its inclusion here is meant to address this lacuna.[4] Second, land and territory are essential in understanding the origin, progression, and consequences of the civil war. Spanish soil was not merely part of the military strategy—for example: offensives, the role of river systems, the successful split of the Spanish peninsula by Nationalist troops and the eventual taking of Barcelona and, finally, Madrid—but also one of the key causes of the war. The characteristic tensions of prewar Spanish society were bound up with what critics have called "the agrarian question," discussed below.[5] Moreover, the Spanish landscape, which lay in ruins after the war, was for the Spanish people a continuing reminder of the ideological schisms that persisted in Spain's postwar society—just as it was for Benet's readers, who were repeatedly confronted with its devastation through his fiction.

Origins: Struggles over Land and Territory

In what is widely considered the most important book on the background of the Spanish Civil War, historian Gerald Brenan identifies what he calls "the fundamental problem in Spain"—devoting over forty pages to discussion of "the agrarian question."[6] For Brenan, it is necessary to begin with this matter if the tensions surrounding the Spanish Republic (1931–36), and thus those governing the war itself, are to be understood.[7] "The first thing to notice," he writes in that text from 1943,

> is that Spain is one of those countries with an undeveloped, primitive economy which is divided by a fairly definite line into two sections. Above are the upper and middle classes, say one fifth of the population, who vote, read newspapers, compete for Government jobs and generally manage the affairs of the nation. Beneath are the peasants and workmen, who in ordinary times take no interest in politics, frequently do not know how to read and keep strictly to their own affairs. Between these two completely different worlds there is a gulf, imperfectly filled by the small shop-keepers and artisans.[8]

The large class of "those who worked with their hands" was not powerless, and Spanish history in fact shows that many times peasant workers had risen up to expel what they saw as "a foreign body which provoked and irritated them"—social bodies such as the Jews, the Moors, the Austrians, and the French were victims of this process, dating back hundreds of years.[9]

It follows that, traditionally, the Spanish (Catholic) *pueblo* was seen as "the great repository of the virtues of the race."[10] Nevertheless, as a way of explaining what happened in the years leading up to the Civil War, Brenan points to "the gradual transfer of the allegiance of the peasants and workers from the Church to revolutionary ideologies hostile to it."[11] This transfer was, in fact, the direct result of the conditions governing this class's relationship with the land.

Although Spain was a predominantly agricultural and pastoral country, containing some areas of cultivated and even highly productive land, the majority of the Spanish Peninsula was fairly unproductive if not extremely poor as regards conditions for crops and livestock.[12] The nature of the relationships peasants had with the land they worked varied considerably throughout the many regions of Spain—just as the characteristic geography of that land itself varied. In very few cases, however, was this relationship anything but exploitative. In the eighteenth century, of course, the vast majority of Spanish soil was owned by the Catholic Church and the noble class.[13] Yet even by the 1930s—a full century after the forced sale of Church properties—peasant workers, whether tenant farmers or landless laborers, still faced poverty wages and extremely poor living conditions.[14] Historically speaking, the need for substantial agrarian reform was all but ignored by Spanish rulers, such that it is possible for Brenan to conclude that "the refusal of the Spanish upper classes to yield an inch in this [agrarian] question has been the most important single cause of the Civil War."[15] Under these conditions, during the late nineteenth and early twentieth centuries Spain became fertile ground for socialist and anarchist ideologies. These newly introduced ideas were embraced by peasants and tenant farmers in great numbers—not to mention city-dwelling factory workers who largely sympathized with their rural counterparts and had their own reasons for wanting substantial social change—in part because they were a path to realizing the land reforms they badly needed.[16]

The relevance of the agrarian question, however, has more often been overlooked or underemphasized by simplistic understandings of the Spanish Civil War. It is commonly said, for example, that the war should be seen as a mere preamble to World War II—an approach with which Juan Benet himself has vehemently disagreed.[17] Similarly, perhaps as a testament to the power of the latter belief, the Civil War is often regarded primarily as a conflict between fascists and communists, when the reality is much more complex, indeed. As Benet declares in *¿Qué fue la guerra civil?* 18 July 1936 saw the eruption of not one but two revolutions. The young Spanish Republic was pulverized through the "combined and simultaneous occurrence of two extremist revolutions launched against it on the same day"—one revolution from the right seeking (at least initially) to restore monarchic rule, and another revolution from the left seeking a much more radical approach to Spanish democracy than a simple Republican state could provide.[18]

Neither of these revolutions was completely unanticipated, and each found some measure of support in the Spanish peasantry, whose economic problems had been left unaddressed for so long. As Benet notes, the right had been organizing over a number of years and were mobilized in opposition to the successful establishment of the Spanish Republic on 14 April 1931.[19] Specifically, the Republicans had plans to draw up "a wide-ranging program of reforms . . . that could only end by producing vertigo, contortions and ill feeling among the conservative classes"—and Benet continues, noting that "without a single concession and paying no heed to the consequences, the first blows were dealt [by the Republic] to the Church, the Army and landowners."[20] The right actually organized a coup against the democratic government of Spain as early as 10 August 1932, although it failed, an uprising that was led by General Sanjurjo.[21] In fact, Sanjurjo—and not Franco—was to be the army's first choice of leader for the uprising of 18 July 1936 as well, although he died in strange and tragic circumstances that Benet relates with literary flair in his essay on the Spanish Civil War.[22] In the end, the 1936 uprising from the right was instigated, led, fought, and won by the army in collaboration with the conservative and bourgeois segments of Spanish society.[23] Nevertheless—and despite the historical reason for their poor living conditions—the number of Spanish citizens who sided with this revolution from the right was still significant enough to warrant their being called, on occasion, the "fifth column" of the struggle.[24]

Similarly, antecedents for the uprising from the left can be seen in the events leading up to the outbreak of the civil war, events in which Spanish peasants and workers rose up in large numbers to protest their treatment by long-standing and oppressive government policies regarding the land.[25] While socialism was almost unknown in Spain through the 1860s, the split in the Workers' International between Karl Marx and the Russian anarchist Mikhail Bakunin was indeed felt in Spain after 1871, eventually leading to the formation of the Spanish Socialist Party (PSOE) on 2 May 1879 and the Federación Anarquista Ibérica (Iberian Anarchist Federation or FAI) in 1927.[26] The political tensions between workers and the upper-class bourgeois Spaniards led to a number of general strikes during the first two decades of the twentieth century in which large unions (the socialist UGT and the anarchist CNT) played major roles.[27] While the Spanish socialist and anarchist traditions that developed from the 1870s onward might have coincided in recognizing the need for social change in Spain, however, they had different understandings of what those changes entailed.[28] The period spanning 1933–34 provides some illuminating and large-scale examples of how such tensions were still palpable during the turbulent years of the Second Republic. In 1933, an uprising by anarchists in Casas Viejas, Cádiz, was met with severe retaliation by the democratic government when—as Benet himself relates—the Civil Guard of the Spanish Republic, on orders from President Manuel Azaña, squelched the rebellion and shot those involved.[29] In 1934, Benet continues, the "October Revolution" met with tragic consequences in the Northern Province of Asturias where "around 50,000 miners struggled for fifteen days against the forces of the [Republican Government's] Civil Guard, the Army [of the Republic], the Legion and Franco's Regulars."[30]

The results of the elections of February 1936—five months before the Spanish Civil War began—illustrate the polarization that increasingly defined the later period of the Spanish Republic. In *¿Qué fue la guerra civil?* Benet notes that the Popular Front (comprising the Socialist Party [PSOE], Izquierda Republicana [Republican Left], Unión Republicana [Republican Union], Partido Comunista [Communist Party], Esquerra Catalana [Catalan Left], and with the support of the anarchist CNT) won an overwhelming 278 parliamentary seats in these elections while the National Front (made up of Monarchists, Carlists, Falangists, and members of JONS) itself won a substantial number (134 seats).[31] In contrast, the center parties managed to win only 55 seats.[32] The scene was now set for a violent clash. The Nationalist forces, which soon fell under the command of Francisco Franco, fully expected to take the entire country—save perhaps Barcelona and Madrid—within merely a few days.[33] This goal was not realized, however, as Juan Benet takes time to document throughout his historical essay on the war.

During the initial outbreak of the war, the vast majority of the Republican government's armed forces deserted and sided with the Nationalists. As Benet notes: "The experts estimate that after 18 July, of the 15,000 officers under the Army and armed forces, only 200 still obeyed the Government of the Republic that, [rendered] defenseless, in order to repel the aggression, was forced to improvise and seek out an army in the only place it could: in the union and worker contingents, in the people's militias and through the purchase of arms and calls for volunteers from abroad and even when this meant embracing the proletariat revolution that the Government of the Republic would go to great lengths to subdue during its brief and rocky period on the warpath."[34] The relatively young and now divided Republic faced a daunting task, not only that of defending itself against the troops, officers, and equipment that had previously been under its control, but also that of managing the secondary threat of a revolution from the left. While anarchist forces also directed their ire against the Nationalists—with a column of troops led by Buenaventura Durruti attempting to expel the latter from the city of Zaragoza after its immediate occupation with the outbreak of the war, for example—they were also responsible for notable conflicts with the Republic itself.[35] Ultimately, their vision of the Civil War as proletarian revolution was vastly different from that held by members of the existing Republican state—that is, for the more radical segments of Spanish society the conflict was not merely a defense against fascism but rather the "first and most important step in social revolution."[36]

It was the aid sent (or not sent) by other countries, however, that ultimately proved decisive in the Spanish Civil War.[37] That is, the revolution from the right was strongly supported by Italy and Germany, who contributed large numbers of troops, artillery, and equipment to the Nationalist side.[38] The Republican government received far less support. Most of democratic Spain's potential European allies sent delegates to the Non-Intervention Committee (NIC), convened in London, refusing to openly support the Republican forces then struggling in Spain.[39] There were exceptions to this of course. First, for example, France initially promised to assist the Republic, but soon bowed to international pressure, issuing a widely publicized retraction.[40] Second, as is well known, volunteers from a number of countries whose governments had declared themselves neutral fought against the Nationalist troops in both the International Brigades and the Workers' Party of Marxist Unification (POUM), noted English author George Orwell being among the latter.[41] And third, of course, the largest contributor to the Republican cause was the Soviet Union—although this aid was not without its own political complications.[42] The Nationalist forces ultimately proved to be far superior, and the Spanish Civil War ended with Franco's victory over the Republic on 1 April 1939. By this time, Spain's population had been drastically reduced—not only due to the incalculable deaths resulting from the conflict itself, but also as a consequence of mass emigration and exile.[43]

Progression: Major Battles and Campaigns

The initial uprising of 18 July 1936 ended with the Nationalist control of approximately half of Spain's geography.[44] Although they were defeated in the industrial areas and the major cities of Barcelona and Madrid—circumstances which, as Benet notes, provided a further stimulus to the proletarian revolution from the left—the Nationalists triumphed with relative ease in Northern Africa/Morocco (where Franco's division was initially stationed), Western Andalusia, León, New Castile, Galicia, Navarra, Mallorca, Canarias, and part of Aragón.[45] Thus, at the beginning of August 1936, Benet explains, "there were three armies on the warpath in Peninsular Spain positioned to combat the Republic." These were

> the Army of the North, under the command of General Mola, based in Pamplona, whose principal objectives were to conquer the Basque Country and advance toward Madrid through Logroño, Soria, Sigüenza and Guadalajara; the Army of Africa—later called the "Army of the Center"—under the command of General Franco, whose mission was to conquer Extremadura and advance toward Madrid through the Tajo valley; and finally the Army of the South, under the command of General Queipo de Llano—the weakest and least effective of the three—, which would restrict itself to maintaining newly acquired territory and try to bring the uprising to the nearest Andalusian capitals—Córdoba and Málaga—that had declared loyalty to the [Republican] Government.[46]

The capture of Madrid—the center of the government at the outset of the war and a city that was itself not without a large number of unions and workers sympathetic to the Republic—remained central to assuring a Nationalist victory. Initially, the idea was for these armies to converge on Madrid and occupy it as early as was feasible.[47]

Although Nationalist armies managed to engage Madrid in battle within the first several months of the war, Juan Benet's account emphasizes that a decision to rethink the attack was made in Leganés on 23 November 1936 by Franco and other generals.[48] Giving up on the goal of occupying the city and the possibility of strategically bringing the conflict to an end within a relatively short period of time, Franco sought instead "to transform it into a long war of degradation, attrition and utter annihilation."[49] For Benet, this "warrior attitude—which eschewed victory unless accompanied by extermination—necessarily was translated militarily into a series of campaigns of unusual and ambiguous character."[50] In addition, the relatively early seizure of the resisting central-northern territories allowed Franco to gain industrial capital that permitted the manufacture of more equipment and ultimately gave the Nationalists not merely a strategic advantage but moreover the ability to continue this sort of war of attrition.[51] The following brief account of notable battles of the Spanish Civil War privileges those military encounters given priority in Benet's essay.

The Battle of Jarama was a key part of the events of early 1937, as the Nationalists tried (unsuccessfully) to cut Madrid off from Valencia—now not merely another urban Republican stronghold but also the *pro tempore* capital of the government. A Nationalist victory would have meant that Madrid—still an important Republican base—was essentially fenced in by enemy forces. In the end, victory was elusive for both sides, each of which lost some twenty thousand troops in the encounter.[52] Although Jarama also showed that the Nationalists were capable of forms of assault other than the brute frontal attack, for Benet, it displayed the characteristically Nationalist drive not for victory but for total annihilation.[53] Inserted in his multipage description of the details of the battle is a substantial digression regarding military superiority as he makes this case:

> All who are familiar with the Spanish Civil War must agree that after the spring of 1937, and until the end of the conflict, all encounters of importance are characterized by a clear—and at times overwhelming—National superiority and that the potential for closure—favoring, without fail, the cause of the strongest [side]—is never fully and completely exploited [by the Nationalists]. In a war between strangers—and above all in a modern conflict—rarely does one side seek the extermination of the other, being content instead with the negotiation of a peace that provides all the advantages of wartime politics. Countries need each other and all of them—in one way or another—concede [the need for] fellowship; a state of war may result from a modification of the conditions surrounding this fellowship, but never from [a disagreement over] this fellowship itself. [This is not] the case of the Spaniards who launched into a war because they refused to allow for the other's existence and were ready, in the end, to extinguish it through the force of arms.[54]

Although Benet takes pains to elaborate on the many nuances of this argument, he remains fully convinced that the Nationalist side wished not for a quick strategic victory, but rather for a massive cleansing that would wipe all enemies of the Nationalist cause off the map. This idea was to be a major part of his fiction as well. Following Jarama, the Northern Campaign—which proceeded in an orderly fashion from East to West and lasted from June to October of 1937—ended with the Nationalist occupation of such cities as Bilbao, Guernica, Santander, Oviedo, and Gijón and consolidated Franco's control over the Western half of Spain.[55] More important still was the advance of Nationalist troops, also in 1937, all the way to the coast, south of the Ebro River. This move successfully split the Republican forces of Eastern Spain in half—with remaining centers of strength in Barcelona to the north, and Valencia to the south.[56]

Despite the many strategic and tactical successes of the Battle of the Ebro, which he discusses in the essay, Juan Benet regards the 1938 conflict as a last-ditch effort by the Republican forces, an "eminently defensive bat-tle, planned not to defeat the enemy and shift the course of the war toward victory, but rather only to wear him out, to oblige him to abandon the in-tention of achieving an unconditional surrender."[57] Benet describes the bat-tle in great detail over six pages of his essay (including a map), beginning with the river crossing by Republican troops on the night of 24 July. This initial attack ended with the surprise of three sleeping Nationalist divisions and the capture of some four thousand prisoners and much needed equip-ment.[58] Subsequent gains made by the Republicans through incursions into enemy territory were finally met with the first Nationalist counterattack of 8 August, and by 18 November the last Republican soldier had retreated back across the Ebro.[59] Due to the characteristic superiority of their forces, the Nationalists suffered only modest losses in this encounter while the Republicans lost an estimated 50 percent of their troops to death, injury, or capture. Military superiority notwithstanding, the campaign of the Ebro induced widespread anxiety amongst both the Nationalists and their allies. Yet this anxiety—rooted in the unexpected and impressive success of Re-publican troops during the Ebro battle—did not stop the last of the foreign volunteers who had fought alongside the Republicans from leaving Spain (also on 18 November). By the end of 1938, it was clear that an end to the fighting was imminent and, moreover, that the Republicans were certain to lose.[60]

Early the following year—on 26 January 1939—Nationalist troops man-aged to take Barcelona, and the war entered its final months.[61] In the last days of the war, Franco managed to reaffirm his support for a war of anni-hilation one final time. He was presented with—and refused—an armistice proposal offered by two prominent Republican leaders that would have allowed for a period of twenty-five days in which any Spanish civilians or military could leave the country if they so desired.[62] Perceiving that further negotiations were merely being used by the other side as a stalling tactic—in order to facilitate evacuations from the last Republican strongholds of Alicante and Valencia—Franco called for an end to talks and gave the order to advance on all Republican positions on 25 March 1939.[63] Madrid finally fell on 28 March, and within a few days, the remaining Republican forces had been rounded up. On 1 April—the "Day of Victory"—"Generalísimo" Franco finally declared the war over.[64] In the end, the Spanish Civil War had lasted some one thousand days and caused the loss of over one million Spaniards, including those dead, disappeared, and exiled.[65]

For Benet, the legacy of the war is that it plunged Spain into a dark and enigmatic space. This is due not only to the way in which it was car-ried out—the "campaigns of unusual and ambiguous character" that were waged seeking to "annihilate" the enemy of the Nationalists—but in fact more fundamentally to the nature of civil war itself. For Benet, the Spanish Civil War is, at its very core, "unintelligible."[66] The war and the dictatorship that followed effectively froze the existing tensions in Spanish society, rather than resolving them, such that in 1976 he would write that the worst part

> is that politically and socially, these forty years have passed in vain
> . . . that the two groups that fought in 1936 remain in their respec-
> tive positions, hunkering down in the same trenches and ready to
> fire—upon their adversaries or upon whomever appears before
> them—the same shots as back then. That neither side has come up
> with any new, up-to-date, ideas, nor have they been able to look
> around themselves seeking a lesson that they are unable to learn
> on their own. Such is the Spain of today: the same habits of 1936
> fueled by the same fury. The same fight between oppression and an
> imposed order, between the Republic and the Monarchy, between
> an authoritarian state and an elected government; the same parties,
> the same extremisms, the same rankness, almost the same shouts
> and acronyms, and, of course, the same names and nicknames.[67]

That is, although the civil war waged by the Nationalists constituted an attempt to obliterate their opposition, this attempt was ultimately unsuccessful. The tensions that had led to the civil war persisted in the postwar period—despite the dictatorship's continual insistence that Spain was an internally homogeneous community united under Catholicism and conservative values.

In fact, Benet's essay demonstrates a strong opposition to the myopic stance of the Franco dictatorship—reflected in its nation-affirming slogan of "Una, Grande, Libre" (One, Great, Free)—merely by emphasizing the notion of a pluralist Spain. Despite the fact that the regime all but outlawed the very notion of the "Two Spains," Benet's essay in fact uses this phrase specifically twice—once near the beginning and again toward the end.[68] At a certain stage of the war, he writes, each Spain was opposed to the other via a spatial logic—"in a general sense it can be said that the meridian of Madrid came to define the geographic boundary of the 'two Spains': Western Spain embraced the cause of the uprising and Eastern Spain proclaimed itself with the Republic."[69] With the victory of the Nationalists, what had earlier been a strictly spatial division between two opposing camps became much more muddled, indeed. Benet's essay on the war—published only after Franco's death and the end of the regime—is an important attempt by a Spanish writer to once again acknowledge the notion of a specifically Spanish pluralism. *¿Qué fue la guerra civil?* seeks to set the historical record straight, to delineate the opposing camps of Spanish society and point out that they still exist even—and especially—after almost forty years of dictatorship. When placed in their historical context, Benet's novels and essays thus display a keen, if sometimes subtle, awareness of Spain's persisting problems. These run the gamut: from the legacy of inadequate land reform, to the need for an alternative to a narrow Francoist historiography, and most of all to the need to document the devastating effects of the Spanish Civil War.

Consequences: Dictatorship, Landscape, and Benet

"The agrarian question" must be in mind when seeking to understand Spain's postwar years. The decade following the end of the civil war saw both a reduction in the amount of cultivated land and a simultaneous (and necessarily problematic) increase in the population of agricultural laborers. Although there were some relatively ineffective attempts at land reform in Franco's Spain, these remained far from realizing the intentions of the Republican redistribution and collectivization plans that had been annulled by the dictatorship.[70] Indeed, "during the first quarter century of the regime the basic structure of land ownership remained unaltered."[71] This is not at all surprising if one recalls that—as Juan Benet himself noted—the Nationalist uprising from the right had been waged by the military along with the support of the bourgeois segments of Spanish society.[72] In fact, as one scholar has pointed out, "the term Francoism . . . must be understood as an entire system of class domination through which the landowning, the industrialist and the financial sectors exercise direct control of the state apparatus supported by military power."[73] With the socialist and anarchist notions of land reform effectively pushed aside by the Nationalist victory, the growing postwar population of rural Spanish laborers had very little hope of improving their living and working conditions.[74]

The beginning years of the dictatorship were known as the *años del hambre* (years of hunger), and few peasants during those years—whether in the countryside or the cities—were unaffected by problems of food scarcity.[75] This was particularly true of those areas of Spain that had been home to the Republican forces, where many people were viewed by the war's victors and sympathizers with suspicion if not outright contempt.[76] Although the Franco Regime cultivated an almost mythical respect for the life of the countryside—that area of Spain where, in opposition to the urban centers of Madrid and Barcelona, for example, the population had disproportionately embraced the conservative rhetoric of the dictatorship—the first decades of the Regime nonetheless saw mass immigration to the cities, which promised better living conditions.[77] While throughout the 1940s (in both rural and urban areas) there were *guerrillas* who continued to resist the Franco Regime, pressing for social change—whether by centrist Republican, socialist, or anarchist standards—most Spanish citizens settled in and tried to adapt to dictatorial rule rather than be imprisoned or killed outright.[78]

Spain's physical landscape itself was a bleak reminder of the disastrous effects of war. The country lay in ruins, both its major cities and its rural areas. While there is much that may change in forty years, in *¿Qué fue la guerra civil?* Benet pauses during his synopsis of the northern campaign to describe how one town destroyed by the Nationalist advance remained devastated even in 1976: "The ruins of Belchite are still standing, one of the few Spanish landscapes in which the scars of the war are completely preserved; there are not even any insects there; the wind whistles through the holes left by the mortars and a door—hanging by a lone hinge—moans and creaks, ashamed by the presence of a visitor."[79] This digression is of great interest to the reader as it conveys—in the midst of a historical essay—Benet's literary vision and the more poetic qualities of his prose, which can be found also in his descriptions of the landscape of his invented place named Región. Moreover, a similar description appeared in his first novel, *Volverás a Región*. In fact, *¿Qué fue la guerra civil?* boasts many digressions that might be seen as having a more literary tenor—what might be mistaken for a dry historical text is surprisingly full of a respect for irony, mystery, and even humor.[80] This should be seen as a complement to the way in which Benet—in novels such as *Volverás a Región, Saúl ante Samuel,* and *Herrumbrosas lanzas*—"offers long narrative segments on the military strategy of both sides in a way that is indistinguishable from his description of fighting in his history *¿Qué fue la guerra civil?*"[81]

Of course, Benet's characteristic blending of history and fiction—evidenced even and especially in his novels, but also in his essays—must be understood as a particular response to the ideology of the Franco dictatorship.[82] A noted historian has written that Francoism "sought to impose its own view of the nature of the war as a struggle between the barbaric godless hordes of the proletariat and the guardians of traditional Christian values." Within Spain, the result was that, where history was not itself annihilated outright as an academic discipline, it became propaganda.[83] For this reason, the work of Anglophone historians of the Spanish Civil War and the dictatorship that followed—not only Gerald Brenan but also Paul Preston, Gabriel Jackson, and a number of others—has been indispensable for those seeking to understand the war and its effects. Such scholarship is particularly important given the absence of an objective frame of reference among Francoism's official historiographers.[84] The regime's narrow and normative view of history itself and also of its narration—combined with the censorship practices instituted in 1939—meant that Spanish authors could not critique the dictatorship outright.[85] In this context, Benet's approach to literary creation—which was to articulate what one scholar has called "a countervoice to the historiography of the Regime"—is an intriguing one.[86] Regarded by both writers and critics alike as "the spearhead of literary innovation which rejected the tenets of social realism that emerged following the Spanish Civil War," Benet turns away from the articulation of a realist reflection of contemporary Spanish society in his fiction.[87] Even if, as one scholar has written, he "offers scant insight into the rituals of social interaction"—that is, "we know very little of what his characters eat and how they dress," for example—the reader finds that Benet's novels are nonetheless very social, indeed, albeit in a different way.[88] In large part, the social dimensions of his work stem from the "realistic" attention he gives, not to characterization, but to the description of landscape and to the intricacies of civil war.

Landscape (of his fictionalized Región, of course) has a powerful role in Benet's novels that cannot be underestimated. Región's landscape in fact evokes characteristically Spanish problems of the pre- and postwar periods—ranging from inadequate land reform dating back to the Enlightenment to the military campaigns of a not-unfamiliar-sounding civil war, to the destruction left by the war.

The beginning of Benet's first novel, *Volverás a Región,* is devoted to an "exposition of the geographical space of the invented place Benet calls Región—that is, to a rigorous description, tending toward the exhaustive, of its spatial dimensions and properties," an exposition that progresses from "Geography/Geology" to "Climate" to "Effects on Man."[89] Indeed, as one critic has pointed out, "The forbidding landscape of Región makes its presence felt on every page."[90] His initial narration highlights the significance of Región's own "agrarian question" in detail. A lengthy paragraph from the English translation serves to impress upon the reader the importance of the land for Benet, and the resonance of Región's history with that of Spain:

> All the failed attempts at reform in the economy of that land of
> shepherds and rotten boroughs have only served in the end—from
> 1771 to 1836—to exaggerate the poor state of matters concerning
> property, the working force, and rural benefits: the common lands,
> snatched away from a few drowsy communities and put up for
> public auction, were acquired by the same distant and unknown
> potentates who arrived in time to acquire church properties at a
> tempting price. Then the well-known inversion was produced, the

consequence of a law beclouded by the *idée fixe* of the colonization
of uncultivated and amortized lands and the breaking up of large
pasture lands, public or private. The lowlands, the property of the
commune or the church, where in the eighteenth century the people
affected worked and grazed their cattle close to their barns, were
given to the highest bidder, an aristocrat from Castile, Catalonia, or
Estremadura, while the upper pastures, good only for wool-bearing
stock—which were the property of the great lords who controlled
the tableland—were broken up and distributed among the expro-
priated neighbors, with a payment of the monies they had received
in the previous transaction. After fifteen or twenty years of sterile
efforts at feeding a few head of cattle among those brambles or cul-
tivating some rickety rye, bitter, yellow and gritty—responsible for
malnutrition, the degeneration of the race, and the loss of vigor—
the peasant, worn out and ruined, will not hesitate one day to take
advantage of the annual visit of the administrator of the lowland
farms to give him back his mountain property in exchange for being the emphyteuta of an insignificant part of his former property.
So that the law only served—after several years—to convert the former rural smallholder into the tenant farmer of the great lords; and
if it hadn't helped him progress before, what will it be now that he
must share his income with a landowner, who, at the slightest delay
in payment, rescinds the contract?[91]

The invented land of Región is—just as was Spain itself—subject to the
same insufficient and exploitative land reforms that scholars of the Spanish Civil War have underscored as its very cause. Benet's novels are also
equally attentive to the long history of divisiveness that led to the war, at
times describing the origins of the conflict in the nineteenth century, much
as has Gerald Brenan's *The Spanish Labyrinth*.[92]

Read in light of *¿Qué fue la guerra civil?* Región's civil war is a thinly
veiled representation of the Spanish Civil War. This premise is even voiced
directly by the narrator of the first section of *Volverás a Región,* who calls
the war "a paradigm on a lesser scale . . . than peninsular-wide events."[93]
While Región is an invented, novelistic place—certainly akin to invented
Yoknapatawpha County (the invented place of William Faulkner) or Macondo (Columbian Nobel Prize–winning author Gabriel García Márquez's
own invented land)—the English-language reader should understand that
a great deal of the proper nouns and dates circulating in Benet's text draw
their primary meaning from Spain's history. Prominent examples of these
correspondences include phrases such as the "Civil Guard," the "Second

Republic"; the dates in which major battles of the war occur in 1937 and 1938; real-world abbreviations such as "CEDA" and "CTV," and of course real places such as Madrid and Valencia.[94] Around these names and dates of primarily historical importance, Benet constructs a fictional realm that nonetheless continues to parallel the "peninsular-wide" events of the historical civil war on the Spanish Peninsula.[95] In Benet's novels, after a Nationalist uprising—which occurs, unsurprisingly, as did its historical referent, during July of 1936—Región becomes a "remote pocket of resistance" defined by an "unyielding commitment to the Republican cause."[96] Whereas military strategy is a topic of *Volverás a Región* as well, what predominates in that first novel are the effects of the battles fought in Región, and the reader must turn to later works such as *Saúl ante Samuel*—and of course the *Herrumbrosas lanzas* series—for more detailed discussions of the "military strategy involved in the struggle." Therein, as one critic has written, "Benet details the battle plans of the Republican and Nationalist armies as if writing a military manual."[97]

The way the war unfolds in Región presents many commonalities with events from Spanish history. But these historical events are given a fictional ground to the degree that Benet situates the war within the unique (semi-) fictional geography of Región. In *Volverás a Región,* the contrast between neighboring Macerta and the titular Región represents the very notion of the "Two Spains" embraced by Benet explicitly in his essay on the Spanish Civil War. While Macerta is controlled by Nationalists, Región is home to a few prominent liberal families and supports the Republic. This is not due to any sort of revolutionary ideology, as explained in the first section of *Volverás a Región,* where the narrator explores

> a Región, surrounded by silent mountains and small settlements, inhabited by a collectivity that was homogeneous in poverty and lacking a proletariat, which had emigrated ten years before the last barracks-headquarters of the civil guard was closed, and where the most timid attempt at collectivization is considered madness, anti- clericalism will never go beyond a few jokes, trade unionism is a pretension, and anarchy a respect for tradition. . . . It's not that the people of Región had lost interest in politics; in reality they had thought very little about them and even the joyful outcry of April 14th was largely modified because in the whole town there wasn't a single flag to be dyed purple, nor did it enter anyone's head to climb up to the balcony of the town hall—which without a doubt was in a state of ruin and would have collapsed, dying the day with

mourning—to wave it. Politics—or rather the expression of republican joy and merrymaking—took place in a big old car that Eugenio Mazón had acquired, no one knew how.[98]

Seemingly unmotivated by a revolutionary politics, Región supports the Republic nonetheless. While the specific political stance of its inhabitants remains somewhat undefined, its inhabitants hold "a certain tacit popular consensus" supporting "the union of democratic forces, an antifascist line, [and] a return to statism."[99] One Nationalist and one Republican, Macerta and Región are bitter enemies whose social distance is reflected in their geographical separation by a sierra.[100]

The military campaigns of the civil war in Región are an important part of many of Benet's novels, and once again his fiction recalls his description and analysis of the war in *¿Qué fue la guerra civil?*. Even with its characteristically scant resources, the Región Defense Committee at the center of many of his novels is still able to mount offensives against the Nationalists.[101] The *Herrumbrosas lanzas* series, in fact, is "centered around the meetings of the fourteen members of the Republican Committee for the Defense of Región on 8 and 15 February [1938]."[102] Región's offensives against the Nationalists—discussed both in *Volverás a Región* and *Herrumbrosas lanzas,* for example—bear notable resemblances to the Battle of the Ebro in *¿Qué fue la guerra civil?*.[103]

More important still, the Nationalist motivation for the war provides another point of contact between Benet's fiction and *¿Qué fue la guerra civil?*. This is the fundamental basis for comparing Benet's novels and his essay. Just as in *¿Qué fue la guerra civil?*, *Volverás a Región* highlights the Nationalist propensity for waging war via "battles of attrition, in frontal attacks which wear out cadres . . . in long campaigns of useless attrition with the sole object of prolonging to its bitter end a completed war with an establishment of victors who are too numerous."[104] Moreover, the Nationalists of Benet's novels are—just like their historical counterparts—allied with the bourgeois segments of Spanish society.[105] *Volverás a Región* thus emphasizes the "desire for the final liquidation" of the enemies of conservative Spain, noting that "the whole campaign of 1938 could have been resolved with greater economy and in a shorter time with a single attack launched against Región. [The Nationalists] would have—inevitably— taken the place in a few days and—with a show of strength, energy and resolve—placed all the republicans in a situation where they would have had to lay down their arms."[106] Holding true to the notion that events in Región reflect—at a smaller scale—the "peninsular-wide" events of the

Spanish Civil War, the narration of *Volverás a Región* in fact attributes the very same qualities to (fictional) Colonel (later General) Gamallo that Benet's later essay would use in describing the Nationalist forces as a whole. One critic points to the "vile egotism," and the "personal animosity of Colonel Gamallo, who fights for no ideal" underscoring that he "inordinately prolongs his campaign against Región"—qualities that remind the reader of Benet's conclusions. In his fiction, just as in his historical essay, the Spanish Civil War was ultimately an extended war of attrition whose goal was not strategic victory but instead the utter annihilation of the Republican forces. In both cases, Benet regards this conflict as, in the end, "unintelligible," precisely because it was motivated—in Región just as in Spain itself—by "silent impulses—like avarice, incompetence, ambition, and the lack of courage."[107]

One of Benet's most important assertions, whether in his essay or his novels, is that the Spanish Civil War should be judged by its effects—social division, devastation, and of course death. These effects are most consistently symbolized in the author's depiction of Región's landscape. *Volverás a Región* makes clear the intimate relationship between Benet's literary production and his historical take on the Spanish conflict: "Región was left deserted; deserted it will always be, eaten by the leprosy of the bullet marks, roofs full of holes, and sewers open, the wind that swirls and whispers through the openings, the torn drapes, the doors that squeak on their hinges and beat against their frames, incapable of being closed on an age of shame and stupor, sunken in dust and surrounded—like the Nineveh of Jonah—by fire, ash, and flintstone, the woe-begotten emblem of that fratricidal will.[108] In this passage in particular, the novel's description of Región recalls—right down to the whistling wind, holes left by arms fire, squeaky doors, and even feelings of shame—Benet's remarks on the desolate town of Belchite in his essay *¿Qué fue la guerra civil?*.[109] Benet's depiction of the devastation left by the war in his fiction has prompted some scholars to identify an "anti-regime ideology" that "tends to see the war in terms of its effects" The idea is that under the dictatorship—after a certain period of time had passed, of course—the literary quality of novels concerning the war got better precisely because "peninsular fiction began to work out the disastrous effects that the war and its outcome had for all cultural activity in Spain."[110] As one critic has pointed out, "If we read *Volverás a Región* in the double context of Francoist historiography and Benet's theoretical ideas on history, the novel becomes not merely a tale about the mysterious life of Región, but also a vehicle of dissidence that subverts the discursive and historiographic practices of the State."[111] This much has been established by previous criticism—but Juan Benet's fiction is notable not merely for its connection with and reflection upon Spain's history, but also for the interdisciplinary connections its makes possible. These include encounters with civil engineering, Bergsonian philosophy, and cultural geography and spatial theory, all of which have at their base Benet's persistent respect for enigma.

Chapter 2

The Civil Engineer and the Author

Hydraulic Works, Water, and Literature

> Like every art, one had to learn [civil engineering] in the workshop—
> the same as with painting, sculpture or décor—, with daily practice,
> committing errors of all kinds day after day and, above all, having to face
> one's own mistakes. Classroom lessons and the norms and criteria found in
> books served very little; on-the-job experience, due to its individualized and
> instantaneous nature, was more important than any theoretical dictum—
> and only thanks to the resources of imagination and the rules of a reason
> accustomed to think in scientific terms can one acquire an art that in those
> days required in any case much in the way of improvisation.
>
> > Juan Benet, "Ingeniería e intimidad" (Engineering and Intimacy)

Juan Benet was a creative giant who excelled not merely in one but in
two challenging fields. Appropriately, several contributions to the homage
published in the *Revista de Obras Públicas* (Journal of Public Works) in
1994—a year after his death—recognize that Benet in fact straddled two
worlds. One contributor points out that "Juan Benet was both an engineer
and a writer, or if one prefers, a writer and an engineer. It would be difficult
to say which word should come first"; Benet "cultivated his activity or 'his
profession' as a writer and an engineer in equal parts and consistently, and
he not only loved them both equally, but moreover he never renounced
either one of them in order to dedicate himself exclusively to the other."[1]
Others go much further, pointing to the primacy of his engineering work
over his literary production: "[Benet] always professed to be an engineer
who wrote, and I never once heard him invert the order of these words";
"Juan Benet was a civil engineer first and a writer second."[2] It is not that
literary critics have been unaware of Benet's first chosen profession, but
rather that its mention has seldom warranted more than a casual reference
outside of the above remarks—which were made late, after all, and in a

journal devoted to engineering at that.[3] It is significant, in this regard, that as recently as 2009 a volume of Juan Benet's written work on topics related to hydraulic engineering has been edited by the Colegio de Ingenieros de Caminos, Canales y Puertos. This posthumous anthology, appropriately titled *Si yo fuera presidente* (If I Were President), documents Benet's ability to think about hydraulic issues from a perspective that is at once that of the historian, the engineer, and the humanist.[4] To reconcile Benet the engineer with Benet the author, I would emphasize the importance of his civil engineering work—as worthy of attention in its own right and, more significant, as a fundamental part of any attempt to understand his fiction. This is an aspect of his life and work that—while never before discussed in relationship with his literary production—is fundamental if we are to understand Juan Benet as a writer.

Juan Benet, Civil Engineer

It would be shortsighted at best to attempt to understand Juan Benet's literary production without taking his civil engineering work and perspective into account. It is significant that Benet's literary production and his engineering output developed more or less in parallel. That is: after graduating from the Escuela de Ingenieros de Caminos, Canales y Puertos in 1954, he soon began his career as a working civil engineer, signing on with the firm MZOV (Compañía de Ferrocarriles de Medina de Campo a Zamora y de Orense a Vigo) in 1956.[5] From 1956 to 1959, Benet lived in Ponferrada, working on the canals of Queroño and Cornatel; from 1959 to 1961, in Oviedo, working on the line from Lugo de Llanera to Villabona; and from 1961 to 1965, in León, on the Porma reservoir dam—returning to Madrid only in 1966.[6] Also during this same period, he wrote and published the book of stories *Nunca llegarás a nada* (1961), demonstrating important themes and archetypes of his later novels; he composed *Volverás a Región* between 1962 and 1964, although it would not find a publisher until 1967; he penned the book of essays *La inspiración y el estilo,* which appeared in print in 1966; and, as early as 1965, he even began work on his second novel, *Una meditación,* which would win the Biblioteca Breve Prize in 1969.[7]

In fact, Benet continued writing fiction and literary essays throughout the rest of his thirty-five years working with MZOV (later MVOZ Cubiertas).[8] As his reputation in literary circles grew, his standing in the field of his first chosen profession also solidified. This engineering success eventually allowed him to form his own consulting company—the Compañía Hidrocinética Regional—in 1987.[9] Also during the late 1980s he received the highest honor awarded by the Colegio de Ingenieros de Caminos—"Colegiado de Honor" (Member of Honor), giving a speech on that occasion that was published in the School's *Revista de Obras Públicas.*[10] Juan Benet's legacy thus necessarily includes not merely his literary works but also the physical constructions he helped design and build, the essays he wrote on topics germane to civil engineering, and—as he himself noted with some humor in 1989—the some forty pages a week he wrote about concrete as part of his job.[11] Many of the civil engineering essays he published are of potential interest to literary scholars familiar with (or seeking to become familiar with) his novels and are, in addition, quite accessible as well. These include "Ingeniería e intimidad," "Ingeniería y conducta social" (Engineering and Social Conduct), "Política hidráulica" (Hydraulic Politics), and "Hidráulica moderna y regadío antiguo" (Modern Hydraulics and Ancient Irrigation), just to name a handful. Others, of course, are more technical or perhaps of lesser relevance given the present circumstances, but may nonetheless lead to new and interesting future work by Benetian scholars.[12] The reader should note too, that references to engineering appear also in Benet's non-engineering essays.[13]

Apart from his early work on a diverse range of civil projects, most of Benet's career was devoted to works of hydraulic engineering, above all else dams. His major projects included not only the Porma dam—which was posthumously named in his honor—but also civil works at Atazar, Bujeda, Calandra, Eirós, Fervenza, Llauset, Moralets, Rialp, Santa Eugenia, Tajo-Segura, Vegamián, Vellón, and Villalcampo.[14] Bridges, too, held a special meaning for Benet, even if he seldom worked on them professionally.[15] A well-circulated story about Benet notes that he was filled with the desire to become an engineer while visiting the Portuguese city of Oporto—where he caught a glimpse of the Ponte Maria Pia, a bridge designed by the company of famed engineer and constructor Gustav Eiffel.[16] For Benet, devotion to many large-scale professional projects centered on water was not merely a requirement of his job. One can find a similar fondness for water manifested, also, on a smaller scale: in seemingly coincidental details of his life, just as in his everyday behaviors. For example, in Madrid, he chose to live on a street named Pisuerga—which is, it should be noted, the name of one of the Duero River's major tributaries.[17] In addition, poet Blanca Andreu (his second wife) notes that whenever they crossed a river together he would always greet it aloud by its name, "saying, for example, 'Salve, padre Duero.'"[18] Benet's friend, Spanish writer Javier Marías, remembers that "there was nothing he liked more, when he was traveling, than to bathe in unfamiliar rivers."[19] In fact, Juan Benet had always been fascinated by water and by rivers, and civil (hydraulic) engineering provided a wonderful way for him to stay connected to them.[20]

Since one of the prerequisites for his civil engineering work was his having attended the Colegio de Ingenieros de Caminos, Canales y Puertos in Madrid (between 1948 and 1954), it is not surprising that Benet came to embody the colegio's values. One critic has reflected recently on those values in an essay that focuses on the first half-century of the school's existence (from its formation in 1853 through 1899), as read through its widely respected *Revista de Obras Públicas*.[21] Within nineteenth-century Spanish society, engineers came from accommodated families, embodied liberal traditions, and referred to themselves as "children of progress and civilization."[22] As such—and given the fact that they went on to hold government posts after graduation—they were not without their own influence in political and, through their journal, more public matters.[23] Their liberal principles—although somewhat divorced from the world of day-to-day politics—stressed the importance of generalized liberal ideals through discussions of "progress, backwardness and civilization," even though individual engineers might have often disagreed in concrete matters.[24] The historical character of the Colegio de Ingenieros had not changed all that much by Benet's time. Even under the Franco dictatorship's narrow educational policies, the engineering school enjoyed a privileged status, much as before. As Benet wrote, the school itself pertained not to the Ministry of Education but rather the Ministry of Public Works, and accordingly it "was better equipped, run and supplied than any of those centers that depended on the Ministry of Education."[25] Graduates still found employment in government posts, which for Benet meant that his "only options" were either to work in "a project office, or work in the provinces."[26] He opted for the latter, of course, and consistently saw his work in terms that resonate with the nineteenth-century liberal tradition of engineering as a social force pushing for progress and the betterment of civilization.

As Benet makes clear in his engineering essays, he regards water as an important natural resource to which every Spaniard should have access. In "Política hidráulica" he writes: "One should not mince words when it comes to water, it is perhaps the first natural resource that, due to demographic growth and industrial development, must be subjected to a complete and total planning."[27] In "Ingeniería e intimidad" he begins with some remarks on the nineteenth-century history of engineering, but soon launches into its moral dimensions. Benet might as well have been describing himself when he wrote that the professional image engineers enjoyed came with "a certain morality; immersed in the currents of the march of modern times, when he did not constitute the motor and agent of progress, the engineer was imbued with a certain neutrality in the social struggle; he was not very contaminated by politics, he would disdain established interests and impugn the retrograde passivity of those who would not embrace change, but neither would he throw himself into the void of revolutionary ideas. His task was to move progress forward little by little, in agreement with the physical and mechanical laws at the heart of his conception of the world."[28] Benet's own worldview was perhaps very similar. Although he found much to critique, indeed, regarding the Franco dictatorship, he nonetheless also held to the relative neutrality that characterized the lives of nineteenth-century engineers. Within the parameters of that relative neutrality, of course, he could be quite opinionated regarding the current state and future directions of the field.

Benet's perspective on civil engineering itself might be understood as a dissenting opinion of sorts, as—at times—it ran against the grain of widely accepted views of the field held both by members of the wider Spanish society and even by his fellow engineers. In fact, while some of Benet's engineering essays took on historical themes—and still others dealt with technical specifications—there were also those that focused explicitly on the practice of civil engineering itself.[29] Benet saw engineering as an art akin to painting, sculpture, and décor, and not merely as a technical science. Much as with an art, Benet writes, there is no way to learn it other than on-the-job practice. He notes that, while in the Madrid School, students "mastered the 'what,' 'why' and the 'in order that'" of engineering, and "one had to learn how to build things on site, from those with more experience."[30] At the same time that Benet frames engineering as an art, he rails against the lack of imagination and overt technicalism that have come to dominate the field.

> The aristocratic pretensions of engineering have largely been eradicated and not because there are now some 6,000 engineers as opposed to the 600 that existed a half-century ago; not because changing attitudes have done away with their privileges just as has happened to every other caste; not because their activity is now subject to the court of public opinion just as are the activities of any other citizen; *not because the banality and lack of imagination of a few have destroyed the mystery that previously enveloped the profession;* they have been brought down because with progress [engineering] has been reduced to what it always was: *a mediating activity, which rarely pursues its own ends.*[31]

The above passage is instructive in two respects. First, it demonstrates Benet's insistence that engineering, as an art, requires a certain imaginative spark. This is, notably, an attitude that Benet also employs in his book of essays, *La inspiración y el estilo,* where he meditates on the importance of style, inspiration, and even enigma for the creative (literary) process. Yet just as the creation of fiction relies on enigmatic processes which are poorly understood by rational means, even engineering is grounded in the mysterious realm of imagination.

In another essay, "Ingeniería y conducta social," Benet makes this point more clearly, comparing and contrasting the notions of the technician and the engineer. Although in many respects the two are similar, he writes, "in their origin they are two different arts that each correspond to a distinct etymology. While the Greek word *tejné* refers in substance to an established art, that presumes a tradition and rules, and occupies a place in society that is known, fixed and without a doubt fundamental, the Latin root *genô* has a primary meaning that refers to the action of engendering, to produce something new, to cause." From this Latin root, Benet continues—a root underlying the Spanish word *ingeniero* (engineer)—come the notions of invention and ingenuity.[32] As Spanish intellectual and friend Félix de Azúa was to write, reflecting upon Benet's death, "He wouldn't permit the ever greater hypertechnicality or dependence of experts far removed in ever more specialized aspects [of engineering] to lessen his responsibility; he wanted to conserve intact the qualities of a worthy and admirable tradition."[33]

The second thing to note about the extended passage from "Ingeniería e intimidad" (through Benet's original italics) is that engineering must be understood as a necessarily social activity that has unfolded within Spain's unique historical context. In another essay, also published in the *Revista de Obras Públicas,* Benet wrote that water and irrigation works were a primary and historical strength of Spain. In that essay, he links the country's remote past and its present potential: "For me it is beyond question that the long tradition of water and irrigation works in our country—a tradition that goes back to the times of the Roman and Muslim dominations—is largely responsible for habits that, in general, [today] characterize its approach and execution."[34] Throughout his career as a working civil engineer, Benet tirelessly suggested ideas for how Spain might better conserve and transmit its water resources to inhabitants living in the far reaches of the country. Those ideas he elaborated, of course, also have their own history, and stem largely from the hydraulic politics of those figures Benet regarded as forefathers: Joaquín Costa, Manuel Lorenzo Pardo, and Indalecio Prieto. Joaquín Costa (1846–1911) was a prominent intellectual, politician, lawyer, and writer who pushed a regenerationist program for Spain as it entered the twentieth century; Manuel Lorenzo Pardo (1881–1953), a civil engineer who became director of hydraulic works under the Primo de Rivera dictatorship (1923–30) and continued in that role under the Second

Republic (1931–36); and Indalecio Prieto (1883–1962), a socialist politician who was named minister of public works under the Second Republic.[35]

Hydraulic Engineering in Spain

It has been said that, while the first half of Spain's nineteenth century saw the growth of the country's network of roads and the second half may be seen as the era of railways, the first part of the twentieth century was devoted to hydraulic works.[36] This notion is confirmed merely by looking at the Spanish society into which Juan Benet was born in 1927. Manuel Lorenzo Pardo—at that time director of hydraulic works—had already been appointed by Dictator Primo de Rivera to oversee a massive program of irrigation and dam construction—a program which was responsible for completing numerous dams on sections of the Ebro River between 1926 and 1930.[37] Later, under the Second Republic, Indalecio Prieto—minister of public works—reappointed Lorenzo Pardo, who of course continued those programs.[38] As a noted historian relates, "Prieto believed irrigation would be a more effective answer to the land problem of Spain than the expropriation of the existing estates, because it could be done without additional social conflict and because much of the land tied up in great estates was too dry to be successfully farmed by small holders."[39] As this quotation suggests, the liberal—essentially democratic—principles underlying Benet's expansive treatment of the water problem in Spain might also be understood as a way of addressing the country's fundamental agrarian problem—albeit in modified form. Noted historian Pierre Vilar, in fact, writes that the irrigation policy touted by Benet's model Joaquín Costa was "real socialism, in effect."[40] In this light, Benet's ideas on hydraulics, which "squared with the regenerationism of Joaquín Costa or Manuel Lorenzo Pardo," reflected—if not a generalized socialist premise—then at least a democratic vision for improving the lives of those same peasants and tenant farmers who had historically suffered from Spanish historical neglect of the agrarian question.[41]

Although the "democratic" spirit of water reform in Spain during the Primo de Rivera dictatorship and the Republic quickly lost its force, according to the essential work *Las obras hidráulicas en España* (Hydraulic Works in Spain)—written by Manuel Díaz-Marta Pinilla—it was as early as 1926 when Spain saw a "luminous idea" take shape.[42] The prologue to the original 1969 edition of that book made clear that the idea for the creation of a Hydraulic Confederation in Spain was based not on regional borders, nor even on bureaucratic machinations, but rather on existing water-basin resources on the Spanish peninsula: "In theory—I repeat—the intent was to institute an organization that was democratic, dynamic and effective. It is exactly what is being demanded in the name of democracy the world over."[43] One of the great ironies is that this sort of "democratic" hydraulic improvement work was in fact funded by a Francoist state that, during the Spanish Civil War, had fought against socialist and collectivist approaches to resolving the agrarian question—but of course Francoism did not fund these water projects *well*.[44] State funding of hydraulic works had only grown with Spain's passing from the Primo de Rivera dictatorship to the Second Republic, but under Franco, "The percentage of the national budget devoted to public works declined from 14.04 under the Republic to 7.74 during the first postwar years."[45] Nor were the water projects that the Franco dictatorship funded even original, as Benet himself explains. While some writers have criticized the Francoist state's construction of dams as being unnecessary and pharaonic, in 1992 Benet disagreed, seeing them not as a self-aggrandizing practice of the dictatorship, but rather as a neglected but continuing practice inherited from prior Spanish governments. As he asserted in an interview: "That's not how it is. . . . The first rigorous and technical plan for hydraulic works was made by the Republic under Minister of Public Works Indalecio Prieto. And that is the plan, its names and origins stripped away, that the Franco Regime would use over the course of twenty-five years."[46]

In fact, Benet wrote a brief essay titled "Prólogo al Plan Nacional de Obras Hidráulicas 1933" (Prologue to the National Plan of Hydraulic Works 1933)—originally appearing as the prologue to a revised edition overseen by Benet himself and reprinted in the recent 2009 anthology *Si yo fuera presidente*—in which he explores the 1933 plan developed during the Second Republic under both Prieto and Lorenzo Pardo.[47] The essay discusses the plan in detail, noting that it is an obligatory reference for hydraulic professionals of all specialties, whether in administrative (governmental) contexts or private industry.[48] Despite the plan's historical importance and more contemporary relevance, argues Benet, it has been traditionally overlooked during the dictatorship years given its association with the politics of Republican Spain.[49] The "new [postwar] state," he writes, for all intents and purposes scratched Lorenzo Pardo's work from the record, having appropriated his ideas as its own.[50] This is not surprising, given that—as Benet points out—in its day, the plan was suggested in the context of collectivizing land reforms that elicited strong reactions from the Spanish political right.[51]

In turn, of course, the Republic's water plans had been based on previous improvements carried out or at least inspired by Benet's forefather, Joaquín Costa. If in Costa's own words, hydraulic politics was "a sublimated expression of 'agrarian politics,'" then Benet's return to his forefather's basic premise and rhetoric must be read through the same lens.[52]

Benet's 1984 essay "Política hidráulica"—whose very title reflects its author's admiration for Joaquín Costa's (water) regenerationism—goes on to refer to Costa specifically in order to provide a two-stage model that is instructive for understanding Spain's hydraulic progress from the late nineteenth century to the late twentieth.

"The hydraulic politics carried out in Spain since the times of Costa is based on a Water Law dating from 1879 that established the basic principles for the rational use of water thanks in essence to the declaration of natural currents as constituting a public good of the state. Over the course of a century of its application, that law has permitted the state, among other things, to regulate forty thousand cubic hectometers per year, four times the natural capacity that the territory offers its inhabitants for consumption; to create the Hydrographic Confederations; to raise more than seven hundred dams; to palliate to a great degree the ravages of droughts and floods and increase irrigation over almost three million hectares."[53]

While this was substantial and needed improvement, writes Benet, over a century later the 1879 Water Law had run its course, and further improvement would only be possible with the passing of a new Water Law that might provide legal backing for "our country's second hydraulic development."[54] In fact, a new Spanish Water Law was passed in 1985 (and subsequently amended in 1999)—a law on which Benet commented in writing during its draft stage.[55]

Benet's admiration for Costa manifested itself, also, when he directed a book series, Ciencias, Humanidades e Ingeniería (Science, Humanities and Engineering)—published by the Colegio de Ingenieros in Madrid.[56] It should not be overlooked that Benet chose to republish Costa's *La política hidráulica* (1911) as the very first book in that series.[57] He admired that Costa had "dreamt of a country transformed from end to end by planning, with its mountains bored through, enclosed in a mesh of waterways capable of delivering, to any point whatsoever, the common good that 'without charge' is produced in any other point blessed with its overabundance."[58] In the first chapter of his influential early twentieth-century work, Costa had explicitly identified his own thesis in this way: "The fundamental condition for agricultural and social progress in Spain lies in the deliveries and deposits of running and fluvial waters. Those deliveries must be the work of the nation, and the agricultural Congress must address the Parliament and the Government demanding them urgently as the supreme necessity of Spanish agriculture."[59] Benet saw the series that included the reprint of Costa's work as an opportunity to republish texts that were "of a cultural and humanistic character whose topics might be only indirectly related" to professional engineering activity.[60]

To a large degree, Benet's views reactualize the spirit of Costa's critique and continue to underscore the need for extensive water planning in his own Spanish society.[61] One of Benet's contemporaries—Julio Llamazares, also a noted Spanish author—reflected on the hydraulic engineer's vision for resolving Spain's water issues in terms that recall the words with which Juan had described Costa's dream. In the short newspaper piece titled "El sueño de Juan Benet" (Juan Benet's Dream), Llamazares writes of Benet's "idealized vision of a country that he imagined would be different if, as he advised, it could be irrigated completely, linking its rivers, carrying the excess water from the rainy northern regions of the peninsula to the driest parts of the south and east."[62] As with Costa's plan—and the later practices of the Republic and even the remnants of these practices kept alive during the dictatorship—Benet's meditations on hydraulic improvements for Spain were totalizing, perhaps utopian, but certainly egalitarian and essentially democratic in spirit.

While Benet's water goals took into account the entire Spanish population, however, his methods were nonetheless sometimes critiqued for being in line with that same elitist tradition from which he attempted to distance himself. In one instance he even confessed to having held a frustrated desire to be a "hydraulic tyrant," working for the good of all but, according to at least one critic, without accepting or even desiring the input of Spanish citizens.[63] Benet's own brief essay "Si yo fuera presidente" (If I Were President), included in the recently published eponymous anthology, frames his desire to lead in a much more democratic light, writing that, if he were president, "During the first five years—a period of time seen as necessary by experts in order to draft a detailed Plan of Hydraulic Works, of national reach—I would consider the diversity of matters that today affect public opinion, never failing to have different results; some of which are positive, others decidedly disappointing; but in the beginning of the sixth year—and until the end of my presidency—this Plan would be initiated, as a consequence of which not even one single drop of rainfall in Spanish territory would go to waste, except for those sent by nature with catastrophic intention."[64] The gentleman of Pisuerga Street persistently framed his thoughts on public water works in explicitly political terms. In "Política hidráulica" he remarks on how the struggle over water has changed little since the beginning of the twentieth century. Therein he specifies that "today, as in Costa's time, the three families that determine or make hydraulic politics possible (three autonomous and independent families that are nonetheless connected . . .) are: technology, nature and politics."[65]

In the short essay "Hidráulica moderna y regadío antiguo" (1989), Benet concisely points to current uses of technology as constituting, in fact, an obstacle to further modernization. The essay begins with the sentence, "My grandfather's land was cultivated by hand," and he goes on to describe the traditional methods of irrigation and watering employed there.[66] This is, for Benet, an archetypical method of farming; and he writes of how "that [previous] culture was sustained by two sources . . . , the effort of human muscle—guided by a technique elaborated over the course of centuries—and the abundance of water. The former has been completely displaced by a number of activities all relegating the energetic component of work to machines, while the latter constitutes, paradoxically, the greatest obstacle for the modernization of culture and the abandonment of its traditional methods." In fact, he continues, "the scarcity of water has been, universally, the spur for the technification of irrigation with the goal of bringing each plant only that quantity and quality of water that it needs."[67] By this he means that, while in the second half of Spain's twentieth century technology has managed to take over the labor process itself, it has done so without an accompanying large-scale recalibration of Spain's natural water resources.

The result of this neglect, of course, as Benet explains, is that water remains abundant where it has been readily available (subsequently being overused through imprecise technology), and scarce where it has been in short supply. Benet concludes by advocating for the better management and regulation of Spain's water resources, and by stressing yet again the importance of *trasvases* as a way of distributing water to areas in which it has been traditionally lacking. This is a position he sustained over many years, as can be verified by going back to a 1984 interview in which Benet insisted, "The Spanish northwest must provide water for the rest of Spain, that is, in this country it is necessary to regulate water."[68] Likewise, near the end of his brief 1981 lecture titled "El agua en Región" Benet asserted, "For me there is no doubt that there will come a day—although it may be impossible to fix it on the calendar—when the Spanish people will celebrate New Year's Eve with grapes from [the southern region of] Almería, grown with water from the northwest."[69]

In 1992—a year before his death—Benet affirmed the intimate relationship between politics and water rights in writing one last time, making the prediction that "water will be the cause of political struggles of the first magnitude, given that there are zones where it is found in excess and others that are deficient in it. Spain will undoubtedly see conflicts arise, as long as the country still has not learned that water has no owner, that it is a public good, that one cannot talk of an Aragonian water, a Cantabrian water, or an Andalusian water. . . ."[70] Similarly, he writes elsewhere of how, if he were president, "Water would cease to be labeled with local, regional or autonomic ownerships."[71] The relatively recent conflicts that have arisen over water rights in Spain after Benet's death, centering on the National Hydraulic Plan, are thus somewhat unsurprising from a Benetian perspective.[72]

Engineering-Literary Connections

If Benet's civil engineering work was his first profession, then it was no less entertaining for him than was his literary work. Blanca Andreu has remarked that "in fact, engineering and hydraulics, when he was having fun and relaxing, would serve him as stimulation and entertain him in an indisputably literary way."[73] Inversely, if literary creativity was his "hobby"— for lack of a better term—Benet was no less serious about it. Not only was he serious about literature, but he was also serious about those aspects of civil engineering that found their way into literary texts—whether his own or those of others. There is one lengthy but worthwhile anecdote from Benet's friendship with contemporary Spanish writer Javier Marías that best captures this seriousness. In the "Acto de Homenaje a Juan Benet," published in 1994, Marías shares a conversation the two had during a dinner regarding one of his own published novels:

> I also remember above all else an occasion—I bring it up because there is something of an engineer's touch to it—in which during an entire dinner [Benet] torturously held me in suspense over the issue of how to tell me with the most flair that he had enjoyed one of my novels. And on that occasion—on which I remember that Blanca Andreu was present, as well as another friend—he began by telling me "Well then, this novel, yes, it is fine, what's happened is that you've committed a tremendous, truly unpardonable error in this book and, you see, well the book isn't what it might have been." I became terrified, because when someone is your mentor and you take his opinion as the most important response to the appearance of your new book, well, you take in every word; and I began to think that he was going to raise an objection to its structure, or its very conception, that he was going to tell me that its style was horrendous, and he said: "There is a serious problem because there is a moment when you talk about a railway bridge"—and that was the only thing he had written down on the note he had in front of him—"a railway bridge, and you go on to describe it in the following way: 'The wide river of blue waters, broken by the long bridge of diagonally crossed iron'"; he said, "and of course, that cannot be, because, how could you not have realized that this bridge is," and I am very sorry, I don't remember exactly what he said, but he

said something that was completely incomprehensible to me, let's say that he said that the bridge was a bridge of policated beams of blecarian misipication, "And of course if you had said that it was a bridge of policated beams of blecarian misipication, well, then the novel would have been quite different, how great indeed would your novel have been if you had said this."[74]

Of course the funny-sounding nonsense phrase used by Marías to describe the bridge in this anecdote—which, in the original Spanish, reads *un puente de vigas pudeladas de mispiquel a leberquisa*—is not only significant because it pokes fun at the technical engineering vocabulary Benet often employed in a friendly way, but also because it points to the absolute solemnity with which Benet approached literature, civil engineering, and even the intersection of the two.[75] If Benet's fiction consistently references rivers, bridges, dams, and the like, the reader can bet that he has thought quite a bit about their description if not also about their role in the work.[76]

Railroads, another area under the purview of civil engineers (and of course Benet worked on extending rail lines in his early days), appear also in his essays and fiction. In *Herrumbrosas lanzas,* for example, a section of the third book of the first volume (referred to in the table of contents as "Don Tertuliano Herencia and his love of the railroad") devotes a number of pages to the station in Macerta that was at that time the end of the railroad line.[77] Benet's essay *¿Qué fue la guerra civil?* also makes it clear that engineers were a relatively routine part of war operations, and the battle of the Ebro specifically. Therein he mentions "sections of engineers charged with constructing pontoons and bridges (a couple of them were submergible) in order to cross the river and the construction of trenches," railroad construction during the war, and also Goicoechea—an engineer who worked with general Mola of the Nationalist side during the historical conflict.[78] But, in the end, both bridges and rivers are particularly important in Benet's work in that they also become a way of reinforcing the dualistic nature of the struggle between the Nationalists and the Republicans in Región.

One scholarly essay that, in part, reconciles Benet's hydraulic engineering and his fiction also points to the word *río* (river) as the etymological root of the word *rivales* (rivals)—an observation that is quite pertinent to Benet's literary development of the notion of the "Two Spains."[79] Rivers and bridges work as important parts of the narration and evocation of Región, but also as metaphors for the Benetian theme of a Spain divided against itself.[80] The Lerna and the Torce rivers—located in the (Nationalist territory of) Macerta and the (Republican stronghold of) Región, respectively—are a frequent point of pause for Benet in his fiction and come to reflect the sociopolitical "duality" he establishes as early as *Volverás a Región*.[81] These rivers routinely become points of reference for buildings and other landmarks in his novels, as would be expected, but they also receive their own extended attention by the narration.[82] *Volverás a Región,* from the outset, emphasizes the topological characteristics of an area formed by "two parallel valleys" each shaped by a river, and the map included with the first 1983 edition of *Herrumbrosas lanzas* allows the viewer to see concretely (in cartographic representation, of course) how each river valley has been carved out of the larger area's topography.[83]

In his "Breve noticia sobre los ríos españoles" (A Brief Review of Spanish Rivers)—included in both Spanish and English translation as part of the book *El agua en España*—Benet attributes a certain mystery to the connection between human societies and water that is also relevant to his novels. Reflecting on "the great civilizations of antiquity," which derived their stability from the rivers that were central to their agricultural progress, he writes:

> One may think that a farming people living in a climate of perpetually cloudless days and nights would have a markedly different concept of water from one which has always derived the latter from rainfall. It is plausible that the former—who are hardly aware of the nature of rain, do not depend on it for their irrigation and have no reason to associate it with the water flowing down their rivers and waterways—would not see anything divine or mysterious in water, nothing that had not always been related to the earth they tread, regarding it as just another element, like the earth, clay or rock, or the land they live on. This is not, however, the case, since for these people it is sufficient for them to raise their eyes towards their farmlands and then scan the desertified hills and mountain ranges bounding their valley to understand that where there is no water there is no life.[84]

It is easy to make the connection between Benet's description, here, of the mysterious and seemingly divine power expressed through water and the Región-dwelling characters who are similarly bound to "their valley" by the surrounding mountain range. The persistent presence of the Torce and Lerna rivers in Benet's novels add atmospherically to the sense of enigma and mystery that shrouds his invented land. Likewise, a remark in the latter part of Benet's essay—"To the Iberian peninsula, nature has proven to be a provocative, whimsical and unpredictable mother. . . . In hydrographic terms the country is still in a semi-wild state"—suggests yet another possible source of Región's shadowy and enigmatic character.[85]

As a natural extension of his thoughts on water and hydraulic engineering, bridges, for their part, are not without a privileged place in Benet's texts. There is, for example, the Doña Cautiva Bridge, which figures prominently in both *Volverás a Región* and *Herrumbrosas lanzas*. In *Herrumbrosas lanzas* this bridge plays a decisive role in Benet's novelistic description of military strategy unfolding in the war in Región. Circumstances at the end of volume one's third book find the Nationalists within shooting distance of the Republicans at "la casa del Perdón and the Doña Cautiva Bridge, where the defense of the valley was being reorganized."[86] In the fourth book of the first volume of his ambitious narrative, documenting the events of the only partly fictional war campaign in Región, Benet introduces a short history of the bridge into his military-style documentary narration. This is, perhaps, to be expected given his masterful reconciliation of historical and fictional discourse throughout the novel and his writings as a whole. Thus Benet takes a step away from narrating the bloody attempts by Nationalists to gain control of the bridge—a step along the way to defeating the resisting Republicans—in order to discuss the history of this fictional bridge and the surrounding area:

> The construction of the Doña Cautiva Bridge goes back to the final years of the eighteenth century, when an enlightened Magistrate whose name would be engraved in perpetuity in the corresponding tablet on one of the central buttresses, found a way to collect the necessary funds from his district in order to erect the first of those works that would promote the fomentation of the territory of the middle Torce. In spite of the bridge, the El Salvador highway and Socéanos Pass, the canal on the left-most border (there called a dam) and a handful of other works of art, the area never lent itself to being fomented, and the Civil War would have far less impact on it than that esteemed Magistrate, Don Gonzalo Álvarez de Buelnes, who for the greatest honor of his memory and that of Our Lord the King ordered built, in the midst of a fomentary euphoria, two pyramids, each crowned by a lion.[87]

Although this extended reference to the Doña Cautiva bridge is a somewhat isolated episode in *Herrumbrosas lanzas,* a work famously accompanied by a fold-out map of Región and surrounding areas drafted by Benet himself, references to the bridge linger over at least twenty-three pages of his first novel, *Volverás a Región*.[88] This earlier work engages the Bridge of Doña Cautiva in much the same way, as it becomes a strategic point for the Nationalist forces seeking to rout the Republicans.

The location of the bridge is a privileged point even in the larger cartography of Región, as Benet makes clear, and yet its capture is simultaneously instrumental from a purely military strategy.[89] As Benet's narration conveys, the Navarese Nationalist leader Gamallo proposes to capture not merely Región but the entire Torce Valley—and a key part of this plan is to "establish more or less at the site of the Doña Cautiva Bridge a strong and redoubled position that might bring the enemy's attention upon itself and occupy all the forces situated beyond that point."[90] The location of the bridge is, of course, also a key part of Republican strategy and a terrain with which one of Región's commanders, Eugenio Mazón, is quite familiar.[91] A prolonged battle along the river near the bridge in September 1938 shows the Republican forces digging in their heels: "Until the twenty-second they were able, with the concentration of Mazón's whole column in a limited sector facing the abutment of the Bridge—digging trenches on the sides and hiding their mortars in the heather—to hold off the enemy attack, which managed to advance along the esplanade opposite only sporadically and for a few hours."[92] By the twenty-seventh, however, the Republican troops are forced to disband and retreat from the bridge to higher ground, ultimately for good.[93]

The Nationalist capture of the bridge becomes a key loss for the Republican resistance, such that they attempted to retake it later in the year, with combat pushing from November even into the first days of 1939.[94] Led by Constantino, Benet's Republican forces relaunch their attack: "Its immediate objective was the recapture of Doña Cautiva Bridge and ultimately the elimination of all enemy forces on the right bank of the river with an object to regrouping and shaping up a reduced nucleus of resistance upstream from that point, in order to contemporize until the arrival of an honorable peace."[95] Constantino does in fact succeed in recapturing the bridge: "During that same month of November the first objective was reached, the bridge was retaken—in the bloodiest battle waged in the province during the whole war—and the republican troops managed a penetration of several miles along the Burgo Mediano road. And that was all."[96] Although the Navarese general loses the bridge he had won earlier in 1938, Gamallo soon occupies an abandoned Región in December without even having to fire a shot.[97] Even though the Republican captains—who had formerly been fighting separately—reunite after retaking the bridge, the Nationalists are eventually successful as Benet's text shifts abruptly from the narrative action of combat to remembrances of the war after a mere paragraph break.[98]

Significantly, through repetition spanning the entire work (and concentrated in parts I and IV), the bridge becomes from its first capture by the Nationalists one of the symbols of the ruin of Republican Spain, as emphasized at the close of part III: "When they were sunken in that sleep and the first symptoms of Ruin crept in, it must have been understood that fate and time had once more refused to finance an investment that could only be amortized in Teruel, along the Ebro, or at Doña Cautiva Bridge."[99] Here Benet links the (fictional) battle for the bridge with the very real Spanish Civil War battles of Teruel and the Ebro, which he discusses in detail in *¿Qué fue la guerra civil?* thus emphasizing its significance for the war in Región. In this way, the bridge becomes a synecdoche for the historical and ideological tensions of the civil war. Most concretely, the bridge highlights the opposition between the Nationalists and the Republicans, although metaphorically—remembering the etymology of the word rivals discussed above—it symbolizes more universal themes of difference and (potential if frustrated) reconciliation.[100] In sum, Benet's use of rivers and bridges—and, of course, both together in his depiction of Civil War conflicts—reflects at once his persistent interest in both Spain's "peculiar hydrological characteristics" and in its bloody past.[101]

Perhaps unsurprisingly, Benet's thoughts on civil engineering also found their way into other aspects of his literary production in less overt ways. The 2007 republication of his essay "Un extempore" (An Extemporization), for example, is accompanied by a revealing editorial note. As a Benetian scholar has recently pointed out, the original draft of the essay included a remark that pointed to the entanglement of engineering and more philosophical strains of thought in the author's mind. In the midst of an essayistic rumination on mortality and the passing of time—written in 1967, in the wake of his brother Francisco's 1966 death—Benet ponders how much has changed during the previous year: "But the same year that for me (if it were not for your death) would have passed in such a vague way—because memory, immersed in duration, is not a suitable mechanism with which to carry out repeated cuts to its heart—has been marked by nature with ephemeral but unequivocal signs, with one more ring in the cores *of the trees, a fraction of a degree in the endothermic parallax, a dam over the river Guadaliz that now—a year later—has grown from its foundations and in the present moment nears its coronation.*"[102] As the editorial note makes clear—for the first time providing Benet's original text (shown in italics), which had been unpublished in previous editions of the essay—"Benet, in the end, deleted this continuation so characteristic of an engineer."[103] Although in this case the author may have cut a noteworthy reference to engineering, this telling edit reveals in no uncertain terms that the civil engineer and the author of Región's (fictional) history were, of course, one and the same.

Chapter 3

Juan Benet's Bergsonism

Time, Memory, and Knowledge

> I read those three names, let's say, in order of esteem: first Bergson,
> who I think I read in his entirety; Dilthey, I think I read in translation in
> *The Sciences of the Spirit;* and my reading of Ortega took me even to the
> historiological essays of Hegel. . . . In a sense, if someone influenced me
> in those days, it was Bergson.
>
> Juan Benet, quoted in Orringer, "Juan Benet a viva voz"

The French philosopher Henri Bergson (1859–1941)—known for his nuanced juxtaposition of subjective time and *duration* to clock time, of rational and intellectual knowledge to intuition; in sum, of temporality to spatiality—exercised a decisive influence on Benet's thought and literary production. While the Spanish author himself said as much in an interview—and while a handful of scholars have indeed signaled this connection over the years—one cannot hope to understand Juan Benet without also understanding Bergson.[1] This reconciliation of Benet and Bergson, in fact, takes us not merely inward—toward a deeper understanding of the Spaniard's novels—but also outward, toward important interdisciplinary conversations regarding Bergson's work that have been sustained over the last ten to twenty years.

Indeed, we gain much by returning to the Bergsonian aspects of Juan Benet's thought and literary production in today's context. Although his work was somewhat underappreciated both during his own lifetime and throughout most of the twentieth century, there nonetheless exists a significant, contemporary push to return to Bergson's philosophy. This push is due, most of all, to French philosopher Gilles Deleuze (1925–1995). In the 1950s and 1960s, Deleuze called for a "return to Bergson," publishing several essays (and an important book) in French that asserted the relevance of Bergson's legacy for more contemporary readers.[2] During the 1990s and

2000s, no less—greatly indebted to English translations of Deleuze's work, of course—Anglophone critics from a variety of disciplinary frameworks have also found much to admire in Bergson. This renewed interest has, in fact, led to a great number of scholarly monographs devoted to his thought—and to new editions of his original texts themselves (in English translation, as before).[3]

Born in Paris in 1859—to a Polish-Jewish father and an Anglo-Irish mother who frequently spoke to him in English—Bergson was fascinated by mathematics early on, and soon gravitated toward philosophy.[4] He eventually became a member of a number of learned societies, and he received many honors—including even the Nobel Prize for Literature (despite being a philosopher), which he was awarded in the year of Benet's birth (1927).[5] Benet was thus born into a Spanish society that had already been substantially influenced by Bergson. The French philosopher in fact had visited Spain in 1916 as part of a diplomatic mission. In the turbulent context of World War I (1914–18), he was able to visit two prestigious locations frequented by Madrid's intellectuals, writers, and philosophers of the time. The first was the Ateneo—an "Aethenium" that generally reflected Spain's nineteenth-century liberal traditions and historically promoted intellectual discourses of various types—where on the second and sixth days of May he delivered lectures titled "Personality" and "The Human Soul."[6] He also visited the Residencia de Estudiantes—an institution connected with Spain's intriguing educational innovation called the Institución Libre de Enseñanza (Open School of Teaching, founded in 1876)—where he likewise gave a lecture.[7] The list of learned Spaniards in attendance at Bergson's Ateneo lectures alone is an impressive one indeed.[8] These visits, of course, took place well after his ideas had been circulating among Spanish intellectuals— perhaps the most noted of these being poet Antonio Machado and novelist-philosopher Miguel de Unamuno.[9] Bergson's work was being read in Spain by at least 1900, if not in fact as early as 1892, well before Benet was even born.[10]

Although Henri Bergson's influence on Peninsular letters, broadly considered, was great, existing Spanish literary criticism itself has mustered only sporadic references to the French philosopher who served as a touchstone for Benet.[11] Therefore it will be instructive to explore Bergson's direct influence on Benet in general terms, referring to the essays *El ángel del señor abandona a Tobías* and "Un extempore." Next I will look at how key Bergsonian intuitions regarding time and memory were expressed through Benet's fiction, particularly focusing on his second novel, *Una meditación.* While Benet draws strongly from the French philosopher's concepts— providing lengthy passages on memory and recollection that function as fictional illustrations of those concepts and even using Bergson's terms explicitly—he does so in his own way. Last I will fold Bergson's philosophical insights into Benet's remarks on the value of literary discourse itself, drawing from his book of essays *La inspiración y el estilo.*

The Influence of Henri Bergson's Philosophy

Juan Benet was undoubtedly drawn to Bergson's explorations of time (temporality and *duration*), which were engaged explicitly by the Spanish author in selected essays and given expression in the themes and form of his many fictional works. In a sense, even the frequent scholarly comparisons of Benet to Faulkner are also a form of homage to the influence of their "common mentor [Bergson]."[12] Bergson's major texts—which include *Time and Free Will* (1889), *Matter and Memory* (1896), *Creative Evolution* (1907) and *The Two Sources of Morality and Religion* (1932)—persistently highlight a number of dualisms, all of which draw their meaning from the fundamental reality of a temporal experience that is fluid, ever changing, and ultimately irreducible to spatial models. The dualisms explored extensively by Bergson—the primary dualism of space and time; followed by secondary dualisms of matter and memory, intellect and intuition, and static and dynamic religion, respectively—are not simple oppositions but rather complex and overlapping composites.[13] In each case, what is at stake is a more nuanced philosophical model of "two different kinds of reality, the one heterogeneous, that of sensible qualities, the other homogeneous, namely space."[14] As Bergson explains, the subtle interplay of these philosophical dualisms is lost on the human intellect—whose very evolution, for practical reasons, has effected an increasingly greater correspondence between our mental processes and the discrete borders and measurable qualities of space alone.[15] Ultimately space is, for Bergson, a "view taken by mind"—and the unfortunate consequence of this view is that the human intellect "spatializes time."[16]

The "spatialization of time" is a phrase used by Bergson to denote the intellect's routine and practical reduction of a complex and shifting temporal reality to static forms and immobile concepts.[17] Even though the world is inherently and fundamentally mobile, he writes, the intellect persists in understanding this fluid experience in terms of discrete states of consciousness. Using the type of thought Bergson calls intuition—and not intellect—we can nevertheless go beyond the seeming isolation of these individual states toward what he calls "duration":

Pure duration is the form which the succession of our conscious states assumes when our ego lets itself *live,* when it refrains from separating its present state from its former states. For this purpose it need not be entirely absorbed in the passing sensation or idea; for then, on the contrary, it would no longer *endure.* Nor need to forget its former states: it is enough that, in recalling these states, it does not set them alongside its actual state as one point alongside another, but forms both the past and the present states into an organic whole, as happens when we recall the notes of a tune, melting, so to speak, into one another.[18]

Bergson's idea of the fluid and continuous concept of time—as expressed through the notion of duration, which is in a sense the cornerstone of his temporal philosophy—appears both explicitly and implicitly in Benet's essays and fiction.

There is another point of comparison between the two. If Benet indeed read Bergson "in his entirety," as he professed to have done, then he would have come across the many ways in which the French philosopher sought to reconcile scientific thought and philosophical intuition. To wit: the French philosopher intended his work not as an attack on science, but rather as its complement.[19] In the early essay "Introduction to Metaphysics" (1903), he notes that both science and philosophy are necessarily interdependent—a connection evident also in the title of his later work *Creative Evolution* (1907).[20] Bergson also attempted to reconcile his philosophy with more public scientific debates, publishing the book *Duration and Simultaneity* (1922) as a way of dialoguing with Albert Einstein's revolutionary early twentieth-century advances in physics. Another example of Bergson's dialogue with science is an essay ("The Philosophy of Claude Bernard") regarding the classic text *Introduction to Experimental Medicine* (1865), written by a French scientist for whom Juan Benet also expressed esteem.[21]

Benet's awareness and incorporation of Bergson's work is best established by turning, first, to *El ángel del señor abandona a Tobías.* This book-length essay—inspired, ostensibly, in Rembrandt's 1637 painting of the same name—is a difficult text that grapples with questions of grammar, language, signification, science, mathematics, philosophy, religion, politics, and more.[22] One of Benet's very first (and central) observations in that essay concerns the fact that the painting's portrayal of the Lord's Angel in the act of abandoning Tobias has a certain visual immediacy. That is, neither the Lord's Angel nor Tobias stands out as the "protagonist" of the piece.[23] Instead, the subject extracted by the painting's viewer is neither one, nor the other, but rather "the action elaborated between the two and that, in the translation to the lexical order, is manifested in the verb."[24] In his subsequent musings, Benet remarks that the rules and organization of societies have to a certain extent become manifest in the rules and organization of languages and grammars—and thus that language has its limitations.[25] This premise—just as many of the discussions included in the book—is itself a nod to the French philosopher's work. As Benet references Bergson explicitly on a number of pages in *El ángel del señor abandona a Tobías,* we do well to explore the nature of this influence in greater detail.[26] This means seeing how the issue of language is connected with Bergson's own discussions of time.

Bergson's exploration of language in his texts was rooted in his primary intuition regarding an indivisible temporal continuity. For the philosopher— just as for Benet—language introduces divisions into what is a fluid, ever-changing experience of time. In *Creative Evolution,* Bergson wrote that language reflects the main tendency of human knowledge to focus "on a state rather than a change": "Whether the movement be qualitative or evolutionary or extensive, the mind manages to take stable views of the instability. And thence the mind derives, as we have just shown, three kinds of representations: (1) qualities, (2) forms of essences, (3) acts. To these three ways of seeing correspond three categories of words: adjectives, substantives, and verbs, which are the primordial elements of language."[27] Benet's text explicitly cites this Bergsonian notion, highlighting on more than one occasion "that 'disarticulation of the real effected through language,' as Bergson used to say."[28] Benet explains what this means in a sentence that recalls Bergson's words from *Creative Evolution* (cited above): "By applying to each thing and each action a specific signifying term, linguistic perception fragments the real continuum [of experience] into its parts, [and] the flow is interrupted."[29] Referencing the same quotation again later in the book, Benet uses the metaphor of someone attempting to take a picture of a current with a camera and capturing everything "except its variation in time, given that . . . this physical world in continuous mutation is time itself. This is what Bergson was referring to when he spoke of the 'disarticulation of the real effected by language.'"[30] For both Benet and his "mentor," exploring the structure of language is but one way of seeing how temporal experience is nonetheless rendered in decidedly spatial terms by the process of intellection.

Benet's remarks on memory in *El ángel del señor* also reveal a strong Bergsonian inheritance. In *Matter and Memory,* the French philosopher had produced a novel (and still cited) account of memory and temporality, asserting, "Memory is something other than a function of the brain, and there is not merely a difference of degree, but of kind, between perception and recollection."[31] The two types of memory posited by Bergson—the involuntary habit memory ("of motor mechanisms"), upon which we rely for all practical purposes, and also the movement through which we thrust ourselves into the past ("independent recollections")—are also signaled by Benet, who similarly distinguishes "involuntary" and "voluntary" memory.[32] While other numerous aspects of *El ángel del señor* begin to stand out for readers familiar with the French philosopher's work—among them instinct vs. intellection, the human being's evolutionary (mental) adaptation to space, the (false) notion of a homogenous time, ritualized and static religion vs. dynamic religion, and the theme of mystics and mysticism—Bergson's musings on temporality and memory are most clearly relevant to an understanding of Benet's fiction.[33]

These themes of temporality and memory are, in fact, the central concern of another essay by Benet, "Un extempore." Here the French philosopher is not mentioned by name, but is instead present indirectly through the discussion of the theme of time and through Benet's invocation of what is clearly a Bergsonian vocabulary (time as "duration" or "a heterogeneous dimension"; the "current of time").[34] The essay, written in 1967, begins with a meditation on the passing of time since his brother Francisco's death in 1966: "A year has passed since your death. A year that—in contrast to a feeling that is so common and, it seems, accelerates with age—I have found to be enormously long and dilated."[35] Benet implicitly invokes the Bergsonian contrast between clock or calendar time, the time that is routinely measured, divided and quantified, and subjective time—time as experienced and moreover, actually lived and felt. "In truth," he continues, "a year is something purely imaginary that neither flesh nor memory are capable of measuring"; "Memory, I tell myself, desires to know nothing of the measuring of time."[36] This essay expresses the deep feelings and even the sorrow Benet experienced in the wake of Francisco's death, but these emotions nevertheless cohabit with more philosophical reflections as its author explores the very nature of temporality.

For Benet, as explored in "Un extempore," time is inextricably bound to the human experience.[37] In fact, "The human being is a machine that transforms time into existence: the product of that transformation [is] the lived [experience itself] . . . and from this [it follows] that s/he may be capable of transforming the non-quantifiable into something qualitative whose repository is, perhaps, memory. Time has no structure, no form, it lacks transcendence."[38] Key here is the Bergsonian idea that the past is not over, but rather continues, persists, *endures* in the present.[39] As the French philosopher discussed at length in *Matter and Memory*, this past may be actualized by memory, a process that testifies to the interconnection and "mutual support" of involuntary or habit memory and recollection.

Equally, Benet writes of "an omnipresent memory whose data will be incontrovertibly registered and that subsequently, through the force of will or through negligence of the spirit, will be utilized, permanently or intermittently verified or, in further extreme, sepulchered and forgotten."[40]

"Bodily memory," continues Bergson, "is then a quasi-instantaneous memory to which the true memory of the past serves as base."[41] Benet's discussion in "Un extempore" also underscores this process of actualizing (or neglecting) the past from the position of the present: "Forgetting and imagination are the two divergent functions thanks to which that which is remembered and that which is imagined—in their negative aspects, in their shadowy aspects, it might be said—are susceptible to returning and being converted into existence."[42] This existence is moreover—as Benet explains, once again referring implicitly to Bergson's philosophy—either formulaic, repetitive, and remembered, or else it is new—"the new is new precisely because not having been lived nor imagined it is not remembered."[43] The former is a "formula of the happening, known, foreseen and accepted by memory" and the latter is "before anything else a possibility"—a novel possibility that Benet equates with time itself.[44] This is, moreover, a clear nod to Bergson's maxim—introduced in *Creative Evolution*—that "time is invention or it is nothing at all."[45]

As "Un extempore" underscores, however—whether it is taken solely as an articulation of the sorrow he felt during the first year following his brother's death or as a more lasting characterization of the author's thoughts regarding the aporias of time—Benet's perspective on temporality and memory, while still Bergsonian, is more heavily charged with emotion. Bergson had written that it is possible to "detach ourselves from our [present] sensory and motor state" and thus thrust ourselves into "pure recollection."[46] Benet also emphasizes this possible movement, but he imbues it with qualities that are, on the whole, much more negative. Memory, for him, is something of a closed circuit in which his characters are stuck, mired even: "Existence—the transformation of time into existence—is in the end a constant struggle against memory, an attempt to break its circular motion, a hope of returning to find new formulas of conversion."[47] Benet emphasizes the disastrous, even dehumanizing effects of memory: "Memory devours existence; it does not remember the lived but rather reproduces what has been remembered."[48] Ultimately, the way that time and memory are used in Benet's Región fiction references the Bergsonian origins of these concepts—but, at the same time, his novels consistently depict time as "the dimension in which a human being can only be unfortunate, it can't be otherwise."[49]

Time and Memory in Benet's Fictional Narrative

In general terms, Benet's novels—to the extent that they employ a stream-of-consciousness style of narration—thrust the reader into the movement of mental activity, perhaps what one scholar has called "the complexity of the mind's path where diverse moments of time come together."[50] His fiction's characteristic lack (or minimization) of dialogue, action, and plot, together with its frequent use of internal monologues and emphasis on memory all work to create an environment inspired (and even limited) by the contours of subjective time. Whether in relation to Spanish fiction or more generally, existing criticism has confirmed Bergson's importance for the stream-of-consciousness novel. One scholar has written that "the new novelist . . . does not conceive character as a state but as a process of ceaseless becoming in a medium which may be termed Bergson's *durée réelle,*" and another—who focuses specifically on interior monologues in Spanish literature published between 1940 and 1975—has written that the three Bergsonian bases for understanding the stream-of-consciousness novel are "duration, involuntary memory, and intuition."[51]

Much of Benet's fiction highlights his debt to Bergson—via the ubiquitous themes of memory, time, and movement/stasis.[52] Benet's unique perspective seizes upon Bergsonism's fundamental emphasis on change, mobility, and shifting temporality—but with a twist of sorts. His protagonists are stuck in their own psychic remembrances and struggles, unable to move forward. Benet's characters seem to be lost in what Bergson called "pure recollection"—they are unable to act in the present, and instead reflect seemingly without end on past events. Benetian critics have long discussed this aspect of his novels without appropriately seeing it through a Bergsonian lens—routinely noting, for example, that in the fictional land of Región, "Time is frozen," and that "the real action takes place in the psychic lives [of the characters]."[53] The past, as Bergson wrote, survives— *endures*—in the present, of course; but Benet seems to be asking: What happens when people detach from bodily memory and thrust themselves headlong into the sheets of past?

This act of recollection (of the past) proves an alienating if not also dangerous experience for many of Benet's characters, who "feel uneasiness, insecurity, uncertainty and . . . perceive around them enigmas and secrets of unceasing ambiguity" until they manage to reach the "deepest level" of memory.[54] The completion of this task—reaching this deepest level of memory—of course, is something that persistently eludes them.[55] The character of Dr. Sebastián in *Volverás a Región,* for example, epitomizes Benet's own particular invocation of this Bergsonian inheritance. Throughout that first Región novel, the doctor remains "trapped in hesitation, in a decaying house, unable to make decisions."[56] Likewise, Benet's novel *Un viaje de invierno* centers on one party scene alone, as a mother waits for her daughter, Coré, who has seemingly been taken away by the girl's father.[57] Likewise, this Bergsonian influence is felt, also, even in Benet's penultimate novel that—while it does not take place in Región—nevertheless portrays characters who are distanced from the possibility of taking action and even from the reality of change itself. In *En la penumbra* (1989)—a novel that recalls *Un viaje de invierno* in many respects and that one critic has called "the most hermetic of Benet's texts"—all seven chapters center on one single conversation between two women (an aunt and her niece). One critic has summarized the novel concisely by writing: "Late one October afternoon in the half light [*penumbra*] of her study the aunt and her niece each await the arrival of a messenger."[58] The title of that novel itself once again clearly points to the characters' inability to act or to live in Bergsonian time, recalling *Creative Evolution,* for example, wherein the French philosopher wrote: "The idea of change is there, I am willing to grant, but it is hidden *in the penumbra.*"[59]

Benet's second novel, *Una meditación,* unfolds over 440 pages in the original Spanish (more than 360 pages in the English translation) without a single paragraph break, making it the most extreme example of Benet's use of the stream-of-consciousness style. It is also the novel that most clearly admits its Bergsonian inheritance. Bergson's own philosophical vocabulary is evident throughout the book, with words such as *durée* (duration), *élan* ([vital] impetus) and *moral cerrada* (closed morality) appearing sporadically, italicized and in the original French (and alternately also in Spanish, for example as *duración*).[60] The novel begins with the narrator's remembrance of his grandfather's farm in the Torce Valley to the north of Región, and somewhat aimlessly proceeds to detail the lives and histories of Región's families such as the Ruans, the Mazóns, the Corrals, and the narrator's own unnamed lineage—all with a cast of characters too varied and incompletely drawn to explore with any degree of detail here.[61] The effects of the Civil War are clear here as well—just as they are in Benet's first novel—and the narrator reflects, in part, on how in the postwar period "all the wounds of the war were open[,] . . . families [were] divided and scattered," and the "victors . . . every day, at every moment, and on every street corner, flaunted their triumph."[62] The text's relation of specific details regarding the characters and history of Región, however—while important and ongoing—is nevertheless immersed in an endless flow of recollections and reflections, strung together seemingly without any arrangement or ordering principle.[63] Despite the novel's stylistic excess and immense scope, however—it was, in fact, ambitiously composed on one continuous roll of paper—it is nonetheless fairly representative of Benet's novelistic oeuvre as a whole.[64]

We encounter in *Una meditación* the Bergsonian themes of time and memory that constitute the bedrock of Benet's other novels. The excessive stream-of-consciousness style employed in *Una meditación* (just as in others) allows Benet to fully exploit what is a defining characteristic of his novels. That is, existing criticism has pointed out that his novels are very similar in style and subject matter to his philosophical essays. One scholar has written of how he generally folds philosophy and literature together, noting that "Benet creates an image of a discourse which situates itself between literature and thought by means of reconciling the difference between the two."[65] *Una meditación* is no exception to this general rule, in the sense that—very early in the text, indeed—the narration drifts away from the retelling of specific events and remembrances of Región's denizens to meditate at length on the nature of memory and time.

Many of these (titular) "meditations" focus extensively on that process (so well explored by his influence Bergson) through which the past surges up and becomes actualized in the present moment.[66] Benet's narration reflects at length on the Bergsonian notion that the past is preserved as a whole that *endures,* even if it is not accessed through the practical concerns of an involuntary bodily or habit memory.[67] The narrator ponders this notion explicitly on a number of occasions, for example, here using an intriguing geological metaphor for memory. "I have never understood how the temporal disappearance of a memory is attributed to forgetting, refuted by so many phenomena, because in the same way that sedimentary rock holds in its bosom all the traces of beings who left their stamp when it was nothing but soft and impressionable clay, memory can shelter and store up everything that in its day had the necessary consistency to leave an indelible trace."[68] As the narrator of *Una meditación* explores, "Memory holds a trip"—either that trip remains dormant in a state of potential recollection, or else "the bubble comes bursting to the surface, dragging behind it a thousand other details, buried and intact, following it on the way to awareness."[69] Throughout Benet's works, as his characters and narrators grapple with memory and recollection, they live closed lives of quiet despair.[70] In *Una meditación,* however, detachment from the present is taken to the extreme—and the hyperbolic narrative style allows for an ongoing overtly philosophical engagement with Bergson's insights into time and memory.

In fact, Benet repeatedly presents the reader with philosophical segments of text that are indisputably grounded in Bergsonian principles. For example, in the passage that follows, the narrator provides what is in essence a description of that voluntary movement to the past that Bergson equates with "recollection":

> On turning his attention to a remote memory that inexplicably returns to consciousness and the present, with no other will than his having intervened, and after passing through an extensive and shadowy period during which, half-forgotten, a whole area of existence would remain, enwrapping that moment and beginning to take shape little by little on a retina (because the ear rarely accompanies an evocation and respects a strictly silent manner of composing the image, prior to the voice) where, emerging from a disordered and chancy ostracism, reproducing themselves are certain recurrent images that intertwine and refer to each other by means of a law of continuity that memory doesn't know but of which the sense of having lived is aware.[71]

In truth, these seeming digressions on the nature of time and memory constitute the philosophical center of the novel—the Bergsonian conflict between the flow of lived experience and the static concepts that only incompletely attempt to grasp a shifting and complex temporality.

This philosophical core of *Una meditación* is further illustrated through passages that recall both Bergson's idea of the "cinematograph of the mind" and his discussion of the Eleatic paradox of Achilles and the tortoise—both of which are ways of denouncing the fact that the mind approaches change only through static representations and isolated, abstract categories.[72] Two of these categories privileged in Benet's second novel are the psychic and the physical realities of consciousness. As one character notes, "In all of Western thought . . . standing out is that decision to establish once and for all a *quid pro quo* that tries to delimit with rational incisions in the field of the real, man's conscious continuum"; "one must wonder what drove thought to prefer the search for a nonexistent boundary instead of opting for the investigation of that only link that joins physical and psychic phenomena and constitutes the essence of the conscious continuum."[73] Just such a linkage of physical and psychic phenomena is, in fact, at the heart of Bergson's philosophical project. In *Time and Free Will,* he discussed at length the intersection of psychic and physical phenomenon using a model that, while quite nuanced, worked against the commonsensical notion that psychic life and the body were two autonomous areas of experience.[74]

One can see how this insight also influenced Bergson's reconciliation—in *Matter and Memory*—between bodily memory and recollection memory. Through philosophical meditations such as those above, Benet's text explores the notion of "a single ontological unity that, as a first obligation, must fuse the physical world with the world of representation in a single spectrum, between whose strips, no matter how far apart, ontic differences will not exist."[75] Although psychic life and bodily experience may be different, Bergson asserts, there are nonetheless fundamental relationships between both. The narrator of chapter 2 of *Volverás a Región* puts these nuanced Bergsonian relationships well: "Consciousness and reality mutually penetrate each other: they are not isolated, neither are they the same."[76] We do well in considering, as does one of Benet's characters in *Una meditación,* "how habit fixes and encumbers thought, how love alters recognition, how feeling modifies representation in the same way that will denies perception, or creates it."[77]

In addition, the paradox of Achilles and the tortoise—of which Bergson was so fond—also appears in the text. The Eleatic philosopher Zeno described a paradox wherein the hero Achilles races with a tortoise: if Achilles is ten times faster than the tortoise, and if the tortoise is given a head start of ten meters, then Achilles will never be able to catch up. To explain the perceived paradox: Achilles will never catch the tortoise because he will first have to travel one-tenth of the distance (one meter), in which time the animal will also have moved another one-hundredth of the distance. From there, the series continues: $1/100$ for Achilles, $1/1000$ for the tortoise; $1/1000$ for Achilles and $1/10,000$ for the tortoise and so on. Of course, it is clear to us that Achilles will in time overtake the tortoise—Bergson explained the flaw in reasoning inherent to Zeno's paradox by asserting that, although the space covered by both racers is infinitely divisible, the (temporal) movement itself is not. For the French philosopher, this was an instructive point that expressed his primary intuition regarding time—movement is not divisible because it is a temporal process, whereas space is "a view taken by mind" that sees only through a quantitative lens a static snapshot of reality—much like the one discussed by Benet in *El ángel del señor.* In *Una meditación,* the narrator explicitly points to this very same paradox on more than one occasion—for example "(as if between my I and my memory of the I there always existed a distance that was, even though infinitesimal, unbridgeable, the same that separated Achilles from the tortoise)"—all as a way of affirming the fluid reality of temporal experience.[78]

The fundamental Bergsonian distinction between space and time that is reflected in the paradox of Achilles and the tortoise appears in *Una meditación* also in the form of discussions regarding the limits of language and the tyranny of measured clock time—both further manifestations of what the French philosopher called the "spatialization of time." At the same time that the reader is immersed in the chaotic flow of *Una meditación*'s seemingly endless paragraph, the text itself points to the inability of language to capture reality. Recalling the explicit reconciliation of Bergsonian philosophy and language that Benet effected in his book-length essay *El ángel del señor,* the text makes observations such as this one: "There is no verb that defines the action of time flowing to the spell of those moments that whirl and curl."[79] In the same way, the rigid measurement of temporality by clock time is contrasted with the temporal flow that, for Bergson, characterizes lived experience. A great deal of *Una meditación* focuses on the character Cayetano Corral's (frustrated) work restoring clocks and other mechanical objects, "on whose mechanism, sometimes, he worked tirelessly for three or four days in a row."[80] Benet's novelistic descriptions persistently equate the clock with immobility, suggesting that real temporality escapes its measurement: "'It doesn't measure time,' Mr. Corral's first born would say one day, addressing his clock 'time isn't engendered either by stars or clocks, but by tears.'"[81] Although characters may not live fettered by spatialized clock-time, however, given Benet's peculiar application of Bergsonian philosophy, this does not mean that their lives are any less restricted. Escape from clock-time may be liberating in a sense—at one point, Cayetano reflects, "Time was more real now, more absolute, more independent of the hands and the zeal of the master; completely alien to the metric capacity of the clock." More often, however, Benet's characters and narrators remain mired in fear and confusion as they attempt—unsuccessfully—to understand the past that *endures* all around them.

It is essential to understand that for the Spanish novelist time—and not only time but the *awareness* of time—is a defining characteristic of human experience. As he had written in the essay "Un extempore," comparing the human concept of time with an animal's experience of temporality: "all in that kingdom, all except man, live in harmony with the clock and the calendar because, not knowing what time is, I would not dare to suggest that they do not persist in counting that [amount of time] which they have lived, remaining in supine ignorance of the fact that it also has an end. Of the fact that they count it there can be no doubt; whether they are aware that they count it, that is another story."[82] It is this inherently human awareness of the passing and limits of time that feeds the fear and confusion experienced by Benet's characters. At a philosophical level, the importance of memory for them is that it is a way of mediating between two modes of knowledge: as the narrator of *Una meditación* ponders, there is "a first means of knowledge—the series of awareness—on one side desirous of extending its lights to the whole shadowy zone dominated by the second—the series of the flesh"; "one might say that memory is the no man's land that separates both modes of knowledge."[83] In general terms these forms of knowledge might be contrasted in terms of consciousness vs. the body. Memory in this sense reflects the detachment implicated in Bergson's notion of pure recollection, but Benet invokes a memory that is, moreover, deceptive, fragmentary, and lacks the continuity inherent to Bergsonian duration.[84]

In *Una meditación,* Benet's narrator writes that "a frontier doesn't exist between psychic and physical acts and that furthermore, it becomes inappropriate to seek that frontier, wherever it might be found."[85] By plunging themselves headlong into the past, Benet's narrators and characters isolate themselves from others, cut short the very possibility of action in the present, and detach themselves from a shifting and changing duration to relive fragmented moments of the past in isolation from others. This narrative process, one given meaning through the many implicit and explicit references to Bergson in the text of *Una meditación,* is characterized by one critic as the attempt "to conjure up the past, not to mourn or celebrate it, but to interpret, to understand, to define that past's truth and, with it, that of the narrator within the past"—a task that ultimately proves impossible for the characters and narrators who inhabit Benet's Región.[86]

Knowledge and the Art of Literary Composition

Henri Bergson's model of knowledge—as elaborated in *Time and Free Will, Creative Evolution,* and "Introduction to Metaphysics," for example—is a complex one.[87] Notwithstanding, this model may be reduced (for our purposes) to the Bergsonian dualism of intellection vs. intuition. Bergson applies the name "intellect" (a faculty of thought) or "intellection" (its use) to the part of thought that sees the world in spatial terms. Although the essence of lived experience is fluid temporality, the intellect is poorly equipped to *think* this shifting time: in *Creative Evolution* he writes, "Of the discontinuous alone does the intellect form a clear idea"; "Of immobility alone does the intellect form a clear idea."[88] Whereas intellect (through the process of intellection) is a form of knowing that seeks to analyze something—dividing it up, classifying it, making sense of it through established, static categories—intuition, is, on the other hand, a move to coincide with the object of knowledge. Bergson directly contrasts these two forms of knowledge in his essay "Introduction to Metaphysics": "We call intuition here the *sympathy* by which one is transported into the interior of an object in order to coincide with what there is unique and consequently inexpressible in it. Analysis, on the contrary, is the operation which reduces the object to elements already known, that is, common to that object and others. Analyzing then consists in expressing a thing in terms of what is not it. All analysis is thus a translation, a development into symbols, . . . [an] ever incomplete representation. . . . But intuition, if it is possible, is a simple act."[89] In fact, intuition may be accomplished only if the analytical power of the intellect is turned back upon itself—if one can, as he puts it, "bring the human mind to reverse the direction of its customary way of operating, [instead] beginning with change and movement, envisaged as reality itself."[90] Bergson insists that the potential for intuition—for this "direct vision of the mind by the mind"—exists in everyone, but that it is "covered over by functions more useful to life."[91]

While Benet's characters and narrators may be stuck in an intellectual mode—vainly striving to make sense of their lives through detached recollection and unfruitful analysis of the past—it is outside of Benet's fiction, in his essays, where the reader finds greater attention placed on intuition, even if it does not go by that name. Juan Benet's *La inspiración y el estilo*, for example—a book of essays that constitutes an extended meditation on questions related to literary composition and criticism—persistently points to the limitations of what Bergson called "intellectual" thought. In fact, recalling Bergson's assertion that intuition is only possible once the power of intellect has been turned back upon itself, Benet remarks that "(the new writer) will use his own reason to oppose reason, to close off its path using what has not been thought and what is not thinkable, making use of the same rules that are employed by science but that now—let's put it this way—have a different polarity."[92] He asserts that the process through which the writer begins to dominate the work and produce literature is defined and, in truth, only made possible by turning away from the designs of logic and intellection—in a word, certainty.[93]

For Benet, the writer's development of an intuitive style triumphs over processes of logical reasoning. Inspiration comes to a writer only once he has a style, Benet believes, and the work of art can only be assessed by going beyond such limiting notions as "normal behavior," "typical reactions" and "ideological positions."[94] A style is not rational—although it includes rationality—but rather a "zone of shadows" that cannot be reduced by "mathematical reasoning."[95] Benet asserts that, in literary matters, imagination plays a greater role than analysis, which is never sufficient for understanding creative processes. Thoughout *La inspiración y el estilo* we repeatedly encounter his respect for the unknown, as well as his general skepticism that literary criticism may come to completely explain the origins and/or value of a work born of those creative processes.[96] For Benet, either analysis (Bergson's intellection) bases itself on an enigma or else it is "a cozenage that is unlikely to lead to the discovery of things not already known."[97] In fact, in 1982 he would later pose two rhetorical questions that in essence summarize the central premise of that book of essays originally published in 1966. In a prologue that Benet wrote for a book of scholarship exploring his own written work, he asks, "would solving the enigmas and eliminating the difficulties be a vain and counterproductive effort that would ruin that possible value [of a literary work]?"; and also, "may it be that value, enigma, and difficulty are indissolubly united in that work of fiction?"[98] To each of these questions—if *La inspiración y el estilo* is any indication—Benet's answer would be a resounding "yes."

The notions of inspiration and style are key to understanding Benet's fiction precisely because they are connected with processes that are beyond the reach of logical reasoning. This may, in turn, help to explain why his characters are so insufficiently sketched, why the action in his novels takes a back seat to monologue and psychic circumvolutions—in short, why his fiction is so difficult to read.[99] One critic has asserted that "Benet suggests that having clearly defined attitudes and beliefs to communicate (that is, a 'message'), may be an insuperable handicap to the writer."[100] This judgment is not surprising, given that in *La inspiración y el estilo* Benet expresses admiration for what he calls the *grand style* (he cherishes the work of Faulkner and Cervantes) and disdain for the literature that is a product of what he calls "la entrada a la taberna" (the act of entering the tavern). Benet coins this phrase as a way of making clear his derision of that mode of literature whose realist or costumbrist aims leave no space for matters of style.[101] Such literature might be seen as an "intellectual" (in the Bergsonian sense) attempt to capture the world through precise representational techniques.[102] The style Benet prefers, as *La inspiración y el estilo* makes clear (once again using Bergsonian language), is "a style that . . . opens itself to the mind of the reader without demanding of him *an intellection.*"[103] Recalling Bergson's own attempt to go beyond intellection, Benet notes that inspiration "may spring up . . . with a certain independence from knowledge."[104] Similarly, he writes, "It has never been possible—nor is it now—to talk about style with precision"; "that style is not something rational is demonstrated indirectly by the fact that reason has not been capable, up until this moment, of inventing an instrument with which to measure it."[105] For Benet, "the writer begins to refine himself from that very moment in which . . . he allows a great dose of uncertainty to enter into his opinions and doctrines, at the same time that he becomes more rigorous and demanding in his methods and aesthetic criteria."[106] Moved by inspiration—which is dependent on a pre-existing style—and governed by uncertainty, the writer for Benet follows a course that appears to be that of the philosopher for Bergson.

For Bergson, in order to philosophize—that is, in order to escape the abstract categories and strictly spatial designs of a thought that so insufficiently reflects a mobile and ever-changing temporal experience—the mind must begin by "freeing itself from forms and habits that are strictly intellectual."[107] Philosophy is, in this sense, itself an ally of the act of intuition. This act, as Bergson explains—with major consequences for our view of Benet's fiction—is not one that requires a separation of body and mind. Instead, intuition takes place neither outside of time nor outside of the physical world. Intuition is not an act through which consciousness escapes the material world entirely, plunging itself into "pure recollection" for example. Nor does it require a total escape from intellection—for, as Bergson pointed out, intellect is meant to be turned back on itself.[108] Instead, intuition is a "simple act" that requires a certain equilibrium between an intellectual, spatial experience of the body (and its senses) on the one hand, and on the other, a consciousness capable of viewing the world in terms of fluid time and constant change—(in a word, *duration*). Bergson explains in "Introduction to Metaphysics" that "in order to reach intuition it is not necessary to transport ourselves outside the domain of the senses and of consciousness. . . . The time in which we are naturally placed, the change we habitually have before us, are a time and change that our senses and consciousness have reduced to dust in order to facilitate our action upon things. Undo what they have done, bring our perception back to its origins, and we shall have a new kind of knowledge without having been obliged to have recourse to new faculties."[109] In fact, it is Bergson's formulation of this question of knowledge—and not intellectual knowledge but rather the knowledge of the world and of temporality provided by intuition—that provides a touchstone for understanding how Benet's fiction and his essays work together to form an organic whole. To the extent that Benet's fictional characters immerse themselves in "pure recollection"—that is, when they flee from the immediate realm of the senses and temporal consciousness toward remote memories of Región's past (as happens in *Una meditación* and *Volverás a Región*)—they block the road to intuition and thus to the very self-knowledge they may seek. In complementary fashion, Benet shows through his essays that the very creation of those literary characters is in fact made possible precisely by way of employing non-rational thought, uncertainty, and what he calls the "zone of shadows."

Benet's view might be summed up by saying that the text functions as a bridge of sorts between the author and the reader. Each must have an appreciation for the more enigmatic aspects of literary production, whether that is, as his first book of essays suggests, the inspiration that fuels the creative process of the author, or else the style which makes that moment of inspiration possible—and which subsequently (potentially) bewitches the readers of a given work of fiction. Moreover, in Benet's conception of the multidimensional nature of space—mental and physical; conceived, perceived and lived—his move away from closed forms of knowledge, the limitations of rationality, and the static categories of intellection paradoxically makes possible new, more open forms of knowledge.

Chapter 4

Cultural Geography

Landscape, Maps, and Space

> Región is rendered through cartography and narrated, it is drawn and related, it is thought through and constructed following from a single creative impulse that is both temporal and spatial, or if one prefers, it is both idea and cartography.
>
> José Rivero, "Juan Benet," quoted in Baeza, "Acto de Homenaje"

> Whenever I would tell [Juan Benet] that, in truth, he was a geographer, he would nod or disagree emphatically, according to his mood and his feelings in that moment. The years have proven me to be correct.
>
> Clemente Sáenz Ridruejo, quoted in Baeza, "Acto de Homenaje"

Just as easily as we come to attribute Juan Benet's interest in Spain's river systems and landscapes to his role as a practicing civil engineer, we might also be well advised to see him as embodying a contemporary geographical spirit.[1] Maps, regions, borders, topography (rivers, sierras, forests, and the like)—these are nothing if they are not also the domain of the geographer. The fact that his novels are a testament to his professional engagement with his native Spanish soil as an engineer adds something to the equation. In light of the connections that literary scholars have been pursuing in recent decades with what goes by the name of human, cultural, or social geography, Benet's Región fiction illustrates a basic premise of that growing field. That is—for such contemporary geographers—spaces are not purely physical, not purely defined by their material conditions alone (quantitative descriptors of altitude, elevation, rainfall, climate, geology, etc.). Instead, in order to understand individual spaces, we must understand also the human, cultural, or social forces that go into their shaping and into their meaning. In the simplest sense, these geographers ask more qualitative questions of land and territory, questions such as: "What cultural associations do people make with a particular landscape?" "What social forces went into that landscape's formation?" or "How are landscapes implicated in both past and present views of human history?"[2]

These sorts of questions have been asked and answered from numerous points of view, of course; but what the majority of those perspectives all share is a focus on linking the representations of places with those places themselves. There is an ample bibliography of geographical scholarship that has consequences for the nuanced relationships between mental maps, cartographic maps, and their referents.[3] What is even more intriguing—and more novel—is the way in which contemporary literary scholars have brought these questions to bear on the relationship governing fictional representations of space in the written text and the social, cultural, human relationships that span the border between that text and the world external to it. Regarding the study of Spain specifically, for example, a number of Hispanist scholars have brought spatial theory and cultural geography to bear on cultural products depicting Spanish landscapes, whether in novels, films, or other cultural products.[4]

In addition to continuing to explore Benet's invented land of Región, I will refer to three important twentieth-century geographers. Key insights borrowed from these noted figures in cultural geography might aid investigation into the relevance of Benet's literary-cartographic project. A 1925 essay written by landscape theorist Carl Sauer (1889–1975) shows how the contemporary evolution of cultural geography as an academic field has emphasized not merely physical space (topography, geology, land mass, etc.) but also the less tangible but equally important sociocultural elements of landscapes. This perspective is quite relevant to Benet's first novel, which places an equal attention on both landscape and human activity. Benet's work draws from and ultimately contrasts with an earlier text by Brazilian writer Euclides Da Cunha—a connection that has been noted by Benetian scholars and by the writer himself.

Región is a cartographic invention that is at once physical and mental. Noted geographer and spatial theorist David Harvey (1935–) illuminates the significance of Benet's career-spanning Región project for contemporary and interdisciplinary debates surrounding the nature of space. Benet's own development of a Map of Región—originally published with *Herrumbrosas lanzas* in 1983—has a central role in this exploration of space as both mental construct and material reality. Región's space is multidimensional, allowing exploration through the theory of geographer, philosopher, and spatial thinker Henri Lefebvre (1901–1991).[5] In fact, this "new" perspective on Benet's work builds organically from previous Benetian criticism which has signaled the multiple layers of his narrative style and his numerous coexisting themes.

Volverás a Región: A Cultural Geography Perspective

When cultural geographer Carl Sauer published a seminal article titled "The Morphology of Landscape" in 1925, landscape was being approached routinely within a framework known as "environmental determinism." That is, it was generally accepted by geographers that the natural environment determined cultural forms, and that landscape itself was little more than a static backdrop for human history. Instead, as a contemporary cultural geographer reflects, "Sauer's main purpose was to show that environmental determinism had pretty much got it backwards. It wasn't nature that caused culture, but rather [that] culture, working with and on nature, created the contexts of life." For Sauer, landscape was itself a product of culture. It was thus possible for geographers to "read" culture through specific landscapes.[6] Another one of the landscape theorist's relevant insights was that time—or what he called "the fourth dimension of geography"—"is and has been part of geographic understanding. Human geography considers man as a geographic agent, using and changing his environment in nonrecurrent time and according to his skills and wants."[7] Sauer's influence was far-reaching and lasting, such that he is, in fact, considered to be a founder of the geographical subdiscipline known as "cultural geography."[8]

Apart from asserting the importance of culture and temporality for geography in a way that had never been done before, Sauer also "reasserted a renewed importance for descriptive studies . . . of the cultural forms that comprised the landscape."[9] If Sauer put "culture right at the center of geography's project," he consequently also suggested that land and territory cannot be understood without also understanding human activities and societies.[10] In essence, what he accomplished was to do away with a purely physical appreciation of land and to encourage discussions of landscape that were more qualitative.[11] Benet's first novel in fact manages to accomplish much the same shift from quantitative toward qualitative views of landscape.

The first chapter of *Volverás a Región* includes a number of references to those quantitative aspects of landscape study that dominated the field prior to the revolution in cultural geography. The reader is exposed early to all manner of numerical data concerning Región's geography. This occurs, for example, when the narration describes "The Sierra de Región—8,060 feet high at the top of El Monje (according to geodesists who had never climbed it) and 5,411 at its crossing points, the passes of Socéanos and La Requerida"; or when it reports on topographical features of the surrounding area at length, noting "a curvature that increases as it descends toward the west, resting on the eruptive and crystalline formations that, in opposite direction and with convexity, lay down their folds toward the Atlantic."[12] In a lengthy passage that spans pages 28–42 of the English translation, there are numerous references to geological qualities of the land neighboring Región (for example in the Basque Pyrenees, Cantabria, Asturias, and Galicia), to cardinal directions (E-W and NNE-SSW; N-S), to river systems (Torce, Formigoso, Tarrentino brook), and to features such as tectonic plates, valleys, flatlands, summits, geosynclines, and more.[13] Nevertheless, this extended passage is much more than a purely quantitative description of Región. Benet's narration frequently humanizes the landscape through simile—noting, for example, that the "Región range shows itself like an enigmatic witness," or writing of "the summits . . . lined up like the units of a fleet in battle array."[14] The integration of these similes, for example, points to the importance of seeing the relationship between the human, cultural world of Region's inhabitants and their physical landscape.

This relationship between the human and the geological is evident in other ways in that initial passage of *Volverás a Región*. More common than the above similes are Benet's persistent references to a nameless traveler who wanders over Región's terrain. The narration oscillates between noting the human traveler's (hypothetical) movements and depicting the landscape in static terms. Consider the following transition, which might be taken as emblematic of this process. Benet writes: "Suddenly a gulley— the hermetic and impenetrable nature of the terrace is manifest, formed by schists, slate and quartzites, feldspar clay the color of baked brick and placed in rowlocks, covered with a layer of quartz sand a hand thick—puts an end to many hours of traveling that will no longer be able to be recovered or prolonged. The Traveler then notices the reality of the desert where scarcely any traces of man remain."[15] In fact, the entire first chapter of the novel is couched through the vision of this (hypothetical, nameless) traveler. Its very first sentence grounds the reader in this subjective experience of the land, noting, "It's true, the traveler leaving Región who wishes to reach its mountain range by following the old king's highway—because the modern one has ceased to be such—will find himself obliged to cross a small, high desert that seems endless."[16] The result is that even the most quantitative descriptions of territory in the novel are implicitly imbued with a notably human perspective. *Volverás a Región*, throughout, effects a synthesis of the area's landscape and its people—neither is presented in isolation from the other. In this way the static landscape—highlighted through quantitative geological and geographical descriptions—is folded into the human and cultural space of Región.

In order to understand fully the way in which the first chapter of *Volv-erás a Región* works to reposition landscape as inherently connected with human activity, the reader must understand another important literary influence on Benet. Brazilian Euclides Da Cunha (1866–1909) was—like Benet, in fact—a career civil engineer who later took to writing. His most important work was not fiction, but rather a book-length text written in a journalistic or historical style titled *Os sertões* (1902, translated into English as "Rebellion in the Backlands"). *Os sertões* is a lengthy treatment— one, in fact, that possesses many novelistic qualities—of a rebellion fought in the northeast Brazilian territory of Canudos from 1896 to 1897.[17] As one commentator has written, the book is not only "a superb piece of journalism," but also a "treatise of the geography, geology, climatology, and anthropology of the backlands region [of Brazil's northeast]."[18] As Benet himself related in an essay from 1969 published in *Revista de Occidente,* he first came upon Da Cunha's book when he was on an engineering job in Galicia during the early 1950s—well before the publication of *Volverás a Región* in the late 1960s.[19] Therein, he professes a supreme respect for the Brazilian writer and puts him on a par with Latin American authors who are perhaps better known in the Anglophone world—"[Alejo] Carpentier in Cuba; [Juan] Rulfo in Mexico; [Mario] Vargas [Llosa] in Perú and, finally, the sensational [Gabriel] García Márquez in Colombia."[20] Following up on Benet's own remarks on the importance of Da Cunha's influence for the composition of his first novel, existing Benetian scholarship has asserted that a number of parallels exist between the two works.[21]

From a cultural geography perspective, the most important of these parallels has to do with the question of space in Región. One critic has explored in detail the essential similarity of the "narrative spaces" of both books. *Os sertões* begins with a section titled "The Backlands," which is subdivided into a description of the area's geography and climate (titled "The Land") and another section discussing the people inhabiting that region "and how its rugged environment shapes all aspects of their existence" (titled "Man").[22] These same elements of Da Cunha's text appear also in *Volverás a Región,* and "are presented in precisely the same order."[23] This critic has shown how each work thus moves progressively from a discussion of "Geography/Geology," to "Climate," and finally to "Effects on Man"; he argues that, in fact, even the content of these sections is strikingly similar. Each writer breathes life into his respective "imposing narrative ambient," and according to his own style.[24] Although the perspective of "environmental determinism" clearly dominates in *Os sertões,* however—with Da Cunha arguing that people's lives are determined by their physical environment—Benet's invention of a fictitious landscape taken together with his complex novelistic style suggests that seeing *Volverás a Región* from such a perspective is problematic at best. While quantitative descriptions of landscape and territory are plentiful in the early sections of Benet's first novel (for example, "the 42° 45" parallel latitude N, at 2,500 feet altitude"), the frequent interruption of such passages through reference to the unnamed traveler as well as Benet's persistent stylistic rejection of rational meaning indicate that something much more nuanced is taking place.[25]

In *Volverás a Región* there is an interesting synergy between Región's landscape and the people who inhabit it that cannot be reduced to an environmental determinism. Rather than say that the imposing character of Región's landscape shapes the formation of its characters' consciousness, it is more appropriate to say that both landscape and people have reciprocally influenced each other—according to an enigmatic ground that is (purposely) never fully explored by Benet's narrative. Certainly Región is characteristically "dry" and its terrain "impenetrable," but to say that its "violent topography" has determined the paralytic state of its inhabitants any more than has the civil war, its underlying ideological conflicts, or even Spain's historical lack of attention to human disputes over the land—all of which are emphasized in the novel—is short-sighted.[26] If the territory described in *Volverás a Región* is "labyrinthine," the human relationships between Regionites are no less incomprehensible.[27] In the end, the reader is forced to reconcile—in dialectical fashion—the relationship between the facts that, on the one hand, Región's tenants are "fearful of one another, all besieged by the hostility of the geography" and, on the other, that "the people in Región have opted to forget their own history."[28] The complex situation in Región is a product of both geographical concerns and human agency. In fact, Región's imposing geography is best understood as a literary reflection of the human problems (both individual—memory and time; and social—war and conflict) in which its inhabitants are mired.[29]

Moreover, in Benet's fiction, Región is a land subjected to forces that are at once "natural" and "cultural." This reflects a somewhat sophisticated understanding of the interaction between human societies and landscapes. As cultural geography pioneer Carl Sauer has written, "Culture is the agent, the natural area is the medium, the cultural landscape the result. . . . The natural landscape is of course of fundamental importance, for it supplies the materials out of which the cultural landscape is formed. The shaping force, however, lies in the culture itself."[30] In Benet's first novel, the Bergsonian character of his stream-of-consciousness narration is what is fundamental, providing a way of linking the consciousness of his characters with the region they inhabit. This question of style is fundamental, not only for Benet's work as a whole, but also for understanding the relationship of Región's land to the culture of its people. The emphasis on consciousness over objectified terrain creates a style wherein passages of a seemingly objective character that emphasize quantitative data are in effect folded into that primary, subjective vision of people and their relationship to the land. Because of the way *Volverás a Región* presents landscape and people as intimately related to one another, Benet's invented land might even be considered a literary manifestation of what cultural geographer Sauer called "cultural history in its regional articulation."[31]

Benet's Cartographic Vision: The Map of Región

With the publication of *Herrumbrosas lanzas I* in 1983, Juan Benet famously included a fold-out topographic Map of Región that he had designed. Both map and novel have been explored by critics with reference to Benet's characteristic tendency to mix history and fiction, but they also work together, giving shape to the invented land.[32] As one critic has pointed out, the map itself "suggests the concrete and authentic existence of Región," and its "constant use of detail, particularly curves of level and scale, emphasizes the nearness and reality of this province, especially regarding geography."[33] Designed at a scale of 1:150,000, the Map of Región "represents abstract space" and "is based on cartographic conventions."[34] As critics have pointed out, although Región is an invented land, it seems to be situated in the Spanish central-northwest near the province of León. In fact, Región consists of a curious mixture of both fictional places and others that can be verified on a map of Spain.[35] Understanding cartography as a particular kind of spatial representation can help us to see the relationship between this map and Benet's fiction.

It is appropriate to begin with an anecdote involving map reading that appears in Benet's own work, *Herrumbrosas lanzas*. Throughout the novel—which is a literary treatment of the Civil War campaigns in Región— the Republicans are locked in battle with the Nationalists. In the following excerpt, Eugenio Mazón—a Republican leader—attempts to gain strategically important information from one of his countrymen. Spreading a cartographic representation of Región out on a table, Mazón asks the man to pinpoint the location of a certain house on the map.

> When they finished the stew, they cleared the plates from the table where Mazón then laid out the map of the excursionist club, who used it as a guide for their exploratory expeditions. Juan de Tomé and Kerrera each sat to one side while one of the guides remained vigilant at the door. Mazón tried, without success, to get his countryman to signal the position of the house on the map; not only

could he not make sense of it, but moreover, to each question he protested the subsequent objections to all of his indications, and with each name that he was told he would respond that the place in question wasn't over there, that it was on the other side of the mountain.[36]

This concise exercise in map-reading does not result in the information for which Eugenio Mazón is hoping. The man in question—a native of Región—has trouble translating his own personal, subjective experience with the landscape to the seemingly objetive excursionist map with which he is presented. Taken further, however, what this brief story illustrates is that, although we take map-reading for granted as part of our contemporary lives, the relationship between cartographic representations and the knowledge of place built up through subjective experience is not necessarily a close one. Rather than understand this event merely as a minor character's inability to read maps, we do well in seeing that there is a more general property of map-reading and spatial representation at work here.

Maps—both map-making and map-reading—have long been an area of great interest to cultural geographers. There is a great deal of subjectivity involved with both representations of space and their interpretation. As contemporary geographer David Harvey points out, "our subjective experience can take us into realms of perception, imagination fiction and fantasy, which produce mental spaces and maps as so many mirages of the supposedly 'real thing.' We also discover that different societies or sub-groups possess different conceptions [of space]."[37] Maps hardly hold knowledge of an objective or universal character. Instead, "Cartography is about locating, identifying and bounding phenomena and thereby situating events, processes and things within a coherent spatial frame. It imposes spatial order on phenomena."[38] Moreover, the history of maps, as Harvey explains, is wrapped up in the particular textures of modern social and political power. Historically speaking, as modern empires engaged in ever-greater campaigns of spatial domination and colonization—through exploration and conquest—maps took on a new role:[39] "The conquest of space first required that it be conceived of as something usable, malleable and therefore capable of domination through human action. A new chronological net for human exploration and action was created through navigation and map-making. Cadastral survey permitted the unambiguous definition of property rights in land. Space thus came to be represented, like time and value, as abstract, objective, homogeneous, and universal in its qualities."[40] Benet's invention of Región—albeit for literary purposes—points to what cultural geographers have identified as the two sources of the formation of space. Places are constituted both materially—through the physical modification of the existing natural environment—and also through immaterial means. That is—following from Sauer's early twentieth-century insights—they are dependent also on mental conceptions and less tangible cultural understandings of place. In this vein Harvey has written that "It is important to recognize that regions are 'made' or 'constructed' as much in imagination as in material form and that though entity-like, regions crystallize out as a distinctive form from some mix of material, social and mental processes."[41] From this point of view, Benet's region of Región offers a compelling, literary perspective on the way in which our mental ideas about space—whether prior to or even after the modification of a "natural" environment—are just as important as the material conditions that are manifested in a given place.[42]

Existing literary criticism of Benet's work—while it may not have explored the connection with cultural geography explicitly—has nevertheless picked up on the way in which Región is both a material and mental space.[43] One critic, for example, has written that Región is "not only an objectified geographic space but that it is also a space of consciousness . . . a space configured both materially and mentally."[44] Another Benetian scholar who dialogues with cartography—but not necessarily cultural geography—does well in highlighting the constructed nature of all maps, noting that Benet's "cartography is ambiguous paradoxical and enigmatic."[45] Yet another literary critic has written extensively of "various cartographic discrepancies" that exist between the Map of Región and the information conveyed in the Región novels—clarifying also that these "discrepancies, of course, are in line with the aesthetic principles of the author."[46] That is, given Benet's belief in the non-rational nature of creative processes, it would make little sense for his map to do away with the "zone of shadows" that is so central to his novels. It follows that, whether in the Map of Región or in his Región fiction, Benet's "imprecisions . . . call attention toward the process of artistic creation at the same time that they affirm the illusory nature essential to Región's representation."[47] Whether intentional or not, there can be no doubt that imprecision in the realm of fiction is a virtue that Benet holds dear.[48]

The seeming discrepancies between Benet's Map of Región and his Región novels not only reflect his emphasis on enigma, they also come to reconstitute what is his essentially Bergsonian distinction between spatiality and temporality. That is, Benet's Bergsonian roots hold that time is the dimension in which not everything is given at once.[49] As opposed to a spatial reality that is defined by the hard borders of matter, the realm of time is fluid and ever-changing. In this philosophical context, the "discrepancies" and "imprecisions" noted by critics with regard to the Map of Región reflect also the resistance of temporality to spatial representation. Even in the creation of a static map, Benet seems reluctant to embrace fully the strict rationality of intellectual or spatial thought. This reluctance might be understood also as an awareness of what cultural geographers have underscored as an essential characteristic of cartographic representation. David Harvey writes, "Any system of representation, in fact, is a spatialization of sorts which automatically freezes the flow of experience and in so doing distorts what it strives to represent"; and also that "there is, of course, an extended literature on the limitations of cartographic operations and plenty of evaluative materials concerning the uses and abuses of maps."[50] In the end, whether the Map of Región expresses Benet's respect for enigma, his nod to Bergsonian temporality, or an insight into the aporias of cartographic representation specifically—or as is more likely, all three at once—it is clear that space for Benet is complex.

In 1982, Benet recounted having worked with both a physical and a political map of Spain while a youth in school. This anecdote proves instructive given that, as one critic notes, "Región and the cartographic representation that Juan offers us superimposes the two layers mentioned: the physical and the political."[51] The uneasy coexistance of these two ways of representing space points to the complex interaction between space as a material reality (territory, topography, physical geography) and a mental conception (politcal, human forces, and cultural geography). Indeed, as Harvey expresses concisely, "Space, like cartography, is as much a mental as a material construct."[52] Moreover, Benet's revealing anecdote is more broadly reflective of widespread teaching practices that have encouraged a static view of landscape. Similar practices are described by cultural geographer Carl Sauer, in a reflection that squares with Benet's memory. In his essay "The Fourth Dimension of Geography," Sauer wrote that: "Geography as taught in the schools came under the criticism that the pupils were drilled in place names and their location, in river systems, the height of mountains, boundaries and capitals of states. The meaning of toponymy was lost in rote memorizing, it was said. Learning place names and their association on maps was a dull matter, perhaps more so for teacher than student."[53] For Benet, the uneasy coexistence of the political map and the physical map pointed to two different understandings of space.[54] Whereas the rote memorization required of the student in relation to the political map was often "the instrument of the teacher's repression [of the student]," the physical map allowed the student to dream big.[55] The political map represents, for Benet, the tyranny of rationality and intellection. In complementary fashion, the topographical map presents the opportunity for creative processes to express themselves.

In this light, the invention of Región and even the Map of Región accompanying *Herrumbrosas lanzas* offered Benet a unique opportunity to grapple with the intersection of the universal and the particular, of the abstract and the concrete, of rationality and the inexplicable source of creativity. To say that Benet's creation of the mythical and only semi-fictional area called Región is merely the product of two cartographies, however, is insufficient. In fact, as the work of geographer Henri Lefebvre asserts, it is not easy to maintain a strict opposition between physical and political maps. Space is much more complex, indeed. Seen through the lens of cultural geography, Región is ultimately a multidimensional (narrative and cartographical) space in which numerous visions compete, coincide, and overlap.

Multidimensional Space, Narration, and History

Henri Lefebvre is in many respects the cultural geographer, philosopher, and spatial thinker who has most contributed to contemporary academic debates over how space is conceived, represented, and lived. His work sustained a number of connections with the philosophy of Henri Bergson, and his model of space was in turn embraced explicitly by geographer David Harvey.[56] Lefebvre's most recognized work in Anglophone circles has been *The Production of Space,* originally published in French in 1974 and translated into English by Donald Nicholson-Smith in 1991. Literary scholars and cultural geographers alike have latched onto Lefebvre's multidimensional model of space and have employed it in their respective fields. In line with an entire tradition of cultural geography—including also the work of Carl Sauer—the Lefebvrian idea of space is that of a *process* involving both material and immaterial forces. As Lefebvre's triadic model of the production of space outlines, space is conceived, perceived, and actually lived—with representations of space, spaces of representation, and spatial practices all working together to make up a dynamic understanding of space as a movement.[57] As is evident in his stated goal of arriving at a "unitary theory of physical, mental and social space," space is, in fact, multidimensional.[58]

Lefebvre's nuanced and multidimensional understanding of space stems from the fact that it cannot be understood without reference to time. His elaboration of the complex relationship between space and time recalls Bergson's own philosophy, and as such might just as easily be applied in the same way to Benet's emphasis on temporality.[59] For example, Lefebvre explicitly asserts, "Time is distinguishable but not separable from space."[60] Yet there is an explicitly social component in Lefebvre's thought that is lacking in Bergson: "time is known and actualized in space, becoming a social reality by virtue of spatial practice. Similarly, space is known only in and through time."[61] Given the social dimensions of Benet's novels—first and foremost the importance of the civil war for understanding his fiction—literary critics might turn to Lefebvre's work, just as they have to Bergson's, as a way of understanding his novels' emphasis on temporality.

The "spatialization of time," for example, is just as important for Lefebvre as it had been for Bergson. Consider the Bergsonian tenor of his remarks on the notion of clock time: "On a watch or a clock, the mechanical devices subject the cyclical—the hands that turn in sixty seconds or twelve hours—to the linearity of counting. In recent measuring devices, and even watches, the cyclical (the dial) tends to disappear. Fully quantified social time is indifferent to day and night, to the rhythms of impulses."[62] Lefebvre also opposes a quantitative understanding of time (which is a "spatialization of time") to a qualitative notion of time (which is lived time, as duration). The consequences of the quantification of a qualitative temporality are, for the spatial thinker, disastrous.[63] Lefebvre writes, "Time is projected into space through measurement, by being homogenized, by appearing in things and products."[64] This notion might also be harnessed to explain Benet's narration of the mania for working on clocks demonstrated by the character Cayetano Corral in *Una meditación*.

More important, Lefebvre also continues cultural geography's twentieth-century tradition of "reading landscape"—even if his view is more nuanced than, for example, Sauer's, noting that "the fact remains, however, that an already produced space can be decoded, can be *read*."[65] Lefebvre's final work—titled *Rhythmanalysis* and published posthumously—should, in fact, be seen as part of his attempt to establish a more appropriate complex model for reading landscape, sustaining the emphasis that Sauer effectively placed on temporality: "the rhythmanalyst concerns himself with temporalities and their relations within wholes"; "Without omitting the spatial and places, of course, he makes himself more sensitive to times than to spaces. He will come to 'listen' to a house, a street, a town, as an audience listens to a symphony."[66] This multifaceted approach avoids the pitfalls that come with a purely visual approach to space, which may risk reducing the landscape to a static image. Sound is important in the sense that it necessarily imbues investigations of landscape with a temporal character. In this way, the spatial theorist thus sustains cultural geography's traditional emphasis on both landscape and time.

Another significant component of Lefebvre's spatial theory is his incorporation of a healthy (Bergsonian) skepticism that underscores the limitations of what he calls analytical knowledge—which is, in effect, a natural complement to Bergson's rejection of intellection and Benet's suspicion of logical reasoning.[67] Similarly, with great relevance for Benet's approach to the Map of Región (above), he writes, "Knowledge falls into a trap when it makes representations of space the basis for the study of 'life,' for in doing so it reduces lived experience"—specifying that by "representations of space" he means such things as "maps and plans, transport and communication systems, information conveyed by images and signs."[68] Instead, "knowledge must proceed with caution, restraint, respect. It must respect lived experience rather than belabouring it as the domain of ignorance and error, rather than absorbing it into positive knowledge as vanquished ignorance," writes Lefebvre, highlighting the necessity of "understanding lived experience, situating it, and restoring it to the dynamic constellation of concepts."[69] This conception of knowledge resonates with Bergson's philosophy just as clearly as it does with Benet's literary aesthetic. Lefebvre, Bergson, and Benet all eschew the fixity of pre-established spatialized models in favor of the more shadowy zone of shifting temporality and real movement—in sum, emphasizing the unpredictable and imprecise, uncertain elements of lived experience.[70]

Apart from its implicit debt to Bergsonian philosophy and its explicit connections with cultural geography, Lefebvre's theory of space is relevant to Benet's work also as regards the notion of narration. The cultural geographer's multidimensional model of space has been characterized as being constituted by "three dimensions [that] exist in a state of uncertainty"— with uncertainty and complexity being, of course, the basis of the novelist's hallmark literary style.[71] As literary scholars have pointed out, Juan Benet's narrative style is a multidimensional one that suggests an equally complex view of novelistic space. Critics have long suggested that, in *Volverás a Región,* the objective non-focused narration that predominates during the first section of the novel is in fact mixed with multiple, other perspectives, managing to obfuscate an objective perception of events.[72] The high degree of narrative complexity displayed by Benet's first novel functions as a complement to the central premise of cultural geography that space never exists in itself, but rather always in time as lived experience. Moving beyond a dual-layered model of narration in *Volverás a Región,* one critic in particular has asserted that "a better image would be that of the superimposition of multiple transparencies each containing similar but not identical material, and each pertaining to one of the text's multiple narrative visions."[73] This text—as are others in his Región series—is constructed through the interplay of various oppositional voices, each positing its own relationship between temporal consciousness and the unique spatial geography of Benet's semi-fictional land.

And yet, the intimate but complex connection between space, time, and narration in the Región fiction must also involve the primary role of history. As we have seen, Benet's life and literary production were both greatly affected by the events of the Spanish Civil War, and subsequently shaped in direct opposition to the Franco dictatorship's normative and ideological notion of history.[74] Despite the narrative cacophony of his fiction—despite the reluctance of his characters to take action in the present, the fact that they seek shelter, instead, in their past memories—Benet's novels stress the essential importance of space and time as actually *lived*. It is from this essential trait that one may begin to understand their seeming lack of coherence. The negative connotations of this "lack of coherence" are better understood in a positive sense as a respect for complexity. It is this notion of complexity, after all, that the dictatorship viewed as a threat—the incorporations of other existing opinions being viewed with scorn. It may be said that the *golpe de estado* of 18 July 1936 sought to eliminate the complexity of differing opinions through its imposition of the myth of a univocal and homogeneous Spanish people. As one critic has written, Benet's world "is constructed and sustained not via adherence to a concrete reality, but through the construction of an open space where contradiction and uncertainty reign."[75] In addition, it is undeniable that his Región novels form "a reflection on the historical destiny of [Spain] beginning with the Civil War."[76]

In this regard, Lefebvre's remarks on "Time and History" prove instructive also for understanding the fundamental interrelationship between space, time, and history in Benet's fiction. He writes that "Totality eludes the lived, because the lived never reaches it. It should be noted that lived time is not only mental (subjective) time. It is also social time, biological time, physical and cosmic time, cyclic or linear time. Already plural (differential)."[77] Time—as opposed to space, but nevertheless including space—is a complex, heterogeneous, and internally contradictory realm. This notion can be applied to Benet's texts as a way of understanding why the reader encounters a plurality of views on time, all of which co-exist. There is, in Benet's novels, a Bergsonian spatialized or linear time, appearing in Cayetano Corral's clocks, for example. There is, also, the cyclical time of myth, which has been signaled by traditional Benetian scholarship through discussions of Numa, the mysterious guard of the Mantuan forest. There is the mental or subjective time evoked through the interior monologues of Benet's character-narrators (Dr. Sebastián and Marré Gamallo of *Volverás a Región,* for example). There is the physical, geological time of Región's geographic development. There is the social (and biological) time experienced by the families calling Región their home, captured in reflections of youth (in *Una meditación,* for example). And connecting them all is the time and space of war—the Spanish Civil War—which intersects with family histories and manifests itself in the ruins of time and landscape, descriptions of territory, individual memories and reflections, and whose very basis is the country's characteristic, enduring social conflict.

Benet's own remarks on history confirm that it is, for him, a matter of supreme importance. In fact, as he writes in the essay "Sobre el carácter tétrico de la historia" (On the Grave Character of History), "it is the last [subject] that should be taught in school."[78]

> Above all else History should be a prohibited topic because the last thing that the child should learn is how we have gotten to where we are. There are two possibilities: either one teaches it honestly or one does not teach it. . . . But what is impardonable is to teach history with a determined viewpoint, whether that is nationalist, religious or cultural, because that is quite far from what history really is. . . . The history a child studies is, as a rule, a string of imprecisions, a deceptive story that only serves to produce an adult with an incorrect understanding of many essential things: about his era, the era of his parents, about his country, his religion and his culture. About history, in point of fact. And it can't be any other way because history is either summarized and falsified or else it is not taught. Every summary is a falsification.[79]

Benet's views can be partially understood once one recognizes that—as numerous scholars of his work have noted—the Franco dictatorship sought to wipe the deeply rooted conflicts in contemporary society off the map of Spain. One Benetian scholar who has focused on the interrelationship of history and fiction in his texts has written that under Francoism "dissonance has been expurgated from history." Contextualizing his argument within the work of both Spanish and non-Spanish historians, he argues that "Francoist historiography is resolutely shaped by a conception of truth and temporality in which history is viewed less as a complex web of diachronic and synchronic relationships, both formed and revealed through narration, than as an unfolding of time that is repetitive, deterministic and radically unchangeable."[80]

This view of history can help us to understand how both space and time converge in Benet's work and how, through the complex act of narration, they create an open space opposed not merely to Francoist history itself, but moreover, to any univocal perspective on history. That is, all narrowly conceived histories—Spanish or otherwise—are reductions of lived experience, simplifications of what Lefebvre called totality.[81] In this sense, Benet's fiction is perhaps best understood as a chaotic attempt to represent plurality itself. Through the complex act of narration, Benet brings the notion of "dissonance" back into the picture and necessarily connects it with the textures of an identifiable *Spanish* history. The strength of his novels is to have combined an abstract philosophy of time with the concreteness of place. In his semi-fictional land of Región, time and landscape, memory and maps, imagination and history all converge in a decidedly social arena—and negotiating this complex academic terrain is, in fact, what cultural geography is all about.

If—as is clearly stated at the beginning of *Volverás a Región*—the people of his invented land "have opted to forget their own history," then perhaps this needs to be explained through recourse to Benet's own remarks on the subject.[82] If his essay "Sobre el carácter tétrico de la historia" is any guide, the inhabitants of Región would rather forget their history than simplify it; they would opt to forget it rather than live in a falsification. In doing so, however, they move fully into the shadowy zone of the enigmatic that so captivated Juan Benet and that constitutes the shifting ground of his worldview.

Epilogue

The Role of Enigma

> Literature, philosophy or science amount to little more than man's feigned accommodation to the kingdom of fate under the mask of knowledge.
>
> Juan Benet, *Cartografía personal*

In the essay from the collection *En ciernes* titled "Incertidumbre, memoria, fatalidad y temor" (Uncertainty, Memory, Fatality and Dread), Juan Benet writes of "men of letters" who are moved "to abandon an area—one of the few—in which the human spirit feels stable." As he goes on to explain, these travelers are in fact those who embrace the uncertainty that characterizes the field of literature. Literature, he writes, is an enigmatic terrain. It is commonly drenched in all manner of ambiguities, ambiguities that concern everything from the word to the sentence, from grammar to syntax, from content and argument to the entirety of discourse in general, and in light of which it becomes difficult and awkward to affirm not only what is the principle that sustains them, but moreover whether there even exists a principle capable of being expressed by means of any of the resources and methods that are furnished by the literary art.[1]

This comment alone perhaps explains the difficult style of his impenetrable novels—but there is much more at stake. Enigma is the core tenet of the Benetian worldview. For those of literary cut, he insists, "the world, nature, society and man will always be enigmas."[2] In fact, if his essays and fiction are any indication, there is very little from Benet's perspective that is not forced—at one time or another—to make concessions to enigma. Indeed, this notion lies at the base of his nuanced understanding of space, his appropriation of Bergson's philosophy of time, his approach to civil engineering, and even—perhaps even particularly—in his understanding of the Spanish Civil War.

All Is Enigma

Motivated by Benet's own frequent and direct invocations of the notion of enigma, Benetian scholars have traditionally signaled its importance. One critic alone has applied the word to Benet's "enigmatic symbols" the "enigmatic, impenetrable reality" of his first two novels, the "enigmatic clock" worked on by Cayetano Corral in *Una Meditación,* and "the enigmas of inspiration," among many others.[3] Even where the word *enigma* or *enigmatic* is not used, it is implicit, as in one scholar's assertion that Benet's strength is its "rhetoric of ambiguity."[4] It is useful to see how this concept lies at the base of each of this book's chapters. In every case, the notion of enigma conveys a lack of traditional understanding, delimiting a zone of shadows into which reason cannot venture—but it also holds a promise of sorts unfolding from the recognition that things are more complex, and also more open, than they may appear.

Chapter 4 applied the unique understanding of space developed over the twentieth century by the field of cultural geography to an understanding of Benet's fiction. Enigma results from the mysterious slippages between the Map of Región and his fiction, just as it oozes from the mysterious landscape of his invented land itself. "The Región range shows itself like an enigmatic witness," Benet writes in *Volverás a Región.*[5] Through the invention of Región, the Spanish landscape is itself an enigma—it is an area governed by mysterious forces, plagued by distant gunshots and in fact defined by ruin.[6] His characters, trapped in decaying houses, are hardly at ease in their country and remain at the mercy of events that unfold independently of any action of their own. The unnamed traveler who haunts Benet's first novel, leaving Región to roam over its geography, serves as a questioner of sorts, interrogating the relationship between the landscape, its inhabitants, and a history that they "have opted to forget." Like Benet's novels, the field of cultural geography seeks to synthesize the two opposing forces—material and immaterial—that make up our complex and enigmatic social world.

Chapter 3 explored the Bergsonian inheritance of Benet's essays and fiction. At the base of this connection is a respect for enigma and the unknown, which play a role in time, memory, knowledge, and language. For Bergson, time is the dimension in which not everything is given or known at once, a fact that plunges Benet's characters into the trap of (recollection) memory and a disconnection from the present. Rationality, as expressed in both intellectual thought and language itself, is also a zone of shadows. "Human reason," writes Benet, "is complete and competent in the sense that it knows how to find a solution to the problems that reason itself, through its being, poses. But it is incomplete and incompetent in that in order to resolve those problems, it requires another mode of being."[7] Similarly, in *El ángel del señor abandona a Tobías* Benet writes: "All enigma stems from the capacity of reason to take in a wider temporality than that of the present."[8] It is thought itself, temporal knowledge, that plunges Región's characters into an abyss from which they cannot easily escape. In Bergsonian fashion, it is the reason that turns back upon itself—better understood as intuition—that is truly necessary. Although intuition eschews the hard lines and borders of intellectual thought, its enigmatic ground paradoxically shows a way forward.

Chapter 2 asserted the importance of Benet's first chosen profession, civil (hydraulic) engineering. His active participation in the construction of numerous civil works projects (dams, canals, and the like) went hand in hand with a well-defined position regarding the history of water resources in Spain. Imagining—at one time—what he would do if president of his nation, he suggested a way forward that assured access to water resources as a right of everyone living in Spain. His thoughts on the field of engineering itself show remarkable similarities with his remarks in his other, more literary-themed essays—for example in "Ingeniería e intimidad." Instead of seeking refuge in the seemingly quantitative nature of engineering, he sought out the more enigmatic ground where the sciences commingle with the humanities. To that effect, he criticized other engineers for their hyperspecialization and even oversaw a series of books reconciling civil-engineering thought with matters of more widespread debate, a series titled Ciencias, Humanidades e Ingeniería (CHI). In addition, as Benet was never content to remain restricted by disciplinary boundaries, it is no surprise that his hydraulic-engineering work and love for water found its way into his Región fiction—through its presentation of waters, bridges, and even dams. Water itself was a source of mysterious wonder for Benet, as he made clear in his book *El agua en España*.

At the base of all the enigmas discussed is the primary enigma—Spain itself. Chapter 1 explored the numerous debates over Spanish soil and territory—Spain's landscape as both a cause of and a theater for the Civil War. Both Benet's fiction and his essay *¿Qué fue la guerra civil?* portray his home country as destroyed, and pervaded by suspicions and human antagonisms. As he writes in *Volverás a Región,* the war boasts "several enigmas, many things that are not understood if they are analyzed solely through the prism of the economics of war."[9] In yet another essay, published in the collection *La moviola de Eurípides,* Benet explains this enigmatic nature of Spain in no uncertain terms: "Spain . . . continues to be an enigma, a reality incomprehensible for many; maintaining many of its enchantments fresh, having preserved in good measure the originality of its culture and enjoying a few peculiarities that distinguish Spanish life from that of its neighbors and relatives, our country seems to conserve whole and semi-hidden all of its tragic and recurrent power for disappointment and revenge."[10]

This essay, written and published in 1980, some five years after the death of dictator Francisco Franco, alleges that Spain's enigma is—at its root—a historical circumstance. This historical circumstance, of course, invites historical understanding, but not necessarily historical explanation. The civil war is—for Benet—"unintelligible," but so too is humankind.[11] Spain provides a specific example of how our base instincts and capacity for revenge come to rear their head in political and social arenas. As Benet persistently suggests through his fiction and essays, it is very hard indeed to come to terms with Spain's history—even harder given the way history came to be co-opted by the Francoist state.[12]

Conclusion

It is clear that the act of *Understanding Juan Benet* requires a certain flexibility in our approach. In his complex work *Aesthetic Theory,* renowned cultural theorist Theodor Adorno discusses what Robert Hullot-Kentor (the book's translator) has rendered in English as "enigmaticalness." "Artworks are enigmas," Adorno writes, "They contain the potential for the solution; the solution is not objectively given. Every artwork is a picture puzzle, a puzzle to be solved, but this puzzle is constituted in such a fashion that it remains a vexation, the pre-established routing of its observer."[13] One must remember that Benet's works of fiction are works born of artistic process. One must also remember that he saw civil engineering, too, as an art.[14] From this perspective, it is unwise for us to purport to "solve" the "problem" posed by Juan Benet through his enigmatic novels and essays.

Rather than give us a problem to solve, Benet has—through his creative process—given us an invitation of sorts. It is an invitation to rethink our approach, to allow for imprecisions and errors, to allow for nuance in our methods, and for complexity in our models. Adorno continues, "Understanding is itself a problematic category in the face of art's enigmaticalness."[15] In the end, Benet's own particular "enigmaticalness" is a positive force. It is a recognition of the complexity of human experience, and an invitation for us to see the limitations of existing ways of thinking and the potential for rethinking what may have previously gone unnoticed.

This has, of course, been the central insight motivating *Understanding Juan Benet: New Perspectives.* It is worth reiterating that there remains much in Benet's oeuvre—his work as both an author and an engineer—to be explored by future critics. Existing scholarship has only scratched the surface of the Benetian enigma—one that has survived recent interdisciplinary changes in literary studies and that will assuredly survive future collisions between the humanities, the social sciences, and even the sciences themselves.

Notes

Introduction

1. The preface written for the 1984 compilation *Critical Approaches to the Writing of Juan Benet* points to this now canonical characterization: "Complex, difficult and enigmatic—these and like adjectives have been the weapons wielded both by those seeking to praise and, at times, to condemn Benet. Few would argue that Benet's works are easily penetrated, and readers have on occasion turned away from them in nonplussed frustration" (Manteiga, Herzberger, and Compitello, *Critical Approaches,* ix–x).

2. *Volverás a Región* was supposed to be published in 1967 with Destino, but as Benet himself relates in an essay from *La moviola de Eurípides*—"La historia editorial y judicial de *Volverás a Región*" (The Editorial and Legal History of *Return to Región*)— its publication was delayed until 1968.

3. As Herzberger notes in his review of Cabrera's 1983 book, when published it was already five years out of date with Benet's existing literary production as it only covered texts up until 1978 ("*Juan Benet,* by Vicente Cabrera," 441).

4. The period from 1874 to the start of the Spanish Civil War is covered comprehensively by Gerald Brenan in his book *The Spanish Labyrinth.* I make references to other texts as appropriate.

5. See Carr, *Spain: A History,* chapter 8; also *Spain 1808–1939;* Graham and Labanyi, *Spanish Cultural Studies,* 21–52.

6. Benet, *La moviola de Eurípides,* 24 (in the essay "La novela en la España de hoy" (1980).

7. Carr, *Spain: A History,* 220.

8. See Ullman, *The Tragic Week.*

9. Carr, *Spain 1809–1939,* 574. In his first speech to the country, Primo de Rivera declared his aim "to open a brief parenthesis in the constitutional life of Spain and to re-establish it as soon as the country offers us men uncontaminated by the vices of political organization" (qtd. in Carr, *Spain 1809–1939,* 564).

10. Carr, *Spain 1808–1939,* 580–81.

11. On the end of the monarchy, see Graham and Labanyi, *Spanish Cultural Studies,* 133. On the Republic, see Carr, *Spain: A History; Spain 1808–1939;* Graham and Labanyi, *Spanish Cultural Studies;* Cantarino, *Civilización y cultura de España.*

12. Luis López Guerra puts it well: "The Civil War obviously did not arise suddenly out of a single casual event or spontaneous circumstance. As Miguel Delibes so graphically puts it in his latest novel on the Civil War published in 1987, everyone had known for a long time that 'la gorda' ('the big one') was about to blow. The war was essentially the violent accumulation of a series of historical tensions" ("The Legacy of the Spanish Civil War Today," 256). I have sketched out these tensions in the main text. See also Brenan, *The Spanish Labyrinth.*

13. See Brenan, *The Spanish Labyrinth.*

14. As Benet discussed in his *¿Qué fue la guerra civil?* (What Was the Civil War?)—and as will be discussed in chapter 1 of the present work—the civil war was actually the product of two simultaneous uprisings, one by the political right and one by the political left.

15. Qtd. in Núñez, "Encuentro con Juan Benet," 18; see also Compitello, *Ordering the Evidence,* 41n1.

16. Benet, *Cartografía personal,* 316.

17. Benet, *Cartografía personal,* 265.

18. For example: Compitello (*Ordering the Evidence,* 43n7) cites two articles by Isaac Montero in which it is alleged that Benet's turn from social realism was said to represent "an ethical ambivalence and tacit support of the reactionary ideology of the francoist regime."

19. On Benet's anarchist sympathies, see *Cartografía personal,* 285. The details mentioned in the text are important for understanding the political commitments of his enigmatic fiction—commitments that have not always seemed clear to many critics. In a review of Vicente Cabrera's *Juan Benet,* for example, David Herzberger takes the critic to task for remaining vague about the political dimensions of Benet's literary vision and view of the war (*"Juan Benet,* by Vicente Cabrera," 441). Regarding the wine, Benet has said: "I was here, in Madrid, in this house. When it happened, at five or six in the morning, I woke all of the kids up and we opened a bottle of Rioja that we had set aside, from the harvest of 36. Someone—I don't remember who—had given it to me saying: 'Drink it on the day that Franco dies.' And there it was, a bottle with no label; and we finished it off. The wine tasted incredible" (*Cartografía personal,* 319).

20. Compitello, "The Paradoxes of Praxis," 16. The critic goes on to say that the misunderstandings surrounding Benet's position have been fueled by the "scant [critical] attention" paid to Benet's essay *¿Qué fue la guerra civil?* and that Benet's first novel is "in my estimation, the most complex and literarily challenging condemnation of Francoism produced from within Spain during the postwar period" ("The Paradoxes of Praxis," 17). See also Compitello (*Ordering the Evidence,* 53–59, 65–70; "Bibliography: Juan Benet and His Critics") where Benet's distaste for Francoist ideology is discussed at length. Also of note is that, in an essay published in the *Revista de Obras Públicas* after Franco's death, Benet wrote: "I have never had, nor do I have now, much fondness for a State that does not reflect my tastes" ("Ingeniería e intimidad," 75).

21. This anecdote appears in the essay "Sobre la cartografía elemental," published as the first section of *Cartografía personal* (9–12). For discussions of maps and cartography, see also Wood, "Una aproximación"; Rivero, "Juan Benet"; and chapter 4.

22. Benet, *Cartografía personal,* 11.

23. Benet, *Cartografía personal,* 11–12.

24. His remark regarding writing is quoted in Núñez, "Encuentro con Juan Benet," 17.

25. See particularly Compitello, "Región's Brazilian Backlands"; Wood, "Una aproximación." This will be discussed extensively in chapter 4.

26. There will also be historical space and fictional space, mythic space, mental space, conceived space, lived space, and so on.

27. The statist and Catholic character of education under the dictatorship has been dramatized in numerous Spanish films—most recently the 2008 filmic adaptation of *Los girasoles ciegos* (The Blind Sunflowers) by director José Luis Cuerda.

28. See Benet, "Barojiana" (included in *Otoño en Madrid*); and Compitello, *Ordering the Evidence,* 41.

29. Benet, *Cartografía personal,* 316–17. Benet remarks that he learned English precisely in order to read Faulkner (120), while his other professed literary influences include Sterne, Henry James, Melville (in Núñez, "Encuentro con Juan Benet," 21); and Poe, Proust, and Euclides Da Cunha (in *Cartografía personal,* 315–17). Vicente Cabrera cites Proust, Joyce, Melville, Sartre, Malraux, and Camus (*Juan Benet,* 2) as influences, although Benet mentions elsewhere that he dislikes Jean-Paul Sartre as well as Dostoievski and Tolstoi (Benet, *Cartografía personal,* 80). Benet states that, although *odio* (hate) is too strong a word, authors like Lezama, Fuentes, Asturias, Joyce, Borges, and so forth are not to his liking (80).

30. "My brother, who always found a way to lord over me the fact that he was, from birth, a year ahead of me, had met Baroja a year earlier merely by deciding to visit him at his house and telling him that he had read all of his work (which even then had already exceeded 120 titles) with enthusiasm and eagerness" (rpt. in Benet, *Otoño en Madrid,* 19). Benet makes a similar remark about his brother preceding him in everything by a year in the essay "Un extempore" (87).

31. Benet, *Cartografía personal,* 318–19.

32. Qtd. in Núñez, "Encuentro con Juan Benet," 17. Benet, *Cartografía personal,* 318.

33. The quote comes from Núñez, "Encuentro con Juan Benet," 17. Benet reflects on the connection between his engineering work and literary production of this period in a short essay, "A Short Biographia Literaria," published in English translation in the posthumously published collection *Una biografía literaria,* 175–79.

34. Benet discusses the origins of *Una meditación* in Núñez, "Encuentro con Juan Benet," 22.

35. It was José Antonio Fernández Ordóñez who invited Benet to China with him in 1976, and Blanca Andreu once noted the enormous impact this trip had

on Benet, who wrote that the trip "made history" for him, and that Benet always wanted to write something about it. See Baeza, "Acto de Homenaje," 73.

36. Kathleen M. Vernon reflects in the introduction to her edited volume on the international reception of Benet's work: "In fact, one of the most interesting aspects of what Ricardo Gullón has termed the 'Benet phenomenon' is the great interest incited among North American Hispanists with regards to Benet's narrative work; his work has inspired four books of criticism in English without even a single book in Spanish having appeared" (Vernon, *Juan Benet,* 10–11).

37. A fourth volume of *Herrumbrosas lanzas* remained unfinished upon Benet's death in 1993.

38 *Cartografía personal,* 207. Benet shares that he had already built up an "extensive library concerning the Civil War."

39 *Cartografía personal,* 207.

40. These last novels were not part of the Región cycle, but as Compitello notes in regard to *En la penumbra:* "Although the final version of this text did not appear until 1989, Benet published a first version of a portion of it in 1982. Its creative gestation coincides with that of the *lanzas* texts" ("Benet and Spanish Postmodernism," 261). Margenot also classifies *En el estado* (1977) as a novel outside of the Región series (*Zonas y sombras,* 57).

41. Benet had published in the field of civil engineering as far back as an essay from 1976, "Ingeniería e intimidad" (Engineering and Intimacy), and even his essay "Soluciones constructivas en obras de regadío" (Constructive Solutions In Irrigation Work), for example, which was published in the *Revista de Obras Públicas* in 1965 (113.3001: 406–17). The work on tunnels was titled "Panorama actual en las relaciones contracturales en la construcción de túneles en España y su posible desarrollo futuro" (The Current State of Contractual Relations in the Construction of Tunnels in Spain and Its Possible Future Development). See the 2009 publication (a posthumously published anthology of Benet's engineering work) titled *Si yo fuera presidente* (If I Were President).

42. See Herzberger, "Juan Benet's Death." Also Margenot, "Introducción" to *Saúl ante Samuel* for the collaboration between Benet and the critic on a new edition of *Saúl ante Samuel* that was cut short due to Benet's untimely death. Margenot nonetheless went on to publish the new edition with Cátedra in 1994 as originally agreed, having had access to Benet's original manuscript.

43. On January 6 and 7, 1993, a number of articles paying homage to Benet's life and work appeared in prominent Spanish newspapers such as *El País, ABC,* and *Diario 16* (Margenot, "Preface" to *Juan Benet,* ix). He was also honored with special issues in his honor published in *El ojo de la aguja* ("Juan Benet Goitia," 76) and the journal *El Crítico,* published by Juan Carlos Suñén, who also would edit a collection of Benet's writings titled *Prosas civiles.*

44. See also Baltanas, in Baeza, "Acto de Homenaje," 66–67. Molina Ortega notes, "Benet was far from suspecting the controversy that would be raised, after his death, over the intent to give his name to the reservoir on which he worked during those years, a subject on which the locals refused to give way, persisting,

whoever the named person was, in calling the reservoir the Porma" (*Las otras regiones de Juan Benet*, 9n3).

45. Spanish poet Miguel Hernández was imprisoned for his criticism of the dictatorship and died behind bars in 1942. As regards exiled authors: Antonio Machado and Max Aub fled to France; Ramón Sender and Jorge Guillén to the United States; Juan Ramón Jiménez to Cuba, Puerto Rico, and the United States; Rafael Alberti to France and then Chile; Francisco Ayala to the United States and Latin America; Maria Zambrano to Cuba, Puerto Rico, and France, among other places; Rosa Chacel to Brazil and Argentina. See also Michael Ugarte's *Literatura española en el exilio*, 1999.

46. This widely recognized political characterization of Spanish intellectuals comes from Blanco Aguinaga et al., *Historia social de la literatura española*, 16. The rigorous censorship of Spanish literature that was put into effect by the Francoist dictatorship in 1939 with the end of the war is noted by Herzberger (*The Novelistic World of Juan Benet*, 6).

47. Qtd. in Núñez, "Encuentro con Juan Benet," 19. Several long paragraphs were in fact cut from Benet's *Una meditación* (Martínez Torrón, "Introducción," 21), for example.

48. See G. G. Brown, *Historia de la literatura española*, 234.

49. As Benet shares in "Barojiana," his brother Paco in fact did this very thing. See chapter 5 of Andrés Trapiello's *Las armas y las letras: Literatura y Guerra Civil (1936–1939)* for a look at the importance of postwar Paris as a center for exiled Spanish intellectuals.

50. The quotation is from critic Frederick R. Benson in his introduction to his *Writers in Arms: The Literary Impact of the Spanish Civil War*, xxv–xxvi.

51. This is the assessment of Sanz Villanueva (*Historia de la literatura española*, 17). Readers interested in censorship may consult books by Eduardo Ruiz Bautista (*Los señores del libro*) and Manuel L. Abellán (*Censura y creación literaria en España 1939–1976*).

52. The first chapter of Herzberger, *The Novelistic World of Juan Benet*, 5–19, provides a much more thorough accounting of the literary trends and history of the postwar period. The sketch I provide here is necessarily brief.

53. Sobejano, *Novela española de nuestro tiempo*, 15. Juan Benet gives his own brief assessment of the literature produced between 1939 and 1975 in an essay written in 1986 and republished as "La literatura durante el período 1939–1975" in Benet, *Infidelidad del regreso*, 105–19.

54. Sobejano, *Novela española de nuestro tiempo*, 16.

55. Hooper, *The New Spaniards* 18–19; García Delgado, "La economía española durante el franquismo," www.vespito.net/historia/franco/ecofran.html, accessed 10 July 2010.

56. One scholar lists authors of the New Novel as being Benet, Cela, Goytisolo, Torrente-Ballester, Julián Ríos, José María Carrascal, and others (Durán, "Juan Benet y la Nueva Novela," 229). See also Herzberger, "Theoretical Approaches to the New Novel." The "New Novel" was a term that had already been applied to

French authors of the 1950s and early 1960s such as Alain Robbe-Grillet and Marguerite Duras. It is worth noting Michael Ugarte's comments on this phenomenon in his essay "Hispanism's Crisis and the Compitello Generation."

57. See the essay "Luis Martín-Santos, un memento" in Benet, *Otoño en Madrid*, 120.

58. See Sobejano, *Novela española de nuestro tiempo*, 371–96.

59. Compitello notes that "while this change led to the production of a more sophisticated type of narrative fiction, it did not signal an abrogation of socially critical intent. From a straight-forward denunciation of ills through the work's content, more recent fiction has moved to a subtler type of denunciation. Such a change implies a redirection of readership as well. No longer bent on attempting to change Spanish society through the medium of his novel, the writer now directed his message at an intellectual elite with the requisite literary competence to understand complexly structured narrative messages. This indirect manner of criticism may be viewed by some as an abandonment of social goals, or as an attempt to achieve more universal appeal. Yet much of the best Spanish narrative is still, in my opinion, inexorably linked to the socio-political climate in Spain. Its main point of reference is, either directly or indirectly, the specificity of its own socio-political environment" (*Ordering the Evidence*, 21).

60. See Spires, "Juan Benet's Poetics of Open Spaces" for a brief contextualization of Benet, Martín-Santos, and Goytisolo in relation to previous Spanish literature.

61. Alvar et al., *Breve historia de la literatura española*, 655.

62. Benet, author's note to English translation of *Volverás a Región/Return to Región*, vii. In that same note Benet writes of how a couple of rejection letters he received "took pleasure in pointing out to me the vices into which I had fallen as a storyteller. 'Your novel,' one said, 'lacks dialogue. Don't forget that almost all the public reads is dialogue, which is also the best exponent of a novelist's skill'" (Benet, *Return to Región*, viii).

63. Spires, "Juan Benet's Poetics of Open Spaces," 3.

64. These include, for example, a series of connecting lines representing the characters' relationships to each other. Compitello (*Ordering the Evidence*, 79) provides a schematic of this sort; other schematics appear on 84, 87, 89, 91, 92, 96, 101, 110, 115, 130, and 131.

65. Fraser, "The Art of Engineering," 173.

66. Benet in Núñez, "Encuentro con Juan Benet," 22. Gimferrer, "Notas sobre Juan Benet," 47, notes that an early draft of *Volverás* was similar—but that it was suggested to him by his friend Dionisio Ridruejo that he split it up into four extensive chapters. Benet discusses Ridruejo in *Otoño en Madrid* and in the essay "Valedictoria a Dionisio," part of the collection *Dionisio Ridruejo: de la Falange a la oposición.*

67. Sobejano, *Novela española de nuestro tiempo*, 383. Sobejano writes also that "The Civil War is like the [novel's] temporal axis, but it does not divide the novel in a [time] before and an after, instead the remembered events revolve around this axis, some appearing in the forward rotation and others in the movement backward. The

temporal puzzle never becomes coherent: time is evoked with no order other than that subjective [order] provided by consciousness" (*Novela española de nuestro tiempo*, 389).

68. Vásquez, "The Creative Task," 64.

69. These include essays collected in *Una biografía literaria* ("William Faulkner," "Las palmeras salvajes," "Dos guías sobre Faulkner," and "Una vida con Faulkner"). As is to be expected, literary critics have often mentioned and explored this connection. In particular, see Pope's essay ("Benet, Faulkner"), the book *Faulkner en España* by María Elena Bravo, and Cabrera's *Juan Benet*. Benet professed admiration for many of Faulkner's novels, not least of which were *Light in August* and *As I Lay Dying*.

70. Benet, "William Faulkner," in *Una biografía literaria*, 78–79.

71. Benet, *La inspiración y el estilo*, 157. The term "good literature" is used by Compitello in his essay "The Paradoxes of Praxis."

72. See Compitello's discussion of this concept in *Ordering the Evidence* (48–53), as well as his interpretation of Benet's meaning in "The Paradoxes of Praxis." See also Benet, *La inspiración y el estilo*, 87–112. As Margenot relates, the development of the grand style, for Benet, stems from the Bible, particularly the Old Testament (Margenot, "Introducción," 28).

73. On the "discovery" of Juan Benet see Herzberger, "How Malcolm Alan Compitello Discovered and Explained Juan Benet."

74. Noted edited volumes include *Critical Approaches to the Writings of Juan Benet*, ed. Manteiga, Herzberger, and Compitello (1984), *Juan Benet: El escritor y la crítica*, ed. K. Vernon (1986), and *Juan Benet: A Critical Reappraisal of His Fiction*, ed. J. Margenot (1997). The following are foundational texts for understanding Juan Benet: David Herzberger's *The Novelistic World of Juan Benet* (1976), Malcolm Alan Compitello's *Ordering the Evidence: Volverás a Región and Civil War Fiction* (1983), and John B. Margenot III's *Zonas y sombras: aproximación a Región de Juan Benet* (1991).

75. Most of the characteristic themes of Benetian scholarship were already noted in 1976 by the very first book-length study of his work, David Herzberger's *The Novelistic World of Juan Benet*. Herzberger discusses aspects central to Benet's literary theory such as notions of style, inspiration, and enigma (22–25); literature and reason (25–28); form and content (28–31); history and poetry (31); metaphor and hyperbole (31–36); epic and lyric (36–41); and in the context of discussing Benet's specific novels—*Volverás a Región/Return to Región* for example—he works through the notion of Región (44–49), the theme of decadence and ruin (49–51), the importance of time (51–56), fatalism and destiny (56–59), the importance of the Civil War (59–62), and instinct vs. reason (62–64). Herzberger's chapter on *Una meditación/A Meditation* looks also at narrative structure and technique (74–80), time and memory (80–86), eros, love, and sex (86–91), and of course, style once again (91–100).

76. Two of these were published in *The American Hispanist* in 1979: Esther Nelson's "Narrative Perspective in *Volverás a Región*" and Malcolm Alan Compitello's

"*Volverás a Región,* the Critics and the Spanish Civil War: A Socio-Poetic Reappraisal." Compitello's book *Ordering the Evidence* expands upon this earlier essay's investigation of narrative structure.

77. These approaches refer to works by Tzvetan Todorov and Gérard Genette that were quite popular among 1960s and 1970s literary scholars. See Compitello, "*Volverás a Región,* the Critics," 14–15. The technical vocabulary that appears in the text is employed by Compitello in "*Volverás a Región,* the Critics and the Spanish Civil War" and *Ordering the Evidence* as well as "The Paradoxes of Praxis." The more recent book by Antonia María Molina Ortega continues to pay homage to this kind of scholarship, containing a dense section exploring the various narrators used by Benet: the extradiegetic, intradiegetic, homodiegetic, and the implied author as well (*Las otras regiones de Juan Benet,* 197–238).

78. As Compitello notes in the first line from his 1983 book, "It is current practice in many quarters to view literary criticism and theory as mutually exclusive. I do not share this belief, but rather see them as activities existing at different levels of analytical conception" (*Ordering the Evidence,* 17).

79. See Nelson, "Narrative Perspective in Volverás a Región" (*American Hispanist*), 3.

80. See Cibreiro, "Narrators and their Narrations," 129.

81. See, for example, Herzberger, "Theoretical Approaches to the New Novel," "La aparición de Juan Benet"; Lupinacci Wescott, "Benet's Theoretical Essays"; Compitello, "Reflexiones sobre el acto de narrar." Also, Bravo, "Región una crónica del discurso literario"; Burunat, *El monólogo interior como forma narrative en la novela española (1940–1975);* García Pérez, "*La inspiración y el estilo*"; Lupinacci Wescott, *Creation and Structure of Enigma;* Manteiga, "Time, Space and Narration"; Margenot, "Los cordajes del discurso en *Saúl ante Samuel*"; Pérez, "The Rhetoric of Ambiguity"; Pope, "Benet, Faulkner, and Bergson's Memory"; Rivkin, "La búsqueda literaria en *Una meditación*"; Sobejano, "Teoría de la novela en la novela española última (Martín-Santos, Benet, Juan y Luis Goytisolo)"; Walkowiak, *A Study of the Narrative Structure of Una meditación.*

82. The quote is from Cabrera, *Juan Benet,* 47.

83. Compitello, *Ordering the Evidence,* chapter 4. Frazer's work was first published in two volumes in 1890 and reached some twelve volumes in subsequent editions.

84. In the author's note to a 1974 edition of *Volverás a Región* (included in the English translation by Rabassa), Benet writes "The truth is that around 1951, and under the influence of reading [Frazer's] *The Golden Bough,* I began to write a novel—which I would finish a couple of years later—in which I narrated some events in a single rural environment (which for lack of a precise geographical determination I baptized with the name of Región) dominated by the distant, nocturnal, and omnipresent figure of the guard of a country estate, a kind of vicar in our lands of the guardian of the sacred wood of Nemi" (Benet, *Return to Región,* v). See also Labanyi, *Myth and History in the Contemporary Spanish Novel,* 253n1; Compitello, *Ordering the Evidence,* 157; Spires, *La novela española de posguerra,*

237–45. One example of Benet's explicit mention of Frazer's text occurs in *El ángel del señor,* 114.

85. See Compitello, *Ordering the Evidence,* 158–59. The quoted material is from 163 and 165, respectively. Also Herzberger, "Enigma as Narrative Determinant in the Novels of Juan Benet," 154; Molina Ortega, *Las otras regiones de Juan Benet,* 45–54.

86. Labanyi writes in the introduction to her book: "My starting point is the assumption that the literary use of myth inevitably—and particularly in the context of fascist ideology—has political connotations. One of the impulses behind this book has been a growing irritation with the school of myth criticism, largely practiced in the United States under the aegis of Northrop Frye, which sets out to prove that the whole of world literature is the manifestation of a timeless universal scheme of symbolic archetypes located in the collective unconscious, dissociated from the particularities of history" (*Myth and History in the Contemporary Spanish Novel,* 2).

87. Labanyi, *Myth and History in the Contemporary Spanish Novel,* 95. Other relevant articles include Orringer, "Epic in a Paralytic State"; Rodríguez, "Reason, Desire and Language"; Martínez Sarrión, "Juan Benet"; and Sobejano, *Novela española de nuestro tiempo,* who calls Benet's work a "mythic transfiguration of reality" (380) whose central theme is ruin. See Margenot, *Zonas y sombras,* chapter 4, "The Return and the Search: Stages of Mythic Process" (my translation).

88. Herzberger, in "Benet y la historia," points to Juan Benet's 1985 review of a newly edited version of an important work by Spanish historian Américo Castro (*España en su historia,* originally published in 1948) as an indicator of this sort of open critique. While it is difficult to approach Benet's works without at least giving an implicit nod toward the history/fiction dichotomy, the critic most invested in this type of analysis has clearly been Herzberger; see "Benet y la historia," *Narrating the Past,* "Splitting the Reference," "Nuevo historicismo," "Juan Benet and the Spanish Civil War," and of course *The Novelistic World of Juan Benet.* See also Compitello, "*Volverás a Región,* the Critics and the Spanish Civil War"; *Ordering the Evidence;* Minardi, "Hacer la Historia"; Molinaro, "Other Knowledge, Other History and *La otra casa de Mazón*"; Navajas, "Intertextuality and the Reappropriation of History in Contemporary Spanish Fiction and Film."

89. As Herzberger has pointed out: "Francoist historians assert and subsequently sustain their dominion over time and narration, so that history systematically emerges as myth; and historians of the Regime draw forth meaning from history that stands resolutely as the equal of truth. In this way they create a powerful master discourse for history, supported by the certitudes of myth, from which no deviations seem possible" (Herzberger, "Splitting the Reference," 128).

90. Herzberger, "Nuevo historicismo," 145. This sort of analysis is also the structuring critique of Labanyi's *Myth and History in the Contemporary Spanish Novel.*

91. Bravo, "Juan Benet before History," 155.

92. On Faulkner and Proust see Manteiga, "Time, Space and Narration in Juan Benet's Short Stories," 121; also Pope, who remarks at the close of his insightful

but brief article, "It is impossible to define further which in Benet are Faulknerian influences and which ideas are derived from his direct reading of Bergson" ("Benet, Faulkner, and Bergson's Memory," 118); cf. Fraser, *Encounters with Bergson(ism) in Spain*, chapter 3.

93. Pérez Magallón, "Tiempo y tiempos en *Volverás a Región,* de Juan Benet"; Solana, "Temporal Shifting in *Herrumbrosas lanzas.*"

94. English translation of Benet's remark provided by Solana, "Temporal Shifting in *Herrumbrosas lanzas,*" 170; the original reference comes from Benet, *En ciernes,* 16–17. See also Shiv Kumar's *Bergson and the Stream of Consciousness Novel* for the genre's general characteristics.

95. "Interior lives": Ortega writes that "the true action [of *Volverás a Región*] takes place in the psychic life of [the characters]" (*Ensayos de la novela española moderna,* 142). See also Sobejano, *Novela española de nuestro tiempo,* 391; Manteiga, "Time, Space and Narration in Juan Benet's Short Stories," 135. "Contrast": Ferrán, *Working through Memory,* 106, drawing on Benet, *El ángel del señor abandona a Tobías.* "Past and present": Ortega, "Estudios sobre la obra de Juan Benet," 71; also Ferrán, *Working through Memory.*

96. Gullón, "Esperando a Coré," 143.

97. On the self: see Vásquez, "The Creative Task." On desire and sexuality: see Epps, "The Cold Furnace of Desire"; also Benet, "Ingeniería y conducta social." On biblical references: see Herzberger, "The Theme of Warring Brothers in 'Saúl ante Samuel'"; Orringer, "The Biblical Perspective on Civil War in Benet's *Saúl ante Samuel*"; Sobejano, "*Saúl ante Samuel,* historia de un fratricidio." On politics: see Mota, "Sobre la obra de Juan Benet en los años de la transición"; Minardi, "Hacer la Historia"; also Compitello, "The Paradoxes of Praxis." On modernism and postmodernism: see Compitello, "Benet and Spanish Postmodernism"; Bravo, "De modernismo a posmodernismo." On binaries: see Epps, "The Cold Furnace of Desire"; González, "Tecnología y Arcadia en *Volverás a Región*"; Lupinacci Wescott, "Benet's Theoretical Essays"; also Fraser, "The Art of Engineering."

Chapter 1

1. The "royal pardon" Benet mentions in the epigraph was also known as the Amnesty Act of 30 July 1976, which proclaimed: "Since Spain is headed toward full democratic normalization, the moment has arrived to conclude this process by laying to rest the legacy of any past discrimination whatsoever in the name of the fraternal social fellowship of Spaniards" ("Real Decreto-Ley 10/1976 de 30 de julio." Accessed 20 March 2012. www.boe.es/boe/dias/1976/08/04/pdfs/A15097–15098 .pdf.) Benet mentions this pardon also on page 28 of *Qué fue la guerra civil?*

2. See Brenan, *The Spanish Labyrinth;* Preston, "The Agrarian War in the South"; and Jackson, who writes concisely that "The Civil War came as the climactic release of the political passions of a century" (*The Spanish Republic,* 493).

3. The canonical description of the tensions leading to the Spanish Civil War is Gerald Brenan's *The Spanish Labyrinth,* originally published in 1943. See also

Preston, *The Coming of the Spanish Civil War*; Carr, *Spain 1808–1939*; Graham and Labanyi, *Spanish Cultural Studies*.

4. Malcolm Alan Compitello noted this gap in Benetian scholarship in an essay from 1984 ("The Paradoxes of Praxis," 16), and it persists even today.

5. According to Paul Preston, "The foundations of all modern scholarship on the Spanish Republic and Civil War were laid by Gerald Brenan in 1843"; "Brenan perceived that it was a fundamentally Spanish affair, rooted in the agrarian question and comprehensible only in terms of the previous hundred years of Spanish development" ("War of Words," 5, 5–6). See also Preston, *The Coming of the Spanish Civil War*; "The Agrarian War in the South"; Matthews, *Half of Spain Died*, 27.

6. Brenan, *The Spanish Labyrinth*, 87. See also, for example, Vilar, *Historia de España*, 96–100.

7. Brenan, *The Spanish Labyrinth*, 87.

8. Brenan, *The Spanish Labyrinth*, 87–88. Brenan's analysis in these pages draws a sharp contrast between countries such as England and France, where social mobility was possible, and Spain, where it was not.

9. Brenan, *The Spanish Labyrinth*, 88–89.

10. Brenan, *The Spanish Labyrinth*, 89.

11. Brenan, *The Spanish Labyrinth*, 90.

12. Brenan writes, "The fact that certain small irrigated regions scattered round the edges of the Peninsula contain the most productive land in Europe must not make one forget that a large part of the centre consists of heath, thin steppe pasture or desert. The area of cultivated land in Spain in 1928 was between 50 and 60 million acres: that of pasture and underwood was somewhat larger, whilst 15 million acres were totally unproductive. Of the pasture land more than one half was extremely poor—incapable, that is, of maintaining more than two sheep per acre" (*The Spanish Labyrinth*, 90–91).

13. Brenan, *The Spanish Labyrinth*, 106.

14. Brenan, *The Spanish Labyrinth*, 120–21. The gravity of the situation is signaled by Brenan's mention of the fact that three quarters of the population were landless *braceros* who went without work during almost half of each year. The desamortizacion process actually begins in 1798 and continues during the nineteenth century.

15. Brenan, *The Spanish Labyrinth*, 124.

16. Brenan makes this case for the connection between the plights of both rural and urban workers (*The Spanish Labyrinth*, 124–25) and draws this very conclusion (126), leading into detailed sections on anarchists, anarcho-syndicalists, Carlists, and socialists—all of which follow from his discussion of the agrarian question.

17. Benet, *¿Qué fue la guerra civil?* 26–27.

18. Benet, *¿Qué fue la guerra civil?* 29. See also Jackson ("Introduction," 11), who regards this theory as unique. Benet writes: "That I know of, history has never seen a comparable case. A state generally has sufficient resources to deal with one revolution; two on the same day seems too much" (*¿Qué fue la guerra civil?* 29; see

also 47, 137). Benet's fiction also sustains this assertion: see for example *Herrumbrosas lanzas,* 118.

19. Benet, *¿Qué fue la guerra civil?* 32: "Confronted with the unexpected Republican triumph of 14 April [1931], met by the entire country with great and spontaneous jubilation, the opposition were convinced of the necessity to strengthen, regroup, and mount a counterattack. On their own, the first groups of the extreme right had formed in 1928, 1930 and 1931 around figures like Giménez Caballero, Doctor Albiñana ('the first Spanish fascist'), Ramiro Ledesma Ramos, a certain intellectual seduced by Nazi ideology, and Onésimo Redondo, a ringleader from Valladolid who soon united with the former to form the Juntas Ofensivas Nacional Sindicalistas (JONS). Separately, José Antonio Primo de Rivera, the son of the recently deceased dictator, founded Falange Española (FE) on 29 October 1933."

20. Benet, *¿Qué fue la guerra civil?* 33.

21. See Benet, *¿Qué fue la guerra civil?* 31.

22. As Benet relates, Sanjurjo, exiled in Estoril (outside of Lisbon, Portugal), was chosen as the leader of the technical (if not political) uprising of 1936 and died in an airplane shortly after take-off as the novelist explains, in the process highlighting the leader's tragic vanity as if the event were fictional. The pilot "Ansaldo—who would later describe the event in a book saturated with bitterness and deception—was stricken with terror by Sanjurjo's luggage, a trunk stuffed full of all his harnesses, uniforms, boots, hats and medals, which the general refused to lighten, insisting on the necessity of appearing in Burgos with all of his regalia and medals. During takeoff, the plane grazed some trees, turned over and crashed—quite appropriately—into the Boca do Inferno [Mouth of Hell volcano], where the general met his death, covered in flames, charred right along with his regalia and medals" (*¿Qué fue la guerra civil?* 46).

23. Benet, *¿Qué fue la guerra civil?* 67: "The haute-bourgeoisie—naturally—sided with Franco." In *Volverás a Región,* Benet notes that the uprising from the right "counted on the rancor of the privileged classes" (57).

24. Benet uses this phrase on page 68 of *¿Qué fue la guerra civil?* and explains its intention to refer to "clandestine supporters of the uprising [from the right]." The word "column" commonly refers to a group of army troops and is here appropriated to designate the role of (seemingly unaffiliated) common citizens in the war. See also Yglesias, *The Franco Years,* 6. In addition, the aims of the group known as "Carlists" squared relatively well with the uprising from the right. The name "Carlist" comes from the first Carlist war of 1833–40 when, after the death of King Ferdinand VII (who fathered no male heir to the Spanish throne), the *carlistas* opposed the notion that his daughter Isabel should succeed him, favoring instead Ferdinand's brother Carlos. See Brenan, *The Spanish Labyrinth,* chapter 9.

25. For example, Brenan mentions the "large peasant risings in Castile and Aragon and above all in Andalusia" in 1840, 1855, 1857, 1861, and 1865 (*The Spanish Labyrinth,* 138–39).

26. Brenan cites an uprising of 1857 where Spaniards identified themselves as "Socialists" (*The Spanish Labyrinth,* 138–39) but points out that existing Federalist

traditions in Spain established many points of contact with newer socialist ideals. On the 1871 split in the International, see Brenan, *The Spanish Labyrinth,* 143. On the creation of the Socialist Party, the Partido Democrático Socialista Obrero (PSOE), see Brenan, *The Spanish Labyrinth,* 215. On the FAI, see Brenan, *The Spanish Labyrinth,* 184.

27. See Brenan, *The Spanish Labyrinth,* 220–21.

28. See Murray Bookchin, *The Spanish Anarchists.*

29. Benet, *¿Qué fue la guerra civil?* 34. This event, as Benet points out, contributed to political advantages gained by the Spanish right in the elections of November 1933.

30. Benet, *¿Qué fue la guerra civil?* 34. Benet continues, "Following the repression, summary judgments and executions [of 1934], the moment seemed to have arrived for the military coup that many [on the right] had long desired" (34). See also Shubert, "The Epic Failure."

31. Benet, *¿Qué fue la guerra civil?* 35. On the Falangist approach to the elections, see Payne, *Falange,* chapter 8. See also Jackson, *The Spanish Republic and the Civil War,* chapter 10.

32. Benet, *¿Qué fue la guerra civil?* 35.

33. Brenan, *The Spanish Labyrinth,* 316.

34. Benet, *¿Qué fue la guerra civil?* 45.

35. Benet, *¿Qué fue la guerra civil?* 47, also 58 on the death of Durruti; and of course Bookchin, *The Spanish Anarchists.* Benet discusses the fighting between socialist and anarchist forces in Catalunya and Barcelona in *¿Qué fue la guerra civil?* 66, 82.

36. Brenan: "The Anarchists, on the other hand, had a policy of collectivizing both land and industry which they did their utmost to push through. For them it was the first and most important step in social revolution. Far from regarding the war as a mere war against Fascism, they saw in it the opportunity for which they had long been waiting to create a new type of society. . . . Moreover, they believed that the war could only be waged successfully if it was accompanied by social revolution behind the lines" (*The Spanish Labyrinth,* 319).

37. According to Brenan, "The result of the war was decided by the question of foreign help" (*The Spanish Labyrinth,* 317).

38. In *¿Qué fue la guerra civil?* Benet mentions the German and Italian interventions against the Republic in general (55, 86) and singles out the well-known bombing of the Basque city of Guernica by the Condor Legion (91) and the fact that, following Franco's pact with Italy, the number of Italian troops on Spanish soil reached 50,000 (66).

39. Benet makes the following judgment against the countries participating in the NIC, which was "charged with maintaining the arms embargo and overseeing the lack of direct intervention in the Spanish conflict by the parties signing the agreement"; he writes, "Thanks to the pusillanimity of the Western powers who were fearful of offending the dictators of Germany and Italy and to the blameworthy hypocrisy of the secretary from Quai d'Orsay (one Saint-Léger, who was just as

shady in diplomacy as he was sugary with the pen, a future Nobel Prize winner), the Non-Intervention Committee would become the organism that, rendering the intervention of democratic powers impossible, would allow the open intervention of totalitarian powers" (59). Graham, in *The Spanish Republic,* xi, makes the same claim. See Margenot's edition of Benet's *Saúl ante Samuel* for one example of how the NIC found its way into Benet's fiction (371n315).

40. Benet, *¿Qué fue la guerra civil?* 59.

41. One of the most notable books on this subject is British writer George Orwell's *Homage to Catalonia,* which describes his first-hand experiences with the POUM.

42. Benet notes that party communists attempted to depose Largo Caballero, president of the Republic from 1936 to 1937, an event that must be understood as part of an attempt by the Soviet Union not necessarily to aid Spain but rather to exert its own influence (*¿Qué fue la guerra civil?* 81).

43. The title of a book by Herbert L. Matthews alleges that *Half of Spain Died* in the war, for example. As Gabriel Jackson also points out, nearly half a million Spaniards fled across the French border during merely two weeks as a direct consequence of a Nationalist victory in 1939 that ended with the taking of Barcelona ("Introduction," 19). For the most comprehensive discussion of the number of "Deaths Attributable to the Civil War," see Jackson, *The Spanish Republic,* 526–40.

44. Benet illustrates his essay with a number of maps. See *¿Qué fue la guerra civil?* 43 for one detailing the initial results of the uprising from the right.

45. Benet, *¿Qué fue la guerra civil?* 43.

46. Benet, *¿Qué fue la guerra civil?* 49.

47. Benet, *¿Qué fue la guerra civil?* 48. "As long as the Republic managed to conserve the capital in its hands—even once the capital was moved elsewhere—the war could continue and it only ended a short two days after Franco's troops entered [the city] through the Puerta del Sol" (48).

48. This event found its way into Benet's fiction as well—in *Saúl ante Samuel,* for example, as noted by Margenot's note on page 172 of the 1994 edition.

49. Benet, *¿Qué fue la guerra civil?* 58; see also 138–41. For more on 23 November, see Benet, "Tres fechas," 160. The idea of a war of attrition figures also into Benet's fiction, for example in *Herrumbrosas lanzas,* 201–2.

50. Benet, *¿Qué fue la guerra civil?* 73.

51. Benet, *¿Qué fue la guerra civil?* 102.

52. Benet, *¿Qué fue la guerra civil?* 74–75; also 66.

53. Benet, *¿Qué fue la guerra civil?* 71–72.

54. Benet, *¿Qué fue la guerra civil?* 71–73.

55. Benet, *¿Qué fue la guerra civil?* 92, 97, 102.

56. Benet, *¿Qué fue la guerra civil?* 119.

57. Benet, *¿Qué fue la guerra civil?* 123. Benet reasons that his "opinion is that the Battle of the Ebro was a military success of the Republic" in that it prolonged the war for another eight months when no one would have anticipated it would last another two weeks. "Without a doubt its army was annihilated after that last stand

but does not the greater value of an army lie in this kind of sacrifice?" For more on the Ebro, see Benet, "Tres fechas," 168.

58. Benet, *¿Qué fue la guerra civil?* 126.

59. Benet, *¿Qué fue la guerra civil?* 127–28. See also Graham, *The Spanish Republic at War,* 391.

60. Benet, *¿Qué fue la guerra civil?* 128.

61. See Graham, *The Spanish Republic at War,* 395–97. Also Jones, "The Catalan Question Since the Civil War," 236.

62. See Benet, *¿Qué fue la guerra civil?* 135. These were Segismundo Casado—the leader of the Republican Army—and Julián Besteiro—a prominent socialist and former president of the UGT.

63. Benet, *¿Qué fue la guerra civil?* 135.

64. See Jackson, "Introduction," 19.

65. Benet, *¿Qué fue la guerra civil?* 136.

66. He writes, for example: "General Duval was correct when he asserted that civil war tends to become unintelligible. The Hegelian march of the spirit and reason through history is only demonstrable when it is reason—a written and obvious one—that moves the muscles of the runner. When they are moved by silent impulses—like avarice, incompetence, ambition, and the lack of courage—that march becomes unintelligible and, therefore, investigable. It is worth saying, belatedly and uselessly investigable" (Benet, "Tres fechas," 170; this English translation is by Malcolm Alan Compitello, published in *Rewriting the Good Fight* as Benet, "Military Strategy in the Civil War," 22). See also Compitello, "Benet and Spanish Postmodernism," 262.

67. Benet, *¿Qué fue la guerra civil?* 29. See also Preston, *The Triumph of Democracy in Spain,* 1.

68. Herzberger: "Long countenanced by Spanish historiography as an abstract of liberal and conservative divisiveness in Spain since the Enlightenment, the idea of two Spains as a sound historiographic precept is quickly discarded by the Regime. When discussed at all, it is viewed as a perversion of true Spanish history in the context of the nation's universal mission" (*Narrating the Past,* 29). Benet uses this phrase also in the text of *Herrumbrosas lanzas,* Vol. III, 569. In *En agua en España,* he writes of the "two Spains" from yet another perspective: "It is certainly a historical cliché to talk of the two Spains—the dry and the moist" (161).

69. Benet, *¿Qué fue la guerra civil?* 41; the phrase also appears on page 131. The notion of the two Spains is also, of course, implicit in the numerous contrasts he draws between the Nationalists and the Republicans.

70. Payne, *The Franco Regime 1936–1975,* 388.

71. Payne, *The Franco Regime 1936–1975,* 480.

72. Benet, *¿Qué fue la guerra civil?* 67.

73. Sevilla-Guzmán, "The Peasantry and the Franco Régime," 102. See also Preston, who writes, "Landowners wished to preserve the existing structure of landed property; capitalists wished to safeguard their right to run industry and the banks without trade union interference; the army wished to defend the centralized

organization of the Spanish State and the Church wished to conserve its ideological hegemony" (*The Triumph of Democracy in Spain,* 4), and also underscores "Francoism's function as the defender of capitalism" (17).

74. "The main objective of the government agrarian policy [from 1939 to 1951] was to maintain the dependence of the labourers on the large land-owners who controlled the labour market" (Sevilla-Guzmán, "The Peasantry and the Franco Régime," 103–4).

75. Hooper, who notes also that, "but for the loans granted by the Argentine dictator, General Perón, it is possible that there would have been a full-scale famine" (*The New Spaniards,* 15).

76. This is the case of the eastern and particularly the southern areas of the country. There were, in fact, "savage reprisals against those labourers who had shown leftist sympathies or even independence of spirit before the war" (Sevilla-Guzmán, "The Peasantry and the Franco Régime," 104).

77. The cities seldom delivered on that promise. See Hooper, *The New Spaniards,* 15–17; also Sevilla-Guzmán, "The Peasantry and the Franco Régime," 104.

78. See Preston, "The Urban and Rural *Guerrilla* of the 1940s." Preston writes that "the regime executed nearly 200,000 Republicans and imprisoned over 400,000" (230). The postwar resistance figures, of course, also into Benet's novels—for example in the figure of Constantino who is described in *A Meditation* as a "guerrilla fighter" who flees into the Región mountains after the civil war (64).

79. Benet, *¿Qué fue la guerra civil?* 100. Belchite was also famously described by *New York Times* reporter Herbert Matthews as a "fetid mass of wreckage" (Jackson, *The Spanish Republic,* 397; also 407).

80. The more humorous parts of *¿Qué fue la guerra civil?* include Benet's extended description of a Nationalist who starts the uprising too early and reluctantly goes home, confused (39), his mention of the funny term "cuñadísimo" (most brother in-law-ness) (89) for the brother in-law of Franco (who was called the "generalísimo") (62). His description of the death of Sanjurjo shortly after his flight took off is somewhat humorous (Benet makes much of the fact that he dies by crashing into the "Mouth of Hell" volcano) and also turns on the tragic vanity of a general who couldn't return to Spain without his regalia, which ultimately caused the plane to crash (46). Throughout, Benet is attentive to the mysterious and enigmatic aspects of Spanish history.

81. Herzberger, *Narrating the Past,* 101. See also Benson, "La poética de Juan Benet y sus implicaciones pragmáticas," 79.

82. Herzberger writes that Benet is "the postwar novelist who focuses his work most compellingly on the relationship between history and fiction" (*Narrating the Past,* 12), noting also that his work "forges a unique narrative intimacy between history and fiction" (13). This opinion is widely accepted.

83. Preston, "War of Words," 2.

84. "The Francoists in contrast not only carry the responsibility for turning history into propaganda but, much more seriously, are guilty of trying to annihilate history as an academic discipline. The great historians of pre-war Spain were hounded into exile. Those who remained were forced into a kind of inner exile,

compelled to take up other jobs or else to work on periods earlier, and therefore less 'political', than the ones which interested them. The consequence of this has been that, until after Franco's death, the main burden of writing the history of twentieth-century Spain has fallen on foreigners, particularly Anglo-Saxons" (Preston, "War of Words," 5). As late as 1990, Juan Benet himself testified to the importance of these non-Spanish scholars when he cited (and critiqued) Stanley Payne in his essay "Tres fechas," 151–52. See also Payne, *The Franco Regime.* Anglophone scholars had distance enough to see the Spanish conflict for what it was, but they often were incapable of understanding subtle differences resulting from the distance between "inside" and "outside" perspectives. For example, Gabriel Jackson disagreed with the pessimism of Benet's statements in *¿Qué fue la guerra civil?* even while he admired his opinions and reputations, attributing them to the "moment in which he was writing" (Jackson, "Prólogo," 19)—but we might just as easily attribute Jackson's own statement to the fact that he viewed the end of the dictatorship from outside Spain.

85. On the regime's normative strategies, see Herzberger, *Narrating the Past,* 16–17.

86. Herzberger, *Narrating the Past,* 107.

87. The quotation is from Margenot, "Preface" to *Juan Benet,* ix, while the latter judgment is from Herzberger, *Narrating the Past,* 112. See also Herzberger, *The Novelistic World of Juan Benet,* 2.

88. Herzberger, *Narrating the Past,* 112. The critic goes on to explain that, "after all, Benet is one of the greatest Spanish social novelists of the twentieth century. But he is social in the same way that Faulkner and Joyce are social. His placing of people and events in Región is a way not of localizing meaning but of enlarging it" (Herzberger, *Narrating the Past,* 113). Elsewhere Herzberger describes Benet's novels by saying that "events and characters do not come into clear focus" ("Enigma as Narrative Determinant in the novels of Juan Benet," 149). See also Compitello, "The Paradoxes of Praxis," 17. Lupinacci Wescott discusses at length the fact that Benet's characters subvert conventions and are defined by "uncertainty" ("Subversion of Character Conventions in Benet's Trilogy," 73).

89. The quotation is from Fraser, *Encounters with Bergson(ism) in Spain,* 125; this aspect of the novel has been best explored by Compitello, who employs a comparative approach in which Benet's novel parallels *Os Sertões* by Brazilian writer Euclides Da Cunha ("Región's Brazilian Backlands"). On Da Cunha, see chapter 4.

90. Orringer, "Epic in a Paralytic State," 42.

91. Benet, *Return to Región,* 39. All English passages from this novel come from the translation by Gregory Rabassa of 1985. As Solana points out, *Herrumbrosas lanzas* reflects not only on Región's need to get rid of the fascists, but also to reverse the ills of the private ownership of land ("Temporal Shifting in *Herrumbrosas lanzas,*" 168–69).

92. Particularly in *Una meditación, Herrumbrosas lanzas* and *Saúl ante Samuel.* See Molina Ortega, *Las otras regiones de Juan Benet,* 86n101, as well as 86–87.

93. Benet: "The whole course of the civil war in the Región sector begins to be seen clearly when one understands that, in more than one aspect, it is a paradigm

on a lesser scale and with a slower rhythm than peninsular-wide events; its development is like the unfolding of dancing images that, on being projected at a slower speed than is proper, loses intensity, color and contrast. Because in Región there was no coincidence of dates; the republican aim of smothering a military uprising was not simultaneous with the proletarian revolution that pawned its resources to bring about the first. . . . The proletarian revolution that was to change the face of half of Spain during that bloody summer came to be repeated, through an act of mimicry, with the soft and withered tones of autumn" (*Return to Región,* 63–64). A similar statement appears again in *Herrumbrosas lanzas,* as noted by Wasmuth ("Polifonía y armonía de los espacios en *Herrumbrosas lanzas,*" 239–40). Cibreiro has written that "*Una meditación* offers, on the one hand, a retelling of the Spanish postwar by way of a group of characters from a specific region" ("Narrators and Their Narrations," 129). See also Molina Ortega, *Las otras regiones de Juan Benet,* 30.

94. The chosen examples occur in *Return to Región:* "Civil Guard" (43); "Second Republic" (57); the dates of 1937, 1938 (63); "CEDA" (25) refers to the coalition party of Catholic conservatives and Falangists, the Confederación Española de Derechas Autónomas (Spanish Confederation of the Autonomous Right), which was active under the Second Republic and persisted into the civil war years; "CTV" (55) refers to the Italian forces sent to aid the Nationalists, Corpo Truppe Volontarie (Corps of Volunteer Troops), whose acronym Benet humorously explains as meaning "¿Cuándo Te Vas?" (When are you leaving?) in *¿Qué fue la guerra civil?* (75; as CTV on 66, 70). Other abbreviations, although perhaps fictional ("CRT, TIR, TDAP, UTE" 25), coexist with the real as Benet's way of pointing to the ideological divisions under the war. On page 55 of *Return to Región,* the narrator mentions troops coming from "Valladolid, Galicia, Navarre" which were destined to enter "Madrid, Valencia and Región."

95. As Compitello notes, "Among the place names that are a product of his imagination, Benet intersperses references to the real, if somewhat obscure locations in Spain. A check of a detailed atlas reveals that places such as Rañeces, Mampodre, Láncara and la Liébana do, in fact, exist" ("Región's Brazilian Backlands," 44n17). See also Fraser, *Encounters with Bergson(ism) in Spain,* 126–27. As discussed in depth by Molina Ortega (*Las otras regiones de Juan Benet,* 30n75), various critics have attempted to situate Región in Spanish soil as "a real place located between León and Asturias with imaginary names"—the latter quotation being from Oliart, "Viaje a Región," 226–27. See also chapter 4.

96. The "uprising of 18 July" is discussed in the second of the twelve finished books (not volumes) of *Herrumbrosas lanzas* (Wasmuth, "Polifonía y armonía de los espacios en *Herrumbrosas lanzas,*" 242). The quotations are from Solana, "Temporal Shifting in *Herrumbrosas lanzas,*" 174 and 169.

97. Herzberger, "The Theme of Warring Brothers in 'Saúl ante Samuel,'" 103.

98. Benet, *Return to Región,* 64–65. "April 14th" refers to the proclamation of the Second Republic following antimonarchical elections of 1936, and the color purple is significant as it was added to the traditional yellow and red Spanish flag by the Republican State.

99. Benet, *Return to Región,* 65. *Volverás* mentions the prominent liberal families of Región on page 27: "the "Asiáns, the Mazóns and the Roberts." Compare with Solana, "Temporal Shifting in *Herrumbrosas lanzas,*" 168–69.

100. *Volverás a Región* emphasizes discussion of the sierra from page 1, and a notable battle for the Socéanos Pass occurs there during November of 1936 (for example, *Return to Región,* 28). Benet's treatment of the Civil War in his essay similarly points out that the sierra was an important part of the conflict (*¿Qué fue la guerra civil?* 53).

101. Región's scant resources—which of course parallel the Republic's scant resources after the desertion of the vast majority of the army to the Nationalist cause—are highlighted early in *Return to Región* (28). The Defense Committee is mentioned early as well (*Return to Región,* 27) and takes on greater prominence in *Herrumbrosas lanzas.* *Return to Región* mentioned that the Nationalists had "the aim of carrying out . . . a full-scale war against a Región that, with its scant resources and dying energies, had decided to remain faithful to the cause of the republican government" (*Return to Región,* 21).

102. Lupinacci Wescott, "*Herrumbrosas Lanzas I,*" 14. See also Solana, "Temporal Shifting in *Herrumbrosas lanzas,*" 171.

103. Solana describes an attack on Macerta from Región narrated in *Herrumbrosas lanzas* that bears resemblance to the context in which the Battle of the Ebro was waged ("Temporal Shifting in *Herrumbrosas lanzas,*" 180). In *Volverás a Región,* the assault on the Doña Cautiva Bridge suggests similarities with the Ebro offensive, occurring in fact during the same month of November 1938 and leading into the final months of the war. There are, notably, echoes of Benet's respect for the Republican troops that fought in the Ebro: "It was one of those massive counterattacks, launched with unsuspected drive and maintained with courage, which even when they lead nowhere—not even with victorious tactics—have to be organized and executed during the final hours of a campaign whose results could not be altered by anything anymore" (*Return to Región,* 261). Existing scholarship has drawn numerous parallels between Benet's essay on the civil war and his fiction, including not merely generalities, but also specifics. For example, Herzberger (in "Nuevo historicismo," 142), draws a comparison between both in terms of "style, technique and intention"—particularly comparing the battle for Jarama and the battle for Región. For more specific comparisons, see Solana, "Temporal Shifting in *Herrumbrosas lanzas*"; Lupinacci Wescott, "*Herrumbrosas Lanzas I.*"

104. Benet, *Return to Región,* 54.

105. "In the first place, they counted on the rancor of the privileged classes, on the hesitation of an inexpert and timid government, and on the brutality of uncivilized and ingenuous masses, clumsy and bloodthirsty, less than satisfied with leaving the accounts of four centuries settled with the arson and murder of one anticlerical night" (Benet, *Return to Región,* 57).

106. Benet, *Return to Región,* 69. Also, Gamallo's offensive sought to capture Región and occupy the middle valley of the Torce through simultaneous attacks—"by that plan Gamallo hoped, in a matter of no more than ten days, not only to

occupy all the middle valley—for some twenty miles—but also to damage the whole republican defense and reduce its strength to a couple of pockets cut off from the rest of the country, obliged to surrender or continue their resistance in the heart of the mountains. It seems obvious that his intentions were not dictated exclusively by the best strategy for the occupation of Región; if that had been his only aim, it would have been enough for him—in those days—either to launch a single frontal attack instead of spreading it out and breaking it up into three phases or to repeat the old techniques" (*Return to Región,* 69).

107. The qualities of Gamallo are suggested by Orringer ("Epic in a Paralytic State," 45) while Benet's comments on the "silent impulses" motivating the war come from "Tres fechas," 170. The source of this English translation is Compitello (Benet, "Military Strategy in the Civil War"). As Compitello mentions, this sort of description is continued in *Herrumbrosas lanzas* ("Benet and Spanish Postmodernism," 262). In *Volverás a Región* (56–58) there is an extended discussion of these qualities.

108. Benet, *Return to Región,* 74.

109. The remarks on Belchite appear in this chapter and come from *¿Qué fue la guerra civil?* 100. Of course, Benet's focus on devastation and ruin is a part of many of his short stories as well. As noted by critic Janet Díaz, the early story "Baalbec" is a "saga of ruin," an "account of decay and degeneration [that] anticipates a leitmotif of the Región cycle" ("Variations on the Theme of Death in the Short Fiction of Juan Benet," 7).

110. Compitello, "*Volverás a Región,* the Critics and the Spanish Civil War," 12.

111. Herzberger, "Nuevo historicismo," 141, my translation. Compitello ("Reflexiones sobre el acto de narrar," 22) downplays the idea that the political tension in Benet's work might have been intentional, although elsewhere he rightly supports a political interpretation of the works nonetheless ("*Volverás a Región,* the Critics and the Spanish Civil War"). Compitello reflects on history and fiction in Benet more generally in "Benet and Spanish Postmodernism," 260–63.

Chapter 2

1. The author of the quoted words is José Antonio Torroja Cavanillas (see Baeza, "Acto de Homenaje," 63, 63–64), who also wrote: "I am not in a position to say whether his engineering activities prevented him from developing more as a writer; what I can say is that his writing never prevented him from exercising his role as an engineer" (in Baeza, "Acto de Homenaje," 64). Consider also the words of Adrian Baltanas, who writes of Benet's "double engineer-writer personality" (in Baeza, "Acto de Homenaje," 65). José Antonio Fernández Ordóñez notes also, "His life is an equilibrium between these antagonistic impulses" (in Baeza, "Acto de Homenaje," 72). This notion is continued in the 2009 collection of Benet's essays *Si yo fuera presidente* (If I Were President), where—in two introductory homages—Antonio Papell calls him "A bidimensional man" and Juan Guillamón asks the question, "A writer who worked as an engineer or an engineer who wrote?" (7, also 12).

2. Respectively, the authors of these words are noted Spanish intellectuals Félix Azúa (qtd. in Baeza, "Acto de Homenaje," 65) and Vicente Molina Foix (qtd. in Baeza, "Acto de Homenaje," 75).

3. Cabrera's canonical volume on Benet's literary production mentions that he was an engineer in passing merely on one page, in only one sentence (*Juan Benet*, 2). With very few exceptions—notable among those is a recent essay by Tatjana Gajic ("*Fronteras líquidas*," 36–38)—critics have hardly ever attempted to explore the links between Benet's fiction and engineering work seriously. See Fraser, "The Art of Engineering"; also Gimferrer, "Notas sobre Juan Benet." María Elena Bravo expresses what might be seen as a view widespread among literary scholars: "Juan Benet was a scientist by training and an engineer by profession, but his true nature and his real creativity belonged to art" ("Juan Benet before History," 147).

4. The book was published by the branch of the engineering school in Murcia, and includes a prologue, introduction, and a number of brief essays (both published and unpublished) that run the gamut, addressing technical matters of construction as well as broader social perspectives on water use and programs. Some of these essays are referenced in this chapter's notes.

5. Benet describes himself as a poor student, and the school itself as elitist: "I was intelligent enough to get in, but the School was quite boring. It was a career, in those days, directed toward the production of State functionaries. It was an elitist career, and they were very close to teaching us how to drink tea with a *marquesa*." After graduating he found it hard to find a job, and finally landed an assignment in Ponferrada (*Cartografía personal*, 221).

6. Benet, *Cartografía personal*, 318.

7. In 1984, Benet alleged that he only began to write (prose) while living in Oviedo (*Cartografía personal*, 222).

8. In the brief essay "Los comienzos" (The Beginnings), included in *Si yo fuera presidente*, Benet notes that the company is "today incorporated into CMZ" (31).

9. The revealing name of Benet's company is itself a sign that there might be a reciprocal influence of his literary passion on his engineering work. Joaquín Díez-Cascón explains the story behind the name as it was related to him by Benet himself: "It's a name that has its mystery. 'Compañía' comes from 'the company.' He always worked, not in a firm, but rather in a company. He worked in the Compañía Ferrocarriles de Medina del Campo a Zamora y de Orense a Vigo, abbreviated MZOV, but it was always 'Where are you going?' 'I'm off to the company.' For that reason he used the word 'compañía.' 'Regional' comes from the name of Región. The case of 'Hidrocinética' always baffled me. And one day I asked him, 'Why the word "Hidrocinética?'" and he told me: 'I don't know. I had a car and one day I heard that it had a "homocinetic" gasket, and it seemed to me such a good word that I coined "hidrocinética"—"hidro" coming from water.' And there's its origin, that is the story he told me" ("Conference at the Colegio Oficial de Ingenieros," 6). The date of 1987 comes also from that source. See also *Cartografía personal*, 304.

10. Torroja Cavanillas, in Baeza, "Acto de Homenaje," 64. See also Benet, "Discurso leido en el acto de su nombramiento como colegiado de honor." The

Catalunyan School of Civil Engineers, for its part, honored Benet with the "Ildefons Cerdà" medal in 1991 ("Juan Benet Goitia"). One might read his remarks upon receiving the medal of honor (Benet, "Discurso leido en el acto de su nombramiento como colegiado de honor," 77) as reflecting on the union or mutual dependence of his engineering and literary sides. For more on Cerdà, see Fraser, *Henri Lefebvre and the Spanish Urban Experience.*

11. In 1989 he remarked, "It is true that in my life I have written more technical pages than literary ones. I write forty pages about concrete every week" (*Cartografía personal,* 265). Elsewhere, a longer list of Benet's engineering accomplishments can be found: "As a civil engineer, he always decdicated himself to the conceptualization and contruction of great public works, above all else, hydraulic ones, among which can be cited the canals at Cornatel and Quereño, the Porma dam, the Eirós dam, the Atazar dam, that of Santa Eugenia or that of Llauset" ("La trayectoria de Juan Benet como ingeniero de Caminos"). See also Enrique Pérez Galdós's contribution to the 1994 Homage to Benet (in Baeza, "Acto de Homenaje") and Díez Cascón, "Conference at the Colegio Oficial de Ingenieros," for more of Benet's accomplishments.

12. This includes, for example, his "Soluciones constructivas en obras de regadío" (Construction Solutions in Irrigation Works), which is of interest, even though it includes engineering specifications and terminology that may not be familiar or even accessible to all readers (see Benet, *Si yo fuera presidente,* 149–70). See also Benet's contribution to a volume on English photographer Charles Clifford's images of public works under Isabel II titled "Un punto de vista extranjero" (A Stranger's Point of View), which is republished in *Si yo fuera presidente* (137–46). Benet's lecture to the Centro de Estudios Hidrográficos de Madrid on 16 January 1981 titled "El agua en Región" (Water in Región) and published in *La moviola de Eurípides* is interesting, but perhaps misleading in the sense that his remarks are somewhat general. What is indeed of note is that the lecture does describe a few intriguing examples of "Fantastic Hydraulics" that he says were dreamed up during the time in which he was writing *Volverás a Región.* He says that although he never published them, he did put them down on paper under the title "Notas concernientes a ciertas estructuras hidráulicas basadas en la fantasía" (Notes Concerning Certain Hydraulic Structures Based in Fantasy) (*La moviola de Eurípides,* 72).

13. One intriguing example can be found in *El ángel del señor abandona a Tobías,* where Benet—during a discussion of Socrates and revolutionary politics—introduces the simile "like a hydraulic circuit" and goes on to explain the comparison to his argument in detail (126).

14. In addition to the rail lines and practical experience abroad in Finland and Sweden, he also worked on the widening of the Pajares highway and the railway tunnel between Lugo de Llanera and Villabona ("Juan Benet Goitia," 75). Baltanas mentions "El Vellón, Porma, Moralets, Santa Eugenia, etc. various stretches of the Tajo–Segura Aqueduct, the design of several more dams at least, his ongoing work as member of the Comité Nacional de Grandes Presas, and a whole series of reports, studies and writings dedicated to all aspects of hydraulic engineering" (in Baeza, "Acto de Homenaje," 66).

15. Cubiertas y MZOV did indeed serve as the contractor for the construction of the Rande Bridge over the Ria de Vigo in Southern Gallicia. Information on a limited number of the company's projects is available on a searchable online database, although Juan Benet's name is not specifically mentioned. The database is available at en.structurae.de/structures/data/index.cfm (accessed 20 March 2012).

16. This anecdote, which is very widely known, has appeared most recently in popular press articles in Spanish newspapers *El País* and *El Mundo,* written—presumably—with the hope of luring travelers to Oporto. See the newspaper articles by Montes ("Harry Potter in Oporto") and Fluxá ("Europa ineludible"); also Fraser, "The Art of Engineering."

17. This is reflected also in the title of an article on Benet written by Eduardo Chamorro, "El caballero de Pisuerga."

18. Andreu, in Baeza, "Acto de Homenaje," 74. "Salve" is a greeting in Latin akin to saying "hello." The English equivalent would be "Hello, father Duero." See also Benet's *El agua en España,* 148–49. He mentions the Duero and the Pisuerga on page 157 of *El agua en España.*

19. Marías, "Se va de viaje," 29; cited in Molina Ortega, *Las otras regiones de Juan Benet,* 39.

20. See Molina Ortega, *Las otras regiones de Juan Benet,* 39n80.

21. The essay is "Por los caminos del progreso" by Darina Martykánová (2007). See also Fernández Ordóñez and Navarro Vera, "Una aproximación a la 'Revista de Obras Públicas' 1853–1936."

22. Martykánová, "Por los caminos del progreso," 195. The quoted words come from R. Martín's "Cuestión de vida o muerte" (1875). See also Carr, *Spain 1808–1939:* "the fate of the Corps of Road Engineers, set up in the eighteenth century, was bound up with the fate of liberalism itself; dismantled by Ferdinand VII it was set up by the Liberal Revolution in 1820; dissolved in the reaction of 1823, it was re-established by liberals in 1834" (61).

23. Martykánová, "Por los caminos del progreso," 199–200.

24. Of course while they may have agreed on the importance of those themes they had a range of opinions on specific concerns (See Martykánová, "Por los caminos del progreso," 202; also 209 where she writes of the "apolitical" nature of Spanish engineers). Benet himself writes of the neutrality of engineering as a profession ("Ingeniería e intimidad," 74).

25. Benet, "Ingeniería e intimidad," 74.

26. In 1976, Benet reflected, "The former was little more than a prolongation of School with a greater dose of responsibility and assured the enviable situation of not having to leave Madrid, and thus keep one's girlfriend and await the State's call. As I have never had, nor do I have now, much fondness for a State that does not reflect my tastes, I soon opted for work in the provinces" ("Ingeniería e intimidad," 74–75).

27. Benet, "Política hidráulica," 273.

28. Benet, "Ingeniería e intimidad," 74.

29. Félix de Azúa notes of two of Benet's engineering essays ("Soluciones constructivas en obras de regadío," and "Panorama actual en las relaciones contractuales

en la construcción de túneles en España y su posible desarrollo futuro"), "They are texts of absolute technical relevance, but they are written with the prosody of his novels" (in Baeza, "Acto de Homenaje," 64).

30. Benet, "Ingeniería e intimidad," 75.

31. Benet, "Ingeniería e intimidad," 74. The italics are from Benet's original text.

32. Benet, "Ingeniería y conducta social," 80.

33. Azúa, in Baeza, "Acto de Homenaje," 65. That tradition is also discussed by Blanca Andreu, who writes that Benet "told me that he considered Engineering to be superior to literature because it was the labor not of an individual but of a team, because it ignored the vanity of a signature, and because it served to correct the errors that nature, in its prodigality, had committed" (Andreu, in Baeza, "Acto de Homenaje," 74).

34. Benet, "Soluciones constructivas en obras de regadío."

35. Costa's famous call to "close the tomb of the Cid with seven locks" was part of an effort to move forward and abandon traditional myths on which the country had relied for so long (El Cid [Rodrigo Díaz de Vivar] was a Spaniard who fought in the Reconquest of the Peninsula [711–1492] and achieved legendary fame, becoming a symbol of Spain's past glory). Costa exercised a great influence on the writers known as the Generation of 1898, who made similar claims for moving forward and for national regeneration (such as Miguel de Unamuno).

36. The characterization is from Sáenz Ridruejo, "Los ingenieros de Caminos de la generación del 98," 5. See also Germán Zubero, *Obras públicas e ingenieros en Aragón durante el primer tercio del siglo XX*, who quotes this characterization (28).

37. Jackson, *The Spanish Republic:* "In política hidráulica he [Prieto] carried forward the work of the dictatorship. Primo de Rivera had called upon Manuel Lorenzo Pardo to direct a national program of dam building and irrigation. Between 1926 and 1930 a number of dams were completed along the Ebro River, and detailed plans made for the Levant and the valley of the Guadalquivir. Prieto reappointed Lorenzo Pardo, moved ahead with the existing projects, built two dams on the Guadalquivir and inaugurated a new project in Extremadura (the *Obras de Cíjara*), which was interrupted by the Civil War and completed in 1957 under the new name of *Plan de Badajoz*" (91–92). On Primo, Raymond Carr reflects: "Part of his one-man regenerationism was an ambitious programme of state-financed public works, particularly dams, irrigation and roads" (*Spain: A History*, 241). For a concise but detailed depiction of Lorenzo Pardo's life and work, see Germán Zubero, *Obras públicas e ingenieros en Aragón durante el primer tercio del siglo XX*, 142–46. Also Sáenz García, "Evocación del ingeniero de caminos D. Manuel Lorenzo Pardo, Fundador del Centro de Estudios Hidrográficos."

38. Jackson, *The Spanish Republic*, 91–92.

39. Jackson, *The Spanish Republic*, 92.

40. Vilar, *Spain: A Brief History*, 68 (97 in the Spanish version).

41. The quoted material is from "Juan Benet Goitia," 76. See also Fernández Clemente, "De la utopía de Joaquín Costa a la intervención del Estado," who cites Benet in his discussion of Costa. The essay by Gajic ("*Fronteras líquidas*"), makes this link well on page 27.

42. Díaz-Marta Pinilla, *Las obras hidráulicas en España,* 17; in the prologue written by Manuel Torres Campañá. Díaz-Marta Pinilla was born in Toledo, Spain, and first published the book while in exile in Mexico in 1969. Torres Campañá was also a Spaniard living in Mexico, and at the time was president of the Agrupación Europeísta there. See also Díaz-Marta Pinilla, *Las obras hidráulicas en España,* 87, where the author writes that, with the creation of the Confederation of the Ebro in 1926, "Spain beat the other countries to it"; and conversely that by the "present time [1969], Spain has regressed in its relative position with respect to other countries."

43. Díaz-Marta Pinilla, *Las obras hidráulicas en España,* 87.

44. Improvements for rural Spaniards were rhetorically addressed by the early dictatorship, but, as Eduardo Sevilla-Guzmán points out, although small land-holding peasants were seen as adding to the stability of the regime, "the proclaimed desire to create a nation of small-holders was never carried out" ("The Peasantry and the Franco Régime," 105). See also Vilar, *Spain,* 124.

45. The quote is from Payne, *The Franco Regime,* who notes also, "Increased military expenses and wartime shortages left little for new public works, for example, that might have palliated unemployment" (253). The reference to prior spending comes from Jackson, *The Spanish Republic:* "Primo had spent an average of 50 to 60 million pesetas a year on hydraulic works. The 1932 budget called for 80 million, and the 1933 budget for 175 million" (93).

46. Benet, *Cartografía personal,* 304. See also *Si yo fuera presidente,* 173–74. Jackson writes of the "New-Deal–type public works program of Prieto" signaling that "the debate was exactly like that which took place in all the Western countries in the 1930's concerning deficit financing and government sponsorship of industrial projects in capitalist countries" (*The Spanish Republic,* 480). See also Díaz-Marta Pinilla, *Las obras hidráulicas en España,* 17, where the same comparison is made to the United States, with the assertion that Spain's reforms were carried out years before those of the New Deal.

47. Benet, *Si yo fuera presidente,* 171–86.

48. This is a paraphrasing of a sentence from Benet, *Si yo fuera presidente,* 171.

49. Benet, *Si yo fuera presidente,* 171–72.

50. Benet, *Si yo fuera presidente,* 173.

51. Benet, *Si yo fuera presidente,* 175–76.

52. Costa, *Oligarquía y caciquismo,* 204, cited in Gajic, "*Fronteras líquidas,*" 28.

53. Benet, "Política Hidráulica," 278.

54. Benet, "Política Hidráulica," 278. The road ahead will require much more improvement, Benet suggests, putting to rest the misguided notion that the "'era of reservoirs' is a thing of the past" (279).

55. See Garrido, "Analysis of Spanish Water Law Reform." Benet's remarks appear in *Si yo fuera presidente* as "Apuntes al anteproyecto de la Ley de Aguas de 1985" (Notes on the Draft Bill of the 1985 Water Law) (125–28).

56. See *Si yo fuera presidente* for Benet's remarks on the purpose of the series. Although an essay titled "Colección Ciencias, Humanidades e Ingeniería" (CHI) is included in the book, there is a printing error that results in its appearing only on

pages 223–24, when what should be the remaining pages of the essay (225–38), are mistakenly devoted to another topic.

57. See Baltanas, in Baeza, "Acto de Homenaje," 66.

58. Benet, "Política hidráulica," 274.

59. Costa, *La política hidráulica,* 3–4. See also pages 6–8, where Costa elaborates an enumerated plan for the use of those water resources.

60. Benet, *Si yo fuera presidente,* 223.

61. See Gajic, "*Fronteras líquidas.*"

62. Llamazares, "El sueño de Juan Benet."

63. Benet, "El agua en Región," 118. See also Ayestarán Uriz, "La filosofía tecnocrática del agua." It is tempting to contextualize this in terms of Spain's eighteenth-century legacy of Borbonic *despotismo ilustrado* (enlightened despotism), although I have refrained from doing so in the text. Spain's eighteenth-century royalty, most of all King Carlos III (1759–88), sought actively to improve life for Spanish subjects, but without their input.

64. Benet, *Si yo fuera presidente,* 147–48.

65. Benet, "Política hidráulica," 275.

66. Benet, "Hidráulica moderna y regadío antiguo," 4. The novel *Una meditación* (discussed in chapter 3) begins with the narrator's similar remembrance about his grandfather's farm, which "had scarcely any arable land more than a plot of some five acres, bordering on the fish ponds of the river" (7).

67. Benet, "Hidráulica moderna y regadío antiguo," 5.

68. Benet, interviewed by Sabino Ordás, in *Cartografía personal,* 224. There is an excellent map of Spain titled "Rain distribution: Period Spanning 1921–1930" that illustrates this basic problem included in Díaz-Marta Pinilla, *Las obras hidráulicas en España,* 26 (also 146). Water resources are heavily concentrated in the northwest region of Galicia and run east across the northern Spanish coast and French border, with very few other areas of concentration in the remaining estimated 90 percent of the country. See also the map on page 90, depicting the analogous situation in the year 1969. One might speculate that Benet's preference for the word "septentrional" (in English: "northwesterly" or "northwestern")—which occurs with relative frequency in Benet's fiction, in opposition to the word's relative infrequency in spoken Spanish—might be due, in part, to the word's association with the uneven fluvial geography of Spain about which he thought much during his career as a hydraulic engineer.

69. From Benet, *La moviola de Eurípides,* 75. In Spanish culture, it is traditional to celebrate New Year's Eve by eating twelve grapes in succession along with the twelve bell strikes at midnight.

70. Benet, quoted in Gavela, "El agua y Juan Benet." The words come originally from a prediction voiced in 1992 and published in the Spanish weekly *Dinero,* no. 471.

71. Benet, *Si yo fuera presidente,* 148.

72. See Gajic, "*Fronteras líquidas,*" who refers to battles over the Ebro River, referencing Benet and Costa. As Gajic explores, some of the recent debates surrounding the water problem in Spain emphasize the notion of *trasvases,* or detours, as a

possible solution. Benet stridently held to the notion that *trasvases* were important; see, for example, "Política hidráulica," 277. They were also an important part of the work proposed under the Second Republic by Lorenzo Pardo; see Sáenz García, "Evocación del ingeniero de caminos D. Manuel Lorenzo Pardo, Fundador del Centro de Estudios Hidrográficos," 247.

73. Andreu, in Baeza, "Acto de Homenaje," 74.

74. Marías, in Baeza, "Acto de Homenaje," 69–70.

75. I thank Benetian scholar Dr. John Margenot III for suggesting this anecdote to me—I used it also in Fraser, "The Art of Engineering," although it appears translated into English for the first time here. See also Díez-Cascón, "Conference at the Colegio Oficial de Ingenieros" on Benet's reputation for constantly joking around—which is complemented nicely by Marías's anecdote.

76. Consider, for example, that the narrator of *A Meditation* mentions "the dam and the falls built by the Electra de San Juan—the company founded by my grandfather, Mr. Hocher, and a few other gentlemen of Región (Mr. Corral among them, as I am given to understand)—, straddling the two centuries, for which they had brought an Aragonese construction supervisor, an expert in such works of art. . . . It was a low dam, some eighty yards across at the top, of packed ashlar . . ." (167); or the development of "more ambitious projects based on the hydroelectrical resources of the middle stretch of the Torce [River]" (198).

77. In *Herrumbrosas lanzas,* Benet notes that "Región might have been left out of the national railway network" (106).

78. Benet, *¿Qué fue la guerra civil?* 124, 54, and 78, 93, respectively.

79. Gajic, "*Fronteras líquidas*," 36.

80. These are merely two outstanding examples of how his identity as a civil engineer found its way into his texts, and Benet's texts abound, also, with references to engineers, dams, and more.

81. See Molina Ortega, *Las otras regiones de Juan Benet,* 39: "The duality, which began with the two most important cities: Macerta and Región, is prolonged in their rivers: Lerma and Torce." The former river appears, of course, even on Benet's scale map of Región as the "Lerna" and not as the "Lerma." The critic discusses also examples from Benet's works *Una meditación* and *La otra casa de Mazón.*

82. Molina Ortega, for example, in *Las otras regiones de Juan Benet,* mentions the example of the San Bruno monastery, which lies on the shores of the Torce and is discussed in *La otra casa de Mazón* (35). References to the rivers, of course, abound throughout the Región novels.

83. Benet, *Volverás a Región,* 7.

84. Benet, *El agua en España,* 148–49. Trans. Dominic Currin.

85. Benet, *El agua en España,* 166.

86. Benet, *Herrumbrosas lanzas,* 127.

87. Benet, *Herrumbrosas lanzas,* 158.

88. Benet, *Volverás a Región,* 9, 11, 41, 47, 56, 57, 61, 62, 62, 80, 82, 85, 86, 87, 88, 258, 274, 284, 285–89.

89. Benet, *Volverás a Región,* 41. English translation from *Return to Región:* "at the point of the Doña Cautiva Bridge, less than ten miles to the north of Región,

the [Torce] valley acquires its outline of a closed V, so characteristic of quartzites, and the presence of the range—so clear and neat from the terraces of Región's—is suddenly hidden behind its own outcroppings" (33).

90. Benet, *Volverás a Región,* 80.

91. Benet, *Volverás a Región,* 57, 61.

92. Benet, *Volverás a Región,* 82. English translation from *Return to Región,* 70.

93. Benet, *Volverás a Región,* 85, 88.

94. Benet, *Volverás a Región,* 86, 285–86.

95. Benet, *Volverás a Región,* 286. English translation from *Return to Región,* 261.

96. Benet, *Volverás a Región,* 286. English translation from *Return to Región,* 262. Moreover, there is a certain relevance here to Benet's description in *¿Qué fue la guerra civil?* of the (fleeting) Republican success in the Battle of the Ebro.

97. Benet, *Volverás a Región,* 286.

98. Benet, *Volverás a Región,* 287, 293.

99. Benet, *Volverás a Región,* 258. English translation from *Return to Región,* 234–35.

100. Scholars have traditionally explored fratricide and the biblical story of Abel and Cain in relation to the theme of warring brothers in Benet's texts. See, for example, Herzberger, "The Theme of Warring Brothers in 'Saúl ante Samuel'"; Sobejano, "*Saúl ante Samuel,* historia de un fratricidio"; and Orringer, "The Biblical Perspective on Civil War in Benet's *Saúl ante Samuel.*" As another article on Benet has noted, "the bridge is for him at once material and immaterial, aesthetic, historical and figurative. It is an engineering construction that, particularly foregrounds its own aesthetic dimensions (all the more so when compared with, for example, the dam), but also one whose metaphorical value was not lost on such a great mind. Like a bridge, Benet's narrative is carefully engineered to both juxtapose and bring together opposing planes of existence (whether Nationalists/Republicans, fiction/history, sound/vision or even at a much deeper level, space and time)" (Fraser, "The Art of Engineering," 171).

101. Benet, "Política hidráulica," 275. Rivers have, of course, long been part of military strategy, and not merely in Spain's Civil War. Consider, to that effect, the remarks made by Benet's hydraulic forefather Costa concerning the Ebro: "Twelve wars and six revolutions, good sirs! The Ebro basin would barely contain such blood, spilled in only two generations, and what good have they done?" (Costa, *La política hidráulica,* 168).

102. The unitalicized part of the quotation is from Benet, *Puerta de tierra,* 71; the italicized part is from the 2003 editorial notes, 169n3.

103. From Benet, *Puerta de tierra,* 169n3.

Chapter 3

1. In addition to Orringer, see, for example, Pope, "Benet, Faulkner, and Bergson's Memory"; Manteiga, "Time, Space, and Narration in Juan Benet's Short Stories"; and Fraser, *Encounters with Bergson(ism) in Spain,* chapter 3. Bergson is

mentioned somewhat less extensively in Ferrán, *Working through Memory;* and Herzberger, *Narrating the Past* and *The Novelistic World of Juan Benet.*

2. The quotation is from Deleuze, *Bergsonism,* 115. See also Deleuze's essays "Bergson (1859–1941)" and "Bergson's Conception of Difference" (both from 1956)— republished in *Desert Islands*—and the explicitly Bergsonian foundations of Deleuze's *Cinema I: The Movement-Image* and *Cinema II: The Time-Image.*

3. Among those works that stand out are Mullarky, ed., *The New Bergson* (1999) and *Bergson and Philosophy* (1999); Guerlac, *Thinking in Time* (2006); Grosz, *The Nick of Time* (2004) and *Time Travels* (2005); Pearson, *Philosophy and the Adventure of the Virtual* (2002); Kelly, ed., *Bergson and Phenomenology* (2010); Moulard-Leonard, *Bergson-Deleuze Encounters* (2008); Muldoon, *Tricks of Time* (2006); reissues of his works by both Clinamen Press and Palgrave Macmillan; a special issue in 2003 of the journal *Culture and Organization* devoted to Bergson; and volume 15 of the journal *Pli*'s special section on Bergson titled "Lives of the Real: Bergsonian Perspectives"; not to mention an increasing number of articles. See my *Encounters with Bergson(ism) in Spain* for a more extensive bibliography.

4. Benet was also versed in English and influenced by many Anglophone thinkers as well. See the essays compiled in Benet, *Una biografía literaria*—particularly those grouped as "La deuda inglesa" (The English Debt).

5. Bergson's many societies and honors include the Academia de Ciencias Morales y Políticas de Madrid (1925), the French Academy of the same name in Paris (1901), presidency of the British Society for Psychical Research (1913), membership in the Académie Française (1914), presidency of the Commission of Intellectual Cooperation of the League of Nations (1921–26), the French Legion of Honor (1919), the (honorary) Doctor of Letters from Cambridge in 1920, and of course the Nobel Prize, for which he is most famous.

6. These lectures have been translated into English and appear in the appendix to my book *Encounters with Bergson(ism) in Spain,* 302–46. They have the added advantage of covering in small doses many of the larger points he discussed in depth in his most famous books—thereby serving as a wonderful introduction for the reader unacquainted with Bergson's philosophy.

7. This lecture was published much later after the creation of the journal *Residencia* as Bergson, "Bergson en la Residencia."

8. Mary Jo T. Landeira Brisson's 1979 dissertation in Hispanic studies titled "The Presence of Henri Bergson in Antonio Machado" provides a list of those in attendance: A. Maura, M. Azaña, E. Pardo Bazán, R. Menéndez Pidal, J. Ortega y Gasset, A. Castro, M. de Maeztu, G. Marañón, R. Altamira, and M. García Morente, as well as many others (74). See also Fraser, *Encounters with Bergson(ism) in Spain,* 21–23, where Landeira Brisson's work is a major point of reference.

9. See Fraser, *Encounters with Bergson(ism) in Spain,* 23–26; 77–95.

10. These estimates are provided by Guy, "Ortega y Bergson"; Eoff, *The Modern Spanish Novel;* and Landeira Brisson, "The Presence of Henri Bergson in Antonio Machado."

11. My volume *Encounters with Bergson(ism) in Spain* explores this issue.

12. Discussing both Faulkner and Bergson in his essay on Benet, Randolph Pope writes, "It is impossible to define further which in Benet are Faulknerian influences and which are derived from his direct reading of Bergson" ("Benet, Faulkner, and Bergson's Memory," 118). See also Bravo, *Faulkner en España*, for which Juan Benet himself wrote the foreword.

13. Elizabeth Grosz concurs with this position (upon which I elaborate extensively in *Encounters with Bergson(ism) in Spain*): "Although Bergson is commonly understood as an irredeemable dualist, for whom binary oppositions, such as mind and matter, are given, his position is more complex and less easy to decipher than oppositional models allow" (Grosz, *The Nick of Time*, 163). Common misunderstandings of Bergson are addressed also, more concisely, in Fraser, "Toward a Philosophy of the Urban."

14. Bergson, *Time and Free Will*, 97, also 121–23; Deleuze, *Bergsonism*; Fraser, *Encounters with Bergson(ism) in Spain*. Bergson's nuanced treatment of both "quantitative" and "qualitative" multiplicities—noting that it is through quality that we form the notion of quantity (and thus of "quantitative" numbers) (*Time and Free Will*)—might be seen reflected in Benet's discussion of quality and "quantitative" numbers in the essay "La puerta del lavabo" (The Bathroom Door), from the collection *La moviola de Eurípides*.

15. Bergson, *Creative Evolution*, 206. See also Fraser, "Toward a Philosophy of the Urban."

16. The phrase "view taken by mind" appears in Bergson, *Creative Evolution*, 157.

17. Bergson, *Time and Free Will*: "We may therefore surmise that time, conceived under the form of a homogeneous medium, is some spurious concept, due to the trespassing of the idea of space upon the field of pure consciousness" (98).

18. Bergson, *Time and Free Will*, 100, original emphasis. See also Bergson, *Duration and Simultaneity*, 36; *The Creative Mind*, 70, 129.

19. Compare this with similar statements made by Benet in the book of essays *En ciernes* (for example, page 44, where the literary artist "is the counterpart of the man of science"). See also Margenot, *Zonas y sombras*, on "the inherent dichotomy that exists between art and science" for Benet and citing Benet's essay "Incertidumbre" on "the possibility of contradiction" as a defining feature of art (34).

20. There Bergson writes that "metaphysics cannot get along without the other sciences" (*Creative Evolution*, 168), adding, "But if metaphysics demands and can obtain here an intuition, science has no less need of an analysis. And it is because of a confusion between the roles of analysis and intuition that the dissentions between schools of thought and the conflicts between systems will arise" (*Creative Evolution*, 169). Bergson challenged a simplistic instrumentalist view of science, much like Benet did with civil engineering, saying, for example, "Modern science is neither one nor simple" (*Creative Evolution*, 197).

21. See Benet, *Cartografía personal*, where—in a discussion of the importance of style even in scientific texts—he states: "The *Experimental Method* [of Claude Bernard] is a most beautiful book" (113).

22. Benet refers, in this essay, not merely to Bergson, but also to linguists Saussure, Chomsky, and Hjelmslev; philosophers Hegel, Nietzsche, and Socrates; the book of Tobías, and more still.

23. Benet, *El ángel del señor abandona a Tobías,* 14, also 18. This visual immediacy is referred to in the text as an emblem (*emblée*), recalling the discussion of the second of two types of narration (*argumento* vs. *estampa*) that Benet discusses in his *La inspiración y el estilo.* See, for example, *El ángel del señor abandona a Tobías,* 20, for reference to these very terms. Benet also discusses other works by Rembrandt or about the figure of Tobías in the book.

24. Benet, *El ángel del señor abandona a Tobías,* 14. Benet goes on to suggest that the title might be better with a highlighted verb (or nominalized verb), as in: "Abandona el Ángel del Señor a Tobías" or "Abandono por el Ángel del Señor de Tobías."

25. Benet, *El ángel del señor,* 14–15. This idea appears also in *En ciernes* wherein Benet writes of how "the data provided by language, in spite of its being rich and flexible, will always have its own limitations" (47). Consider how Bergson, for his part, saw language as suspect: "The word turns against the idea"; "The letter kills the spirit," (*Creative Evolution,* 127).

26. The first such reference is on page 31 of *El ángel del señor abandona a Tobías,* and later also on 42, 63, 111. The Bergsonian terms "duration," "Eleatic paradox" and "dynamic religion" appear also on 65, 153, 194, 113, and 146, respectively. It should be noted that there are many other Bergsonian aspects of this essay that are less concisely explicable—for example, Benet's dismissal of a pure science (84, 160, 195) and, throughout, his opposition of a realm of static structures opposed to moving realities (whether in language, architecture, or merely philosophy itself).

27. Bergson, *Creative Evolution,* 303. In his analysis of "Benet, Faulkner, and Bergson's Memory" Pope signals that "to express the experience of a heterogeneous and fluid reality the human being must use a language that by nature is discontinuous and homogeneous" (115).

28. Benet, *El ángel del señor abandona a Tobías,* 31. The same quote from Bergson appears (also attributed directly) on 42 and 63. The notion of language disarticulating experience—dividing it up into discrete segments—while addressed in the above quotation from his *Creative Evolution,* appears also in Bergson's other works, for example *Matter and Memory,* 239.

29. Benet, *El ángel del señor abandona a Tobías,* 31. Language and thought also divide time into present, past, and future (105, 108).

30. Benet, *El ángel del señor abandona a Tobías,* 63. And in fact, the idea of a photograph being insufficient to capture real experience is an apt one, as in *Creative Evolution* Bergson had written of the "cinematograph of the mind" that was, for him, a metaphor of how the mind approached movement only through static frames: "We take snapshots, as it were, of the passing reality. . . . Perception, intellection, language so proceed in general" (Bergson, *Creative Evolution,* 306). Later in the essay, Benet returns to this notion, discussing the "analytic mechanism of thought" (*El ángel del señor abandona a Tobías,* 190).

31. Bergson, *Matter and Memory,* 315. Bergson's theory of memory is still cited by more contemporary scientists. See, for example, the essay by Patrick McNamara, "Bergson's 'Matter and Memory' and Modern Selectionist Theories of Memory," published in the scientific journal *Brain and Cognition.*

32. Bergson, *Matter and Memory,* 86, also 86–105; Benet, *El ángel del señor abandona a Tobías,* 87. These two types of memory are often associated by literary scholars with Marcel Proust, although the latter denied this correspondence, and in all likelihood Proust did not fully understand Bergson's theories. Of course Benet was familiar with Proust (who is mentioned on page 78 of "Un extempore"), as was Bergson, who married Proust's cousin Louise Neuberger in 1891. See Fraser, *Encounters with Bergson(ism) in Spain,* 13, 118. In Benet's novel *Herrumbrosas lanzas,* there is a long passage which describes—as the chapter content list makes clear—"[Enrique] Ruan's Fondness of Reading Marcel Proust" (for example, 176). One of his early stories, "Balbec, a Stain" (translated into English in the collection *You'll Never Get Anywhere*), arguably takes its name from the fictional town employed by Proust in his *In Search of Lost Time* (see Benet, *Herrumbrosas lanzas,* 178).

33. For example, Benet recalls the Bergsonian theses regarding man's thought molding evolutionarily to space (*El ángel del señor abandona a Tobías,* 89; from Bergson, *Creative Evolution*), the distinction between instinct and intellection (*El ángel del señor,* 103, as instinctual time vs. intellectualized time on 105); the act of homogenizing temporality and accompanying notion of "an intellectualized time" (104); ritualized religion vs. dynamic religion (110, 146; from Bergson, *The Two Sources of Morality and Religion*); and the theme, so important to Bergson, of mystics/mysticism (144–47). On the latter, see Fraser, *Encounters with Bergson(ism) in Spain.* Benet explicitly cites Bergson's thoughts on religion: "Religion is not so much a fear as a reaction to fear" (*El ángel del señor abandona a Tobías,* 111). Elsewhere—referring to Bergson's *The Two Sources of Morality and Religion* (297)—Benet mentions "the 'law of twofold frenzy,' so dear to Bergson" (*El ángel del señor abandona a Tobías,* 42, also 196). See Benet, "Ingeniería y conducta social," 80, for another implicit reference to Bergson's *The Two Sources of Morality and Religion.*

34. Benet, "Un extempore," 71, 73, 71, respectively. For Bergson as for Benet, neither duration nor memory is homogeneous (Fraser, *Encounters with Bergson(ism) in Spain,* 119).

35. Benet, "Un extempore," 71.

36. Benet, "Un extempore," 71.

37. Benet, "Un extempore": "Because time is given to the human being—in contrast with any other being—at birth" (72).

38. Benet, "Un extempore," 74; "Time that is transformed into existence is not remembered, not measured, not foreseen, nor anticipated" (75). See also Bergson's "The Possible and the Real" in *The Creative Mind,* and the role of the *élan vital* in *Creative Evolution.*

39. Benet also notes, "The past is not time. . . . Neither is the present time, in its greater part" (*El ángel del señor abandona a Tobías,* 74).

40. Benet, *El ángel del señor abandona a Tobías*, 88.

41. Bergson continues: "Since they are not two separate things, since the first is only, as we have said, the pointed end, ever moving, inserted by the second in the shifting plane of experience, it is natural that the two functions should lend each other a mutual support. So, on the one hand, the memory of the past offers to the sensori-motor mechanisms all the recollections capable of guiding them in their task and of giving to the motor reaction the direction suggested by the lessons of experience. It is in just this that the associations of contiguity and likeness consist. But, on the other hand, the sensori-motor apparatus furnish to ineffective, that is unconscious, memories, the means of taking on a body of materializing themselves, in short of becoming present. For, that a recollection should reappear in consciousness, it is necessary that it should descend from the heights of pure memory down to the precise point where *action* is taking place. In other words, it is from the present that comes the appeal to which memory responds, and it is from the sensori-motor elements of present action that a memory borrows the warmth which gives it life" (*Matter and Memory,* 197, original emphasis; see also 211).

42. Benet, "Un extempore," 76.

43. Benet, "Un extempore," 75; see Bergson, *Matter and Memory,* 93. But for both Bergson and Benet, newness, however, may risk subsequently becoming crystallized (Benet, "Un extempore," 76).

44. Benet writes that "time is before anything else a possibility and the more this possibility is explicated by a formula of the happening, known, foreseen and accepted by memory, the less it is time" ("Un extempore," 75). This is, in essence, a rewriting of Bergson's premise in, among other works, *Creative Evolution.*

45. Bergson, *Creative Evolution,* 341.

46. Bergson, *Matter and Memory,* 211.

47. Benet, "Un extempore," 76.

48. Benet, "Un extempore," 75. The tone of the last paragraph on page 77 is quite heavy indeed.

49. These words are those of the character Dr. Sebastián in *Volverás a Región* at the close of its third chapter (234).

50. Pope, "Benet, Faulkner, and Bergson's Memory," 116.

51. Kumar, *Bergson and the Stream of Consciousness Novel,* 1; Burunat, *El monólogo interior como forma narrativa en la novela española (1940–1975),* 4–5, respectively.

52. These aspects of Benet's work have been highlighted by a number of critics who nonetheless underplay or even ignore the significance of Bergson's work. For example, Margenot in *Zonas y sombras* devotes a section to "Time and Memory" (95–102) in Benet's fiction, mentioning Bergson only in a brief reference to the essay by Pope ("Benet, Faulkner, and Bergson's Memory") but nonetheless using the Bergsonian expression "spatialization of time" (for example, on 101) without a more thorough discussion of the French philosopher's influence.

53. Orringer, "Epic in a Paralytic State," 40, cites Ortega, "Estudios sobre la obra de Juan Benet." The second quotation is from Ortega, *Ensayos de la novela española*

moderna, 142; see also Sobejano, *Novela española de nuestro tiempo,* 391; Vásquez, "The Creative Task"; the title of Compitello's essay "Herrumbrosas plumas: *En la penumbra* and Hermeneutic Paralysis" is also revealing in this regard.

54. Pope, "Benet, Faulkner, and Bergson's Memory," 115.

55. Vásquez, in "The Creative Task," has written that "the task is an impossible one" (65).

56. Fraser, *Encounters with Bergson(ism) in Spain,* 124. Esther Nelson describes the psychic action of *Volverás a Región* in this way: "the interior chronology spans a period from the childhood of Gamallo and Sebastián to the present moment, the 1960s, focusing on certain events in the decades of the 1910s and 1920s and especially of the period of the Civil War, but bypassing almost entirely those of the intervening postwar years" ("Narrative Perspective in *Volverás a Región,*" 33). Dr. Sebastián reappears in *A Meditation* (for example, on 117).

57. See Gullón, "Esperando a Coré," 129.

58. Compitello, "Herrumbrosas plumas," 417. See also Gingerich, "Telling (in) the Half-Light."

59. Bergson, *Creative Evolution,* 303; my emphasis. Benet uses this notion also in *A Meditation,* where he describes it in depth: "That day on which that inexplicable and involuntary immersion of memory takes place, a whole zone of penumbra that seemed forgotten and about which the urge to know had lost all stimulation . . . begins to be lukewarmly illuminated; and the more the lines of that precise instant become clear—deformed in appearance but actually preserved intact by the same oblivion that enwrapped it for such a long time—, the more the chronological shadows that surround it close in, breaking that pretended continuity of a past that isn't a dimensional time but an infinite and limited grouping of quiet instants of light in a dark and mobile continuum" (33–34).

60. See, for example, Benet, *Una meditación,* 279, 373, 236, 397, respectively. In the English translation, *A Meditation,* the word *durée* appears italicized in French on page 228. The word appears also in *Volverás a Región* (*Return to Región,* 83).

61. Benet also begins one of his own civil engineering articles with a remembrance of his grandfather's farm ("Hidráulica moderna y regadío antiguo," 4).

62. Benet, *A Meditation,* 69. See also "the outbreak of the civil war" (43), and explicit mention of the "civil war" on many pages (for example 51, 69, 75, 99, 101, 102), as well as discussion of the small number of liberals who survived, and how they managed to survive (99); that is, by living in "hope." My use of the term "narrator" is due to practical considerations underlying the present book, and should not distract from the more complex and therefore accurate analyses of Vásquez ("The Creative Task") and Sobejano (*Novela española de nuestro tiempo*) who have proposed far more nuanced models of the book's narrative; also Rivkin, "La búsqueda literaria en *Una meditación*"; and in reference to narration in Benet's first novel, Compitello, "*Volverás a Región,* the Critics and the Spanish Civil War."

63. This reflects Cabrera's judgment of the novel: "In *A Meditation* no chronological sequence is followed and no specific order, or priority of ideas, is observed" (*Juan Benet,* 92). Benet himself, of course, professed to have organized the text (*Cartografía personal,* 17).

64. Cited, for example, by both Cabrera (*Juan Benet,* 92) and Fraser (*Encounters with Bergson(ism) in Spain,* 130). Benet's own remarks appear in an interview published in *Cartografía personal:* "I wrote the novel by machine on one continuous roll of paper for reasons of comfort and effectiveness" (17).

65. Gingerich, "Returning to the Originary Enmity of Philosophy and Literature," 335. Although this article focuses on Benet's book *Del Pozo y del Numa,* his assertion speaks to Benet's oeuvre as a whole and is clearly relevant, also, to *Una meditación.* A similar comment appears in Benson, "La poética de Juan Benet y sus implicaciones pragmáticas," 79.

66. For example, Benet writes: "days later, at an unlikely moment, memory brings it to the surface . . ." (*A Meditation,* 37, also 71). Here is a more lengthy example of these philosophical digressions, which are so frequent in Benet's novel: "Days later—and just like the musical phrase that on the first hearing impresses the ear more than the taste and, once heard, soon seems erased from one's memory, which rejects any attempt at repetition, but which, days later, at an unlikely moment (almost always going down steps) comes into bloom, completely and perfectly preserved, putting in evidence the contradictions of a memory that registers and flies away but doesn't remember or obey—that accent would appear" (*A Meditation,* 27).

67. Benet remarks as well on the practical concerns of habit memory: "So that a large part of what is habit does not keep memory so much as a distinct knowledge, related to the plan of existence that every man makes for himself and which, little by little, is translated into habits" (*A Meditation,* 32–33).

68. Benet, *A Meditation,* 31–32. He continues: "I imagine that that thick medium, opaque and impenetrable to investigation and verification, where so many acts of our life remain engraved, is only susceptible to being impressed by the unusual and, on the other hand . . . is capable of putting all of its hardness and tenacity up against the registry of habits" (*A Meditation,* 32).

69. Benet, *A Meditation,* 33. Memory is also referred to repeatedly as a "fixed form" or a "register" (*A Meditation,* 66, 78). Compare with Bergson, who writes, "But let there set in some incident that turns our attention from life; let there take hold a sudden disinterest in life. Then the entire past rushes forth into the present and appears to us in the most minute detail" (from English translation of "The Human Soul," in Fraser, *Encounters with Bergson(ism) in Spain,* 318.)

70. I believe that it is the nature of this particular invocation of Bergsonism that has led critics familiar with the French philosopher's thought to overlook the fundamental influence in question. This is the case, for example with Herzberger's discussion on page 69 of *The Novelistic World of Juan Benet.* It should be noted, of course, that Herzberger's text was published prior to Orringer's interview with the Spanish author ("Juan Benet a viva voz"), from which this chapter's epigraph is taken.

71. Benet, *A Meditation,* 35.

72. For example, Benet, *Una meditación,* 48, 49–50, 91; see also Fraser, *Encounters with Bergson(ism) in Spain,* 131.

73. Benet, *A Meditation,* 228, 229. Also, one conceives "existence in the form of categories, none of which is real" (218).

74. Bergson insists that emotional life (and thus affect) are a way of bridging this entrenched misunderstanding. To that effect, he is being explored by contemporary philosophers focusing on affect.

75. Benet, *A Meditation*, 229.

76. Benet, *Return to Región*, 80. That novel, of course, frequently makes references to memory as well: "because memory—I can see very clearly now—is almost always the vengeance for what it was not—what was is engraved on the body in a substance that our lights never reach" (101); "The rules of memory . . . barely supply any other data than a series of atrocious gestures and exaggerated traits, repeated a thousand times and hypertrophied in a recurrent succession of deceptive contrasts" (277). See also, for example, 163, 230.

77. Benet, *A Meditation*, 231–32.

78. Benet, *A Meditation*, 72. Also Benet, *A Meditation:* "A certain kind of hope plays the same role in the life of man as the tortoise in the parable of Achilles; the terrain over which it advances never goes totally forward and that or those hindermost and miniscule remains are designated by the name of desperation" (306). As this quotation demonstrates, of course, following Bergson's philosophy, Benet's characters would believe hope is desperate because they fundamentally misunderstand their lives. Mistakenly seeing temporality through a spatial lens, they are trapped without hope of advancing.

79. Benet, *A Meditation*, 151, also on 153; "Nor does that other verb exist . . . ," 55–56. See Fraser, *Encounters with Bergson(ism) in Spain*, 132.

80. Benet, *A Meditation*, 82.

81. Benet, *A Meditation*, 78. The discussion centers on the measuring of time throughout pages 85–90, and Benet returns to it intermittently throughout the novel, for example much later, on 205–6. On one occasion the text mentions the "clock, its hands . . . trying to persuade me of the immobility in which I was rooted in spite of my efforts to advance in the chronological direction of time (and even the clock was silent, one might say that its little wooden chest held its breath while I was observing it)" (*A Meditation*, 71–72). Time passes irregularly in Región—whether in *Una meditación* or in *Volverás a Región*—as "un espasmo," "un susto," or "un santiamén" (*Una meditación*, 112; see Fraser, *Encounters with Bergson(ism) in Spain*, 137, 138n25). In *Volverás a Región* the narration reflects on "a time—clocks and calendars don't mark it, as if its own density casts a spell with the pendulums and gears in its bosom" (*Return to Región*, 81) and "the hateful order of time" (101). In that novel, the narration highlights the useless calendar in Dr. Sebastián's house (93); see also 223.

82. Benet, "Un extempore," 73.

83. Benet, *A Meditation*, 131. See also Bergson, *Time and Free Will*, and "The Body and the Soul" in *Mind-Energy*.

84. Benet, *A Meditation:* "the deceits of a memory that retreats back to the first day" (15); "For memory there is no continuity at any moment: a strip of hidden time is devoured by the body and converted into a series of scattered fragments" (34).

85. Benet, *A Meditation*, 173.

86. Vásquez, "The Creative Task," 65. Also Herzberger, *The Novelistic World of Juan Benet,* who brings up the question of Bergsonism but glosses it over, even though he correctly concludes that, "in *Volverás a Región,* however, although the psychological time is much greater than the chronological duration, the characters experience no internal growth (69). Benet relies heavily on Bergsonian ideas, even if he invokes them in his own fashion. It is not that the books are completely Bergsonian, it is that in order to understand them we have to understand the extent to which Bergson influenced Benet.

87. Interested readers might elect to read John Mullarky's *The New Bergson* and *Bergson and Philosophy,* Suzanne Guerlac's *Thinking in Time,* or, with reference to other notable Spanish writers, my own *Encounters with Bergson(ism) in Spain.*

88. Bergson, *Creative Evolution,* 154–55.

89. Bergson, *The Creative Mind,* 161–62.

90. Bergson, *The Creative Mind,* 70. See also Fraser, *Encounters with Bergson-(ism) in Spain,* 106–7. In *Creative Evolution* Bergson writes, "you must thrust intelligence outside itself by an act of will" (193).

91. Bergson, *The Creative Mind,* 42, 47.

92. Benet, *En ciernes,* 50; I have modified the English translation of this passage provided by Lupinacci Wescott ("Benet's Theoretical Essays," 20).

93. Lupinacci Wescott, "Benet's Theoretical Essays," 25. See previous note.

94. The first clause refers to Benet, *La inspiración y el estilo,* 27–28; the second includes quotations from *La inspiración y el estilo* by Lupinacci Wescott, "Benet's Theoretical Essays," 21.

95. Benet, *La inspiración y el estilo,* 72; the phrase "mathematical reasoning" is a phrase used by Benet to refer to Edgar Allan Poe's 1846 essay "The Philosophy of Composition." "To me the thesis of *La filosofía de la composición* is not convincing" (Benet, *La inspiración y el estilo,* 70); "Poe seems to insinuate that imagination, as fertile as it may be, unless it is accompanied and complemented by an analytic capacity is not capable of inventing anything grand" (Benet, *La inspiración y el estilo,* 71). The phrase "zone of shadows" appears also in Benet's later work *En ciernes* and is the implicit inspiration for Margenot's book of criticism titled *Zonas y sombras.*

96. For example, Benet, *La inspiración y el estilo,* 25–26. This is commented upon also by numerous critics, including Compitello, "The Paradoxes of Praxis."

97. Benet, *La inspiración y el estilo,* 72.

98. Benet, "Foreword" to *Critical Approaches,* viii.

99. Benet himself writes, "Hence—it will be said—my work demands mentors; persons who, thanks to hours of study and dedication, will help others get through it, eliminating obstacles and illuminating dark corners" ("Foreword" to *Critical Approaches,* viii).

100. Pérez, "The Rhetoric of Ambiguity," 19.

101. Writes Benet, "the most irresistible style will never be that of the costumbrist author" (*La inspiración y el estilo,* 169, also 174 on costumbrism vs. *grand style*).

102. For example, Benet, *La inspiración y el estilo,* 91.

103. Benet, *La inspiración y el estilo,* 163 (my emphasis).

104. Benet, *La inspiración y el estilo,* 53.

105. Benet, *La inspiración y el estilo,* 157; 158.

106. Benet, *La inspiración y el estilo,* 31.

107. Bergson, *Creative Evolution,* 196.

108. See also *The Creative Mind,* 188–200, wherein Bergson writes: "The truth is that our mind is able to follow the reverse procedure. It can be installed in the mobile reality, adopt its ceaselessly changing direction, in short, grasp it intuitively. But to do that it must do itself violence, reverse the direction of the operation by which it ordinarily thinks, continually upsetting its categories, or rather recasting them. . . . *To philosophize means to reverse the normal direction of the workings of thought.*" (original emphasis).

109. Bergson, "Introduction to Metaphysics," 127–28. There is a certain Bergsonian resonance—albeit a distant one—in the correspondence between Bergson's linkage of intuition and what in English translation becomes the word *dust* on the one hand, and the title of Benet's book of essays (in English translation provided by Vicente Cabrera) *Puerta de tierra* (Door of Dust), which included the essay "Un extempore."

Chapter 4

1. The author of the second epigraph, Sáenz Ridruejo (1928–2006), was named "Civil Engineer of the Year" in 2004. See the bibliographic entry for "Sáenz Ridruejo—blog." Also of interest is that Benet—as head of the book series Ciencias, Humanidades e Ingeniería published by the Civil Engineering School in Madrid— elected to republish a work by Casiano del Prado titled "Descripción física y geográfica de la provincia de Madrid" (Physical and Geographical Description of the Province of Madrid), further indicating his interest in geography (Sáenz Ridruejo, in Baeza, "Acto de Homenaje," 77–78).

2. Ali Madanipour puts the question of space well: "The dilemmas of space appear to lie in the way we relate to it: the way we understand and therefore transform, it. The debates between absolute and relational space, the dilemma between physical and social space, between real and mental space, between space and mass, between function and form, between abstract and differential space, between space and place, between space and time, can all be seen as indicators of a series of open philosophical questions: how do we understand space and relate to it? Does it exist beyond our cognition or is it conditioned by it? Do we relate to it by our reason or our senses? Is space a collection of things and people, a container for them, or are they embedded in it? Is it representing openness or fixity? Do we understand and transform space individually or socially? How do we relate space and time? In our response to these questions, we find ourselves divided between rationalism and empiricism, between materialism and idealism, between objective and subjective understanding, between reason and emotion, between theory and practice, between uniformity and diversity, and between order and disorder" (*Design of Urban Space,* 28–29).

3. Theorists working across many disciplines and from many perspectives—such as Dear, *The Postmodern Urban Condition;* Foucault, *Discipline and Punish;* Harvey, *The Urban Experience, The Condition of Postmodernity, Justice, Nature and the Geography of Difference, Spaces of Hope;* Jessop, "Narrating the Future of the National Economy and the National State"; Latham and McCormack, "Moving Cities"; Lefebvre, *The Production of Space;* Madanipour, *Design of Urban Space,* "Multiple Meanings of Space and the Need for a Dynamic Perspective"; Mitchell, *Cultural Geography;* Marston, "The Social Construction of Scale," "What's Culture Got to Do with It?"; Soja, *Thirdspace;* Thorns, *The Transformation of Cities;* and Tilly, "Epilogue"—all ask trenchant questions of the relationship between mental representations of space and physical space. This is, of course, merely a sample. Don Mitchell's primer *Cultural Geography* is perhaps the best place for literary theorists interested in issues of space to begin.

4. This is the case with Malcolm Compitello and Edward Baker's edited volume *Madrid: de Fortunata a la M-40* (2003), Susan Larson's *Constructing and Resisting Modernity* (2011), Eugenia Afinoguénova and Jaume Martí-Olivella's edited volume *Spain is (Still) Different* and my own *Henri Lefebvre and the Spanish Urban Experience* (2011), for example.

5. Lefebvre was influenced by French philosopher Henri Bergson (featured in chapter 3; see also Fraser, "Toward a Philosophy of the Urban"), and in turn influenced the aforementioned David Harvey.

6. Mitchell, *Cultural Geography,* 21. There were, of course, problems resulting from Sauer's simplistic and certainly unanalyzed conception of what "culture" actually *was* (24); also "'culture' was radically undertheorized in Sauer's own work . . . ; it was the taken-for-granted of human life" (29).

7. Sauer, "The Fourth Dimension," 192. Also, "The fourth dimension, time, was necessary to understanding and could not be replaced by stage, cycle, model, or environmental influence" (191–92).

8. See Mitchell, *Cultural Geography:* "Sauer therefore needs to be recognized as [sic] important founder of not one, but two geographical subdisciplines: cultural ecology and cultural geography" (29).

9. Mitchell, *Cultural Geography,* 28.

10. Mitchell, *Cultural Geography,* 21.

11. Sauer's vision of his own field parallels Benet's rejection of narrow views of engineering ("Ingeniería e intimidad," discussed in chapter 2): "what geographers mainly were doing in the East, which interested me less and less as narrowing professionalism" ("The Fourth Dimension," 191). In fact, Sauer's emphasis on how human activities modify the world puts him in a camp with the corresponding European geographers who were his contemporaries instead of his colleagues working in the United States.

12. Benet, *Return to Región,* 28, 29.

13. Benet, *Return to Región,* 29–32. These discussions are paralleled, for example, by the descriptions of the Iberian Peninsula in *El agua en España,* 151.

14. Benet, *Return to Región,* 31, 33.

15. Benet, *Return to Región,* 33.

16. Benet, *Return to Región,* 1.

17. Evidence of the work's novelistic qualities may be found in Compitello, "Región's Brazilian Backlands."

18. Putnam, *Marvelous Journey,* 203–4; cited in Compitello, "Región's Brazilian Backlands."

19. See Benet, "De Canudos a Macondo," and Compitello, "Región's Brazilian Backlands."

20. Benet, "De Canudos a Macondo," in *Infidelidad del regreso,* 127.

21. Although it is somewhat de rigueur to acknowledge this connection, it has been most directly elaborated by Compitello, "Región's Brazilian Backlands," 27. These parallels include the portrayal of General Gamallo by Benet and of (de facto military leader) Antonio Conselheiro in Da Cunha as well as similarities in message, structure, and narrative space (28).

22. Compitello, "Región's Brazilian Backlands," 28. There is certainly reason to consider Da Cunha's achievement as more broadly reflective of the "environmental determinism" that structured geographical thought prior to the early twentieth century.

23. Compitello, "Región's Brazilian Backlands," 29.

24. Compitello, "Región's Brazilian Backlands," 29. A chart on that page compares each of these sections: *Os sertões* [Geog./Geol.] 3–20, [Climate] 20–49, [Effects] 50–169; *Volverás a Región* [Geog./Geol.] 7–10, 36–43, [Climate] 43–48, [Effects] 48–51.

25. Benet, *Return to Región,* 32.

26. Benet, *Return to Región,* 37. See also discussions in this book, chapters 1 and 2.

27. Benet, *Return to Región,* 42.

28. Benet, *Return to Región,* 40, 5, respectively.

29. Consider how the civil war itself—a human conflict—is the cause of many of the problems faced by Benet's characters: *Return to Región* mentions "a kind of abstract indifference and radical distrust that had never been contrasted, at least since the civil war had ended, with a reality—no less unpleasant, of course—that was going to sanction the same source of his reserves in the end" (126).

30. Sauer, "The Morphology of Landscape," qtd. in Mitchell, *Cultural Geography,* 27.

31. Sauer, "The Morphology of Landscape," qtd. in Mitchell, *Cultural Geography,* 28.

32. See my introduction on history vs. fiction; also Margenot, *Zonas y sombras,* 1–40; Wood, "Una aproximación cartográfica a *Herrumbrosas lanzas*"; Wasmuth, "Polifonía y armonía de los espacios en *Herrumbrosas lanzas.*"

33. Margenot, *Zonas y sombras,* 25.

34. Wasmuth, "Polifonía y armonía de los espacios en *Herrumbrosas lanzas,*" 243. Wasmuth maintains that the scale of the map in its 1998 edition is 1:165,000. Rivero writes that the original scale of the 1983 Región map was 1:150,000 ("Juan Benet," 152), and Benet's comments in an interview prior to the publication of the book confirm this scale (Benet, *Cartografía personal,* 211).

35. Compitello notes that "Benet intersperses references to the real, if somewhat obscure locations in Spain. A check of a detailed atlas reveals that such places as Rañeces, Mampodre, Láncara and la Liébana do, in fact, exist" ("Región's Brazilian Backlands," 44n17; see also Fraser, *Encounters with Bergson(ism) in Spain,* 127). Benet's first novel mentions these places early on: "Mampodre to Babia, from Rañeces to Láncara" (*Return to Región,* 30). Readers should be aware that the region called Región also includes a town named Región.

36. Benet, *Herrumbrosas lanzas,* 247. This passage is referred to also in Wasmuth "Polifonía y armonía de los espacios en *Herrumbrosas lanzas,*" 241n4, and in Wood, "Una aproximación cartográfica a *Herrumbrosas lanzas,*" 10.

37. Harvey, *The Condition of Postmodernity,* 203.

38. Harvey, *Spaces of Capital,* 220.

39. In *Spaces of Capital,* Harvey reflects upon how the "connection between geographical knowledge and empire has been a strong topic of commentary in recent years" (217).

40. Harvey, *The Urban Experience,* 176–77; *Spaces of Capital,* 219–20.

41. Harvey, *Spaces of Capital,* 225; see also Fraser, *Encounters with Bergson(ism) in Spain,* 128.

42. Other obligatory references for this general notion are Benedict Anderson's book *Imagined Communities* and Yi-Fu Tuan's *Space and Place.* Of great interest is that Tuan's work is mentioned in Margenot's *Zonas y sombras,* although only in passing (40).

43. My remarks here follow from work originally published in chapter 3 of Fraser, *Encounters.*

44. Wasmuth, "Polifonía y armonía de los espacios en *Herrumbrosas lanzas,*" 246.

45. Wood, "Una aproximación cartográfica a *Herrumbrosas lanzas,*" 17. This in itself might be understood as a response to the fact that, as Harvey notes, "Mapping also turned out to be far from ideologically neutral" (*The Condition of Postmodernity,* 228).

46. Margenot, *Zonas y sombras,* 36, 38; also "the topographical model is full of contradictions when compared with the Región novels" (38).

47. Margenot, *Zonas y sombras,* 39. The critic also notes that the map "lends greater spatial unity and aesthetic coherence to the author's fictional world" (39)—but this coherence, of course, includes the mystery and enigma that are central to his fiction. Wood notes that "the novelesque map is doubly deceitful because it transmits spatial information that is necessarily incomplete regarding an invented land" ("Una aproximación cartográfica a *Herrumbrosas lanzas,*" 11; see also 17).

48. In an interview from 1983, Benet admits that what critics have seen as imprecisions are in reality errors resulting from his lack of attention (Benet, *Cartografía personal,* 211). There is no doubt, however, that whatever the cause, Benet does not see them as a weakness. As he put it in an interview, "One of the privileges of fiction is its sheltering of imprecision. . . . It is a method that comes with its risks and that, of course, has a price that is paid through errors" (211).

49. See Bergson's *Creative Evolution;* also the discussion of Bergsonism in Deleuze's *Bergsonism* and *Cinema I: The Movement-Image;* see also Deleuze's *Cinema II: The Time-Image.*

50. Harvey, *The Condition of Postmodernity,* 206, and Harvey, *Spaces of Capital,* 220, respectively. Harvey continues: "For this reason, Bergson, the great theorist of becoming, of time as flux, was incensed that it took the spatializations of the clock to tell the time" (*The Condition of Postmodernity,* 206). See also Harvey, *The Condition of Modernity,* 223, on the dominance of the sensuous over the intellectual in medieval maps.

51. Rivero, "Juan Benet," 153.

52. Harvey, *Spaces of Capital,* 223. This is, of course, an idea central to cultural geography. Although there are many relevant references here, the topic is explored quite extensively in Doreen Massey's philosophical (and readable) book from 2005 titled *For Space.*

53. Sauer, "The Fourth Dimension," 189. The very study of human geography is traditionally organized regionally. "Regional geography was held to be the main concern . . . natural regions, distinguished by relief or climate, each having an economy proper to its physical nature. Each was delimited by boundaries. . . . The natural region was taken as the basic unit for the study of human geography" (Sauer, "The Fourth Dimension," 190–91). Introduction to regional geography courses abound in the American university system.

54. Benet, *Cartografía personal,* 10–11.

55. Benet, *Cartografía personal,* 11–12.

56. For Bergson's influence on Lefebvre, see Fraser, "Toward a Philosophy of the Urban." On Harvey's debt to Lefebvre, see for example Harvey, *Justice, Nature and the Geography of Difference,* 218–19. As Fraser argues in "Toward a Philosophy of the Urban," although Lefebvre professed to have "hated Bergson's guts" (qtd. from Merrifield, *Henri Lefebvre,* 27), his early explicit rejection of Bergson's philosophy may be attributed to a number of causes and is, at any rate, at odds with his texts' uneasy, if implicit, relationship with Bergsonism's tenets.

57. Lefebvre, *The Production of Space,* 33.

58. Lefebvre, *The Production of Space,* 21.

59. As discussed in chapter 3 with reference to *Una meditación* and other novels and essays.

60. Lefebvre, *The Production of Space,* 175.

61. Lefebvre, *The Production of Space,* 219.

62. Lefebvre, *Critique of Everyday Life,* vol. 3: 130. See also Fraser, *Encounters with Bergson(ism) in Spain,* for passages concerning Bergson, Lefebvre, and Benet.

63. Lefebvre, in *Critique of Everyday Life,* vol. 3, mentions the "splintering of space and time in general homogeneity, and the crushing of natural rhythms and cycles by linearity" (135)—thus the illusion of time as reversible, and from that illusion, the suppression of tragedy and death (133) and the rampant colonization and commodification of daily life. See also Lefebvre, *Critique of Everyday Life,* vols. 1–2; Fraser "Toward a Philosophy of the Urban."

64. Lefebvre, *Critique of Everyday Life,* vol. 3: 133; see also vol. 2.

65. Lefebvre, *The Production of Space,* 17; see also 142. Lefebvrian scholar Stuart Elden elaborates on this in his monograph *Understanding Henri Lefebvre,* 137–38.

66. Lefebvre, *Rhythmanalysis,* 24, 22, respectively.

67. These notions, discussed in chapter 3, are most directly discussed in Bergson, "Introduction to Metaphysics," and Benet, *La inspiración y el estilo,* although in each case they are part and parcel of the thought of each writer.

68. Lefebvre, *The Production of Space,* 230, 233, respectively.

69. Lefebvre, *Critique of Everyday Life,* vol. 3: 17.

70. See also Bergson, *Creative Evolution,* xiii: "theory of knowledge and theory of life seem to us inseparable. . . . It is necessary that these two inquiries, theory of knowledge and a theory of life, should join each other, and, by a circular process, push each other on unceasingly" (original emphasis).

71. Schmid, "Lefebvre's Theory of the Production of Space," 29.

72. See Compitello, "*Volverás a Región,* the Critics and the Spanish Civil War," 16; also Nelson, "Narrative Perspective in *Volverás a Región*"; and González, "Tecnología y Arcadia en *Volverás a región:* Un contraste descriptivo."

73. Compitello, "*Volverás a Región,* the Critics and the Spanish Civil War," 16.

74. Herzberger's *Narrating the Past* is the most comprehensive source on this topic.

75. Herzberger, "Benet y la historia," 24; see also his "Juan Benet and the Spanish Civil War."

76. Gimferrer, "Notas sobre Juan Benet," 49.

77. Lefebvre, "Time and History," 178.

78. Benet, "Sobre el carácter tétrico de la historia," 143.

79. Benet, "Sobre el carácter tétrico de la historia," 143–44.

80. Herzberger, *Narrating the Past,* 33.

81. Lefebvre's notion of totality was decidedly Marxist in origin.

82. Benet, *Return to Región,* 5.

Epilogue

1. Benet, "Incertidumbre," 44.

2. Benet, *En ciernes,* 44. This notion has already been discussed in reference to the book *La inspiración y el estilo.* A concise illustration lies in Benet's identification, therein, of Poe's "The Raven" as "an enigmatic poem" (72).

3. Herzberger, *The Novelistic World of Juan Benet,* 134–35, 84, 23.

4. Pérez, "The Rhetoric of Ambiguity," 18.

5. Benet, *Return to Región,* 31.

6. Herzberger, among others, calls Numa an "enigmatic figure."

7. Benet, "Un extempore," 84; see also the insufficiency of rationality as discussed on page 86. See also *El ángel del señor abandona a Tobías,* 202.

8. Benet, *El ángel del señor abandona a Tobías,* 144.

9. Benet, *Return to Región,* 69.

10. "La novela en la España de hoy (1980)" in Benet, *La moviola de Eurípides,* 23–24.

11. "Nothing is as opposed to the effort of comprehending and formulating the laws that govern the universe, or to a part of it, as the aim of carrying the vitality of man, making use of rational discourse, the idea of his fundamental unintelligibility" (Benet, *En ciernes,* 44–45). Also, the civil war is a war of ambiguity (Herzberger, "The Theme of Warring Brothers in 'Saúl ante Samuel,'" 103). In *A Meditation* the narration notes that all the relationships governing the adult world are "enigmatic" (75).

12. In fact, if one takes into account the class nature of Francoism (as per Sevilla-Guzmán, "The Peasantry and the Franco Régime") it is not surprising that Benet's postdictatorial Región should be a mysterious and enigmatic zone as those who work the land are also alienated from its resources.

13. Adorno, *Aesthetic Theory,* 121.

14. As evidenced in the essay "Ingeniería e intimidad."

15. Adorno, *Aesthetic Theory,* 121.

Bibliography

Primary Literature

Where a different or later publication is cited, years in brackets represent the publication dates of the original Spanish editions.

Existing English Translations

You'll Never Get Anywhere [1961]. Trans. Victoria Hughes. Madrid: Iberia, 1989.
Return to Región [1967]. Trans. Gregory Rabassa. New York: Columbia UP, 1985.
A Meditation [1969]. Trans. Gregory Rabassa. New York: Persea, 1982.
"Military Strategy in the Spanish Civil War" [1976]. Trans. Malcolm Alan Compitello. In *Rewriting the Good Fight*, ed. Brown, Compitello, Howard, and Martin. 3–23.

Novels and Novellas

Volverás a Región [1967]. Barcelona: Destino, 1997.
Una meditación [1969]. Barcelona: Alfaguara, 1990.
Una tumba Numa. [1971]. Madrid: Alfaguara, 1987.
Un viaje de invierno [1972]. Ed. Diego Martínez Torrón. Madrid: Cátedra, 1980.
La otra casa de Mazón. Barcelona: Seix Barral, 1973.
En el estado. Madrid: Alfaguara, 1977.
Del pozo y del Numa. Barcelona: La Gaya Ciencia, 1978.
Saúl ante Samuel [1980]. Ed. John B. Margenot III. Madrid: Cátedra, 1994.
El aire de un crimen. Barcelona: Planeta, 1980.
Herrumbrosas lanzas [1983–86]. Barcelona: Alfaguara, 1999.
En la penumbra. Madrid: Alfaguara, 1989.
El caballero de Sajonia. Barcelona: Planeta, 1991.

Books of Essays

La inspiración y el estilo [1966]. Barcelona: Seix Barral, 1970.
Puerta de tierra. Barcelona: Seix Barral, 1970.
El ángel del señor abandona a Tobías. Barcelona: La Gaya Ciencia, 1976.
En ciernes. Madrid: Taurus, 1976.

¿Qué fue la Guerra Civil? [1976]. Rpt. in *La sombra de la guerra*. Madrid: Taurus, 1999. 21–141.

La moviola de Eurípides. Madrid: Taurus, 1981.

Sobre la incertidumbre. Barcelona: Ariel, 1982.

Artículos I (1962–1977). Madrid: Libertarias, 1983.

Otoño en Madrid hacia 1850. Madrid: Alianza, 1987?

Londres victoriano [1989]. Barcelona: Planeta, 1995.

La construcción de la torre de Babel. Madrid: Siruela, 1990.

Selected Engineering Texts

"Soluciones constructivas en obras de regadío." *Revista de Obras Públicas* 113. 3001 (1965): 406–17.

"Ingeniería e intimidad" [1976]. Rpt. in *Revista de Obras Públicas* 140.3317 (1993): 74–76.

"Ingeniería y conducta social" [1976]. Rpt. in *Revista de Obras Públicas* 140.3317 (1993): 79–82.

"El agua en Región" [1981]. *Páginas impares*. Madrid: Alfaguara, 1996. 113–22.

Ingenieria en la época romántica: Las obras públicas en España alrededor de 1860 [1983]. Ed. Juan Benet. Madrid: Ministerio de Obras Públicas y Urbanismo, 1983.

"Panorama actual en las relaciones contractuales en la construcción de túneles en España y su posible desarrollo futuro." Curso sobre contratación y dirección de túneles. Madrid: Colegio de Ingenieros de Caminos, 1983.

Prosas civiles. Ed. Juan Carlos Suñén. Madrid: Ministerio de Obras Públicas, 1984.

"Política hidráulica." *Agricultura y Sociedad* 32 (1984): 273–80. www.marm.es/ministerio/pags/biblioteca/revistas/pdf_ays/a032_07.pdf.

"Discurso leido en el acto de su nombramiento como colegiado de honor" [1987]. *Revista de Obras Públicas* 149.3317 (1993): 77–78.

"Un punto de vista extranjero." In *Vistas de las obras del Canal de Isabel II fotografiadas por Clifford*. Madrid: J. Soto, 1988. 11–16.

"Hidráulica moderna y regadío antiguo." *OP: Revista del Colegio de Ingenieros de Caminos, Canales y Puertos* 13 (1989): 4–5.

Si yo fuera presidente: La hidráulica como solución a las necesidades hídricas. Murcia: Colegio de Ingenieros de Caminos, Canales y Puertos, 2009.

Short Story Collections

Nunca llegarás a nada [1961]. Madrid: Alianza, 1969.

5 narraciones y 2 fábulas. Barcelona: La Gaya Ciencia, 1972.

Sub Rosa. Barcelona: La Gaya Ciencia, 1973.

Trece fábulas y media. Madrid: Alfaguara, 1981.

Cuentos completos (I&II) [1977; 1981]. Madrid: Alfaguara, 1998.

Selected Individual Essays, Prologues, and Forewords

"Un extempore." *Puerta de tierra*. Valladolid: Ediciones Cuatro, 2003. 69–88.

"De Canudos a Macondo." *Revista de Occidente* 24.70 (1969): 49–57.

"Tres fechas: Sobre la estrategia en la Guerra Civil española." *La sombra de la guerra*. Madrid: Taurus, 1999. 145–70.

"Valedictoria a Dionisio." In *Dionisio Ridruejo: de la Falange a la oposición,* ed. Jesús Aguirre. Madrid: Taurus, 1976. 11–20.

"Foreword." In *Critical Approaches to the Writings of Juan Benet,* ed. Manteiga, Herzberger, and Compitello. vii–viii.

"Prólogo." *Faulkner en España: Perspectivas de la narrativa de postguerra*. María Elena Bravo. Barcelona: Península, 1985. 7–8.

"Los límites de la literatura medieval." In *Edad Media y Literatura,* Benet, Juan, Fernando Fernán Gómez, Jaime Gil de Biedma, Juan Goytisolo, Francisco Rico. Madrid: Trieste, 1985. 89–106.

"Sobre Galdós." In *Juan Benet,* ed. Vernon. 281–88.

"Epílogo" [1987]. In Marías, Javier, *El hombre sentimental*. Madrid: Alfaguara, 1999. 183–85.

"El efecto Barral." *Revista de Occidente* 110–11 (1990): 11–15.

Theater

Max. Revista Española 4: (1953): 409–30.

Agonía confutans. Cuadernos Hispanoamericanos 236 (1969): 307–21.

Teatro. Including *Anastas o el origen de la constitución* (1958), *Agonía confutans* (1966), and *Un caso de conciencia* (1967). Madrid: Siglo XXI, 1970.

Poetry

"Dos poemas: 'En cauria,' 'Un enigma.'" *El Urogallo* 3.19 (1972): 7–8.

Posthumous Collections—Essays and Interviews

Páginas impares. Madrid: Alfaguara, 1996.
Cartografía personal. Valladolid: Ediciones Cuatro, 1997.
Una biografía literaria. Valladolid: Ediciones Cuatro, 2007.
Infidelidad del regreso. Valladolid: Ediciones Cuatro, 2007.

Secondary Literature and Additional References

Abellán, Manuel L. *Censura y creación literaria en España (1939–1976)*. Barcelona: Península, 1980.

Adorno, Theodor. *Aesthetic Theory*. Trans. Robert Hullot-Kentor. Minneapolis: U Minnesota P, 1997.

Alonso, Santos. "*Saúl ante Samuel* (1980) de Juan Benet." *La novela en la transición (1976–1981)*. Madrid: Puerta del Sol, 1983. 159–61.

Altisent, Marta E. "Crimen y compromiso en 'Obiter Dictum' de Juan Benet." *Anales de la Literatura Española Contemporánea* 16.3 (1991): 207–24.

Alvar, Carlos, José-Carlos Mainer and Rosa Navarro. *Breve historia de la literatura española*. Madrid: Alianza, 1997.

Anderson, Benedict. *Imagined Communities: Reflections on the Origin and Spread of Nationalism*. London: Verso 1983.

Aranguren, José Luis. "El mundo novelístico de Juan Benet." *Estudios literarios.* Madrid: Gredos, 1976. 282–93.

Ayestarán Uriz, Ignacio. "La filosofía tecnocrática del agua: ciencia, tecnología y sociedad en Itoitz." Proyecto 'Políticas y Culturas del Agua' IT97/1. Universidad del País Vasco. Accessed 20 March 2012. congreso.us.es/ciberico/archivos _acrobat/zaracomun4ayestaran.pdf.

Azúa, Félix de. "El texto invisible. Juan Benet: *Un viaje de invierno.*" In *Juan Benet,* ed. Vernon. 147–57.

Baeza, Mónica, ed. and coord. "Acto de Homenaje a Juan Benet." *Revista de Obras Públicas* 141.3329 (febrero 1994): 63–80.

Benson, Frederick R. *Writers in Arms: The Literary Impact of the Spanish Civil War.* New York: New York UP, 1967.

Benson, Ken. *Fenomenología del enigma: Juan Benet y el pensamiento literario posestructuralista.* Amsterdam: Rodopi, 2004.

———. "La poética de Juan Benet y sus implicaciones pragmáticas." *Salina: revista de la Facultat de Lletres de Tarragona* 7 (December 1993): 79–88.

———. "Autenticidad y pureza en el discurso de Juan Benet." *Ínsula* 68.559–60 (julio-agosto 1993): 11–13.

———. *Dualidad y espíritu: análisis de la dualidad subyacente en el discurso de Juan Benet.* Stockholm: U of Stockholm, 1989.

Bergson, Henri. "The Philosophy of Claude Bernard." In *The Creative Mind.* Trans. Mabelle L. Andison. New York: Citadel P, 2002. 201–8.

———. "Bergson en la Residencia." *Residencia* 2 (1926): 174–76.

———. *Duration and Simultaneity.* 1922. Ed. Robin Durie. Manchester: Clinamen P, 1999.

———. *The Two Sources of Morality and Religion.* 1932. Trans. R. Ashley Audra and Cloudesley Brereton with assitance of W. Horsfall Carter. Garden City, NY: Doubleday, 1935.

———. *Creative Evolution.* 1907. Trans. A. Mitchell. New York: Dover Publications Inc., 1998.

———. "Introduction to Metaphysics." 1903. In *The Creative Mind.* Trans. Mabelle L. Andison. New York: Citadel P, 2002. 159–200.

———. *Matter and Memory.* 1896. Trans. Nancy Margaret Paul and W. Scott Palmer. New York: Macmillan and Co., 1920.

———. *Time and Free Will: An Essay on the immediate Data of Consciousness.* 1889. Trans. F. L. Pogson, M. A. Mineola. New York: Dover, 2001.

Bernard, Claude. *Introduction to the Study of Experimental Medicine.* 1865. Trans. Henry Copley Greene. Introd. Lawrence J. Henderson. Foreword Bernard Cohen. New York: Dover, 1957.

Blanco Aguinaga, Carlos, Julio Rodríguez Puértolas, and Iris M. Zavala. *Historia social de la Literatura española.* Vol. 3. Madrid: Castalia, 1984.

Bookchin, Murray. *The Spanish Anarchists: The Heroic Years, 1868–1936.* New York: Free Life Editions, 1977.

Bravo, María Elena. "Juan Benet before History: Approaches to Language, Experience and Literary Art in *Herrumbrosas lanzas*." In *Juan Benet: A Critical Reappraisal of his Fiction,* ed. Margenot. 147–65.

———. "Juan Benet: De modernismo a posmodernismo." *Ínsula* 68.559–60 (julio-agosto 1993): 5–7.

———. "*Herrumbrosas lanzas*—bruñidas letras: Juan Benet a la luz de Cervantes." *Discurso: Revista de Estudios Iberoamericanos* 11.2 (1993): 9–24.

———. "Juan Benet a la luz de Cervantes." *Cuadernos Hispanoamericanos* 469–470 (July–August 1989): 304–13.

———. "Región, una crónica del discurso literario." In *Juan Benet,* ed. Vernon. 177–87.

———. "Juan Benet desde la vanguardia: buscando la palabra para Yoknopatawpha y Región." *Prosa hispánica de vanguardia.* Ed. Fernando Burgos. Madrid: Orígenes, 1986. 245–53.

———. *Faulkner en España: Perspectivas de la narrativa de postguerra.* Barcelona: Península, 1985.

Brenan. Gerald. *The Spanish Labyrinth.* 1943. Cambridge: Cambridge UP, 1960.

Brown, Frieda S., Malcolm Alan Compitello, Victor M. Howard, and Robert A. Martin, eds. *Rewriting the Good Fight: Critical Essays on the Literature of the Spanish Civil War.* East Lansing: Michigan State UP, 1989.

Brown, G. G. *Historia de la literatura española.* El siglo XX. Barcelona: Ariel, 1973.

Burunat, Silvia. *El monólogo interior como forma narrativa en la novela española (1940–1975).* Madrid: José Porrúa Turanzas, 1980.

Cabrera, Vicente. *Juan Benet.* Boston: Twayne, 1983.

Cantarino, Vicente. *Civilización y cultura de España.* 5th ed. Upper Saddle River, NJ: Prentice-Hall, 2006.

Carr, Raymond. *Spain: A History.* Oxford, UK: Oxford UP, 2000.

———. *Spain 1808–1939.* 2nd edition. Oxford, UK: Oxford UP, 1970.

Carrasquer, Francisco. "Tres ensayos de Juan Benet." *Ínsula* 68.559–60 (julio–agosto 1993): 9–11.

Chamorro, Eduardo. "El caballero de Pisuerga." *Ínsula* 68.559–60 (julio–agosto 1993): 27–28.

Cibreiro, Estrella. "Narrators and their Narrations: *Una meditación* and *Saúl ante Samuel.*" In *Juan Benet: A Critical Reappraisal of his Fiction,* ed. Margenot. 127–45.

———. "Juan Benet: memoria e irracionalidad en tres obras regionatas." *Ojáncano: Revista de Literatura Española* 7 (abril 1993): 28–39.

Compitello, Malcolm. "Herrumbrosas plumas: *En la penumbra* and Hermeneutic Paralysis." *Letras Peninsulares* 7.2 (1994): 417–34.

———. "Reflexiones sobre el acto de narrar: Benet, Vargas Llosa y Euclides da Cunha." *Ínsula* 68.559–60 (julio–agosto 1993): 19–22.

———. "Bibliography: Juan Benet and His Critics." *Anales De La Novela De Postguerra* 3 (1978): 123-141.

———. "Benet and Spanish Postmodernism." *Revista Hispánica Moderna* 44.2 (1991): 259–73.

———. "Juan Benet and the New Spanish 'novela negra.'" *Monographic Review/ Revista Monográfica* 3.1–2 (1987): 212–20.

———. "The Paradoxes of Praxis: Juan Benet and Modern Poetics." In *Critical Approaches to the Writings of Juan Benet,* ed. Manteiga, Herzberger, and Compitello. 8–17.

———. *Ordering the Evidence: Volverás a Región and Civil War Fiction.* Barcelona: Puvill, 1983.

———. "Región's Brazilian Backlands: The Link between *Volverás a Región* and Euclides Da Cunha's *Os Sertões.*" *Hispanic Journal* 1.2 (1980): 25–45.

———. "*Volverás a Región*, the Critics and the Spanish Civil War: A Sociopoetic Reappraisal." *The American Hispanist* 4.36 (May 1979): 11–20.

Costa, Joaquín. *La política hidráulica (misión social de los riegos en España).* Rev. ed. Madrid: Colegio de Ingenieros de Caminos, Puertos y Canales, 1975.

———. *Oligarquía y caciquismo: Colectivismo agrario y otros escritos.* Antología. Ed. R. P. de la Dehesa. Madrid: Alianza, 1969.

Costa, Luis F. "El lector-viajero en Volverás a Región." *Anales de la Narrativa Española Contemporánea* 4 (1979): 9–19.

Dear, Michael. *The Postmodern Urban Condition.* Oxford, UK: Blackwell, 2000.

Deleuze, Gilles. *Desert Islands and Other Texts 1953–74.* Ed. David Lapoujade. Trans. Michael Taormina. Los Angeles: Semiotext(e), 2004.

———. *Cinema II: The Time-Image.* 1985. Trans. Hugh Tomlinson and Robert Galeta. Minneapolis: U of Minnesota P, 2003.

———. *Cinema I: The Movement-Image.* 1983. Trans. Hugh Tomlinson and Barbara Habberjam. Minneapolis: U of Minnesota P, 2003.

———. *Bergsonism.* 1966. Trans. Hugh Tomlinson and Barbara Habberjam. New York: Zone Books, 2002.

Díaz, Janet. "Variations on the Theme of Death in the Short Fiction of Juan Benet." *The American Hispanist* 4.36 (May 1979): 6–11.

Díaz-Marta Pinilla, Manuel. *Las obras hidráulicas en España.* Aranjuez: Doce Calles, 1997.

Díaz-Migoyo, Gonzalo. "Reading/Writing Ironies in *En el estado.*" In *Critical Approaches to the Writings of Juan Benet,* ed. Manteiga, Herzberger, and Compitello. 88–99.

Díaz Navarro, Epícteto. "Memoria y recuerdo en *Otoño en Madrid hacia 1950.*" *A Ricardo Gullón: sus discípulos.* Ed. Adelaida López de Martínez. Erie, Pa.: Asociación de Licenciados y Doctores Españoles en Estados Unidos, 1995. 81–87.

———. *Del pasado incierto. La narración breve de Juan Benet.* Madrid: Editorial Complutense, 1992.

———. "'Duelo' y 'Viator': Ironía y parodia en los relatos de Juan Benet." *Anales de la Literatura Española Contemporánea* 15.1–3 (1990): 13–27.

Díez-Cascón, Joaquín. "Conference at the Colegio Oficial de Ingenieros." Anonymous transcription. Accessed 21 April 2010. www.catedravmo.com/pdf/conferencies/jdiezcascon.pdf. 1–19.

Durán, Manuel. "Juan Benet y la nueva novela española." In *Juan Benet,* ed. Vernon. 229–42.

Elden, Stuart. *Understanding Henri Lefebvre: Theory and the Possible.* London: Continuum, 2004.

Eoff, Sherman. *The Modern Spanish Novel.* New York: New York UP, 1961.

Epps, Brad. "The Cold Furnace of Desire: The Site of Sexuality in *Volverás a Región.*" In *Juan Benet: A Critical Reappraisal of his Fiction,* ed. Margenot. 33–92.

Fernández Clemente, Eloy. "De la utopía de Joaquín Costa a la intervención del Estado: Un siglo de obras hidráulicas en España." *Contribuciones a la Economía* (mayo 2004). Accessed 20 March 2012. www.eumed.net/ce/2004/efc-jcosta.pdf.

Fernández Insuela, Antonio. "El teatro de Juan Benet." *Ínsula* 68.559–60 (julio–agosto 1993): 17–19.

Fernández Ordóñez, José A., and José Ramón Navarro Vera. "Una aproximación a la 'Revista de Obras Públicas' 1853–1936." *Revista de Obras Públicas* 139.3311 (1992): 11–22.

Ferrán, Ofelia. *Working through Memory.* Lewisburg, PA: Bucknell UP, 2007.

Fluxá, María. "Europa Ineludible: En busca del tiempo perdido." *El Mundo*, suplemento de viajes, núm. 25 (noviembre 2003). Accessed 20 March 2012. www.elmundo.es/viajes/2003/25/1070377811.html.

Foucault, Michel. *Discipline and Punish.* 1975. New York: Penguin Books, 1978.

Fraser, Benjamin. *Henri Lefebvre and the Spanish Urban Experience.* Lewisburg, PA: Bucknell UP, 2011.

———. *Encounters with Bergson(ism) in Spain: Reconciling Philosophy, Literature, Film, and Urban Space.* Chapel Hill: U of North Carolina P, 2010.

———. "The Art of Engineering: The Bridge as Object and Method in Juan Benet's Fiction." *Journal of Spanish Cultural Studies* 11.2 (2010): 167–90.

———. "Toward a Philosophy of the Urban: Henri Lefebvre's Uncomfortable Application of Bergsonism." *Environment and Planning D: Society and Space* 26.2 (2008): 338–58.

Gajic, Tatjana. "*Fronteras líquidas*: Agua y bio-política de la territorialidad en España." *Arizona Journal of Hispanic Cultural Studies* 11 (2007): 25–41.

García, Carlos Javier. "Textura judicial y mediaciones simbólicas en *Volverás a Región* de Juan Benet." *Siglo XXI: Literatura y Cultura Españoles* 2 (nov. 2004): 143–64.

García Delgado, José Luis. "La economía española durante el franquismo." *Temas para el debate.* Accessed July 10, 2010. www.vespito.net/historia/franco/ecofran.html.

García Pastor, José. "El vaticinio de un alma poseída (sobre el arte citativo de Juan Benet." *Ínsula* 68.559–60 (julio–agosto 1993): 25–26.

García Pérez, Francisco. "Prólogo." *Herrumbrosas lanzas.* 1983. Madrid: Alfaguara, 1998. 11–16.

———. "*El aire de un crimen*: A Concession to the Reading Public?" In *Juan Benet: A Critical Reappraisal of his Fiction,* ed. Margenot. 201–20.

———. "*La inspiración y el estilo*: Primeros (y definitivos) pasos de una teoría literaria." *Ínsula* 68.559–60 (julio–agosto 1993): 7–8.

Garrido, Alberto. "Analysis of Spanish Water Law Reform." In *Water Rights Reform: Lesson for Institutional Design,* ed. Bryan Randolph Bruns et al. Washington DC: International Food Policy Research Institute, 2005. 219–35.

Gavela, César. "El agua y Juan Benet." *El País* (27 April 2004). Accessed 8 January 2012. elpais.com/diario/2004/04/27/cvalenciana/1083093510_850215.html.

Germán Zubero, Luis. *Obras públicas e ingenieros en Aragón durante el primer tercio del siglo XX.* Zaragoza: Colegio de Ingenieros de Caminos, Canales y Puertos, 1999.

Gimferrer, Pere. "Notas sobre Juan Benet." In *Juan Benet,* ed. Vernon. 45–58.

———. "En torno a *Volverás a Región* de Juan Benet." *Ínsula* 266 (enero 1969): 14.

———. "Una crónica de la decadencia." *Papeles de Son Armadans* 52.166 (1969): 299–301.

Gingerich, Stephen D. "Telling (in) the Half-Light: Mimetic Poetics and Juan Benet's *En la penumbra.*" *Hispania* 91.3 (2008): 569–78.

———. "Returning to the Originary Enmity of Philosophy and Literature: Juan Benet's *Del pozo y del Numa (Un ensayo y una leyenda).*" *Revista de Estudios Hispánicos* 38.2 (2004): 317–40.

González, Josefina. "Tecnología y Arcadia en *Volverás a región*: Un contraste descriptivo." *Hispania* 78.3 (September 1995): 456–62.

———. "La cárcel como espacio iconoclasta en *El caballero de Sajonia.*" *Monographic Review/Revista Monográfica* 11 (1996): 169–77.

Goytisolo, Juan. *Señas de identidad.* 1966. Madrid: Alianza, 1999.

Goytisolo, Luis. *Antagonía.* 2 vols. 1973. Madrid: Alfaguara, 1998.

Graham, Helen. *The Spanish Republic at War 1936–1939.* Cambridge, UK: Cambridge UP, 2002.

———, and Jo Labanyi. *Spanish Cultural Studies: An Introduction.* Oxford, UK: Oxford UP.

Grosz, Elizabeth. *Time Travels: Feminism, Nature, Power.* Durham, NC: Duke UP, 2005.

———. *The Nick of Time: Politics, Evolution and the Untimely.* Durham, NC: Duke UP, 2004.

Guerlac, Suzanne. *Thinking in Time: An Introduction to Henri Bergson.* Ithaca, NY: Cornell UP, 2006.

Guillermo, Edenia and Juana Amelia Hernández. "Juan Benet. *Volverás a Región.*" *La novelística española de los sesenta.* New York: Eliseo Torres & Sons, 1971. 127–51.

Gullón, Ricardo. "Esperando a Coré." In *Juan Benet,* ed. Vernon. 127–47.

———. "Sobre espectros y tumbas." In *Juan Benet,* ed. Vernon. 206–19.

———. "Sombras de Juan Benet." *Cuadernos Hispanoamericanos* 417 (marzo 1985): 45–70.

———. "Introducción." *Una tumba y otros relatos*. Madrid: Taurus, 1981. 7–50.

———. "Una región laberíntica que bien pudiera llamarse España." *Ínsula* 319 (junio 1973): 3, 10.

Guy, Alain. "Ortega y Bergson." *Revista de Filosofía* 7 (1984): 5–19.

Harvey, David. *Spaces of Capital*. Edinburgh: Edinburgh UP, 2001.

———. *Spaces of Hope*. Berkeley: California UP, 2000.

———. *Justice, Nature and the Geography of Difference*. London: Blackwell, 1996.

———. *The Condition of Postmodernity*. Cambridge, MA: Blackwell, 1990.

———. *The Urban Experience*. Baltimore: Johns Hopkins UP, 1989.

Hernández, José A. "Juan Benet, 1976." *Modern Language Notes* 92.2 (1977): 346–55.

Herzberger, David. "How Malcolm Alan Compitello Discovered and Explained Juan Benet." In *Capital Inscriptions: Essays on Hispanic Literature, Film and Urban Space in Honor of Malcolm Alan Compitello*, ed. Benjamin Fraser. Newark: Juan de la Cuesta, 2012. 53–64.

———. "Nuevo historicismo: 'Construyendo la disidencia: historia y ficción en *Volverás a Región* de Juan Benet.'" In *El hispanismo en los Estados Unidos: Discursos críticos/prácticas textuales*, ed. José M. del Pino y Francisco La Rubia Prado. Madrid: Visor, 1999. 133–47.

———. "History, Apocalypse, and the Triumph of Fiction in the Post-War Spanish Novel." *Revista Hispánica Moderna* 44.2 (1991): 247–58.

———. "Splitting the Reference: Postmodern Fiction and the Idea of History in Francoist Spain." In *Intertextual Pursuits: Literary Meditations in Modern Spanish Narrative*, ed. Jeanne P. Brownlow and John W. Kronik. Cranbury, NJ: Associated University Presses, 1998. 126–42.

———. "Juan Benet's Death." In *Juan Benet: A Critical Reappraisal of his Fiction*, ed. Margenot. 3–18.

———. *Narrating the Past: Fiction and Historiography in Postwar Spain*. Durham, NC: Duke UP, 1995.

———. "Benet y la historia." *Insula* 68.559–60 (julio–agosto 1993): 24–25.

———. "Narrating the Past: History and the Novel of Memory in Postwar Spain." *PMLA* 106.1 (1991): 34–45.

———. "Juan Benet and the Spanish Civil War: History Made of Fiction." In *Rewriting the Good Fight*, ed. Brown, Compitello, Howard, and Martin. 27–44.

———. "Juan Benet's Characters." *Letras Peninsulares* 1.1 (1988): 70–86.

———. "La aparición de Juan Benet: Una nueva alternativa para la novela española." In *Juan Benet*, ed. Vernon. 24–44.

———. "*Juan Benet* by Vicente Cabrera [Book Review]." *Modern Language Notes* 100.2 (1985): 441–43.

———. "Numa and the Nature of the Fantastic in the Fiction of Juan Benet." *Studies in Twentieth-Century Literature* 8.2 (1984): 185–96.

———. "The Theme of Warring Brothers in 'Saúl ante Samuel.'" In *Critical Approaches to the Writings of Juan Benet*, ed. Manteiga, Herzberger, and Compitello. 100–110.

———. "Theoretical Approaches to the New Novel: Juan Benet and Juan Goytisolo." *Revista de Estudios Hispánicos* 14.2 (1980): 3–18.

———. "Enigma as Narrative Determinant in the Novels of Juan Benet." *Hispanic Review* 47.2 (1979): 149–57.

———. "The Theoretical Disparity of Contemporary Spanish Narrative." *Symposium* 33.3 (1979): 215–29.

———. *The Novelistic World of Juan Benet.* Clear Creek, IN: American Hispanist, Inc., 1976.

———. "Juan Benet's *Una tumba.*" *The American Hispanist* 1.9 (1976): 3–6.

Hooper, John. *The New Spaniards.* New York: Penguin, 1995.

Jackson, Gabriel, "Prólogo." *La sombra de la guerra,* by Juan Benet. Madrid: Taurus, 1999. 7–19.

———, ed. *The Spanish Civil War.* Chicago: Quadrangle Books, 1972.

———. "Introduction." *The Spanish Civil War.* Chicago: Quadrangle Books, 1972. 3–22.

———. *The Spanish Republic and the Civil War 1931–1939.* Princeton, NJ: Princeton UP, 1965.

Jalón, Mauricio. "Epílogo." Juan Benet. *Puerta de tierra.* Valladolid: Cuatro, 2003. 160–64.

Jessop, Bob. "Narrating the Future of the National Economy and the National State: Remarks on Remapping Regulation and Reinventing Governance." In *State/Culture: State-Formation after the Cultural Turn,* ed. George Steinmetz. Ithaca, NY: Cornell UP, 1999. 378–405.

Jones, Norman L. "The Catalan Question Since the Civil War." In *Spain in Crisis: The Evolution and Decline of the Franco Régime,* ed. Paul Preston. New York: Harper and Row, 1976. 234–67.

"Juan Benet Goitia." *Ambienta* (julio–agosto 2003): 75–76.

Kelly, Michael, ed. *Bergson and Phenomenology.* New York: Palgrave Macmillan, 2010.

Kumar, Shiv K. *Bergson and the Stream of Consciousness Novel.* Westport, CT: Greenwood P, 1962.

Labanyi, Jo. *Myth and History in the Contemporary Spanish Novel.* Cambridge, UK: 1989.

Landeira Brisson, Mary Jo T. "The Presence of Henri Bergson in Antonio Machado." PhD diss. U of North Carolina, Dept. of Romance Literatures, 1979.

Latham, Alan, and Derek McCormack. "Moving Cities: Rethinking the Materialities of Urban Geographies." *Progress in Human Geography* 28.6 (2004): 701–24.

"La trayectoria de Juan Benet como ingeniero de Caminos." 9 November 2008 by Universidad Politécnica de Madrid. Accessed 20 March 2012. www.universia.es/html_estatico/portada/actualidad/noticia_actualidad/param/noticia/jhiga.html.

Lefebvre, Henri. *Rhythmanalysis: Space, Time and Everyday Life.* 1992. Trans. S. Elden, G. Moore. London: Continuum, 2006.

———. *Critique of Everyday Life,* vol. 3. 1981. Trans. G. Elliott. London: Verso, 2005.

———. *The Production of Space.* 1974. Trans. Donald Nicholson-Smith. Oxford, UK: Blackwell, 1991.

———. "Time and History." 1970. In *Henri Lefebvre: Key Writings.* Ed. S. Elden, E. Lebas, E. Kofman. London; New York: Continuum, 2003. 177–87.

———. *Critique of Everyday Life,* vol. 2. 1961. Trans. J. Moore. London: Verso, 2002.

———. *Critique of Everyday Life,* vol. 1. 1947. Trans. J. Moore. London: Verso, 1991.

Llamazares, Julio. "El sueño de Juan Benet." *El País* (27 January 2009). Accessed 8 January 2012. www.elpais.com/articulo/opinion/sueno/Juan/Benet/elpepiopi/20090127elpepiopi_5/Tes.

López Guerra, Luis. "The Legacy of the Spanish Civil War Today." In *Rewriting the Good Fight,* ed. Brown, Compitello, Howard, and Martin. 243–59.

Lupinacci Wescott, Julia. "Benet's Theoretical Essays: Beneath the Mask of Representation." In *Juan Benet: A Critical Reappraisal of his Fiction,* ed. Margenot. 19–32.

———. "*Herrumbrosas lanzas, I*: Discurso de traición." *Ínsula* 68.559–60 (julio-agosto 1993): 14–16.

———. "Subversion of Character Conventions in Benet's Trilogy." In *Critical Approaches to the Writings of Juan Benet,* ed. Manteiga, Herzberger, and Compitello. 72–87.

———. *Creation and Structure of Enigma: Literary Conventions and Juan Benet's Trilogy.* Boston: U of Massachusetts P, 1982.

———. "Exposition and Pot in Benet's *Volverás a Región.*" *Romance Quarterly* 28.2 (1981): 155–63.

Madanipour, Ali. "Multiple Meanings of Space and the Need for a Dynamic Perspective." In *The Governance of Place,* ed. A. Madanipour, A. Hull, and P. Aldershot Healey. Surrey, UK: Ashgate P, 2001. 154–68.

———. *Design of Urban Space: an Inquiry into a Socio-spatial Process.* Chichester, UK: Wiley, 1996.

Manteiga, Roberto C. "El lector-viajero de Juan Benet." *Ínsula* 68.559–60 (julio-agosto 1993): 23–24.

———. "Time, Space, and Narration in Juan Benet's Short Stories." In *Critical Approaches to the Writings of Juan Benet,* ed. Manteiga, Herzberger, and Compitello. 120–36.

———. "Benet Ventures Beyond Región." *Denver Quarterly* 17.3 (1982): 76–82.

———, David Herzberger, and Malcolm A. Compitello, eds. *Critical Approaches to the Writings of Juan Benet.* Hanover, NH: UP of New England, 1984.

Marías, Javier. "Se va de viaje." *El País* (6 January 1993): 29. Accessed 20 March 2012. elpais.com/diario/1993/01/06/cultura/726274808_850215.html.

Margenot, John B. III. "Gothic Machinery in the Región Novels." *Revista Canadiense de Estudios Hispánicos* 29.3 (primavera 2005): 491–506.

———. "Introducción." *Saúl ante Samuel,* by Juan Benet. Madrid: Cátedra, 1994. 11–84.

———. "Wild Men in the Fiction of Juan Benet." *Forum for Modern Language Studies* 30.2 (1994): 163–74.

———. "Los cordajes del discurso en *Saúl ante Samuel*." *Ínsula* 68.559–60 (julio–agosto 1993): 13–14.

———. "Painting in the Novels of Juan Benet." *Ojáncano: Revista de Literatura Española* 6 (1992): 19–30.

———. "Historia e ideología en las novelas regionatas de Juan Benet." *Cuadernos de ALDEEU* 7.1 (1991): 53–66.

———. *Zonas y sombras: aproximaciones a Región de Juan Benet.* Madrid: Pliegos, 1991.

———. "Demonic Imagery in the Fiction of Juan Benet." *Hispanófila* 33.2 [98]. (1990): 53–70.

———. "Character Questing in Juan Benet's *Volverás a Región*." *Modern Language Studies* 19.3 (1989): 52–62.

———. "Cloisters and Cloisterers in Juan Benet's *Volverás a Región*." *Hispanic Journal* 10.2 (1989): 113–26.

———. "Sacred Spaces and Cloisters in Juan Benet's "Numa, una leyenda" and *Un viaje de invierno*." *The USF Language Quarterly* 27.3 (1989): 43–47.

———. "Cloisters, Doors and Intruders in Juan Benet's *Saúl ante Samuel*." *Symposium* 42.1 (1988): 37–47.

———. "Cartography in the Fiction of Juan Benet." *Letras Peninsulares* 1.3 (1988): 331–44.

———. "The House as Temple of War in Juan Benet's *Saúl ante Samuel. Romance Notes* 29.2 (1988): 119–24.

———, ed. *Juan Benet: A Critical Reappraisal of his Fiction.* West Cornwall, CT: Locust Hill P, 1997.

Marston, Sallie. "What's Culture Got to Do with It? A response to Jakobsen and Van Deusen." *Political Geography* 23.1 (2004): 35–39.

———. "The Social Construction of Scale." *Progress in Human Geography* 24.2 (2000): 219–42.

Martín, R. "Cuestión de vida o muerte." *Revista de Obras Públicas* 12 (1875): 133–34.

Martin, Susan L. "*Saúl ante Samuel* y el círculo hermenéutico." *Explicación de Textos Literarios* 16.2 (1987–88): 57–69.

Martin-Márquez, Susan. "The (En)gendering of *En la penumbra*." In *Juan Benet: A Critical Reappraisal of his Fiction,* ed. Margenot. 93–114.

Martín-Santos, Luis. *Tiempo de silencio.* 1961. Barcelona: Seix Barral, 1997.

Martínez Lázaro, Marisa. "Juan Benet o la incertidumbre como fundamento." *El Urogallo* 11–12 (1971): 175–76.

Martínez Sarrión, Antonio. "Juan Benet: El Numa, mito de Región." *Cuadernos Hispanoamericanos* 684 (June 2007): 115–22.

Martínez Torrón, Diego, ed. "Introducción." *Un viaje de invierno.* Madrid: Cátedra, 1980. 11–102.

Martykánová, Darina. "Por los caminos del progreso. El universo ideológico de los ingenieros de caminos españoles a través de la *Revista de Obras Públicas* (1853–1899)." *Ayer* 68.4 (2007): 193–219.

Massey, Doreen. *For Space*. London: Sage, 2005.

Matthews, Herbert L. *Half of Spain Died: A Reappraisal of the Spanish Civil War*. New York: Charles Scribner's Sons, 1973.

McNamara, Peter. "Bergson's 'Matter and Memory' and Modern Selectionist Theories of Memory." *Brain and Cognition* 30 (1996): 215–31.

Merrifield, Andy. *Henri Lefebvre: A Critical Introduction*. New York: Routledge, 2006.

Minardi, Adriana. "Hacer la Historia: El sentido de práctica discursiva en *Qué fue la guerra civil*, de Juan Benet. La construcción del intelectual después de Franco." *Espéculo: Revista de Estudios Literarios* 32 (March–June 2006). Accessed 20 March 2012. www.ucm.es/info/especulo/numero32/hacerhis.html.

Mitchell, Don. *Cultural Geography: a Critical Introduction*. Oxford: Blackwell, 2000.

Molina Ortega, Antonia María. *Las otras regiones de Juan Benet*. Cáceres: Universidad de Extremadura, 2007.

Molinaro, Nina. "Other Knowledge, Other History, and *La otra casa de Mazón*." In *Juan Benet: A Critical Reappraisal of his Fiction*, ed. Margenot. 115–26.

Montes, Javier. "Harry Potter en Oporto: La librería que inspiró a J. K. Rowling y otros pequeños secretos." *El País* (27 octubre 2007): 4. Accessed 20 March 2012. www.visitportugal.com.

Mota, Carlos. "Sobre la obra de Juan Benet en los años de la transición: Inflexiones, nuevos caminos." *Crítica Hispánica* 27.1 (2005): 37–69.

Mouland-Leonard, Valentine. *Bergson-Deleuze Encounters: Transcendental Experience and the Thought of the Virtual*. Albany: State U of New York P, 2008.

Muldoon, Mark. *Tricks of Time: Bergson, Merleau-Ponty and Ricoer in Search of Time, Self and Meaning*. Pittsburgh: Duquesne UP, 2006.

Mullarky, John. *Bergson and Philosophy*. Edinburgh: Edinburgh UP, 1999.

———, ed. *The New Bergson*. Manchester, UK: Manchester UP, 1999.

Muñoz Alvarez, Javier. "Los ingenieros y las letras." *Ingeniería y Territorio* 78 (2007): 16–23.

Navajas, Gonzalo. "Intertextuality and the Reappropriation of History in Contemporary Spanish Fiction and Film." In *Intertextual Pursuits: Literary Meditations in Modern Spanish Narrative*, ed. Jeanne P. Brownlow and John W. Kronik. Cranbury, NJ: Associated University Presses, 1998. 143–60.

———. "Modernismo, posmodernismo y novela policíaca: *El aire de un crimen* de Juan Benet." *Monographic Review/Revista Monográfica* 3.1–2 (1987): 221–30.

———. "El significado diseminado de *En el estado*." In *Juan Benet*, ed. Vernon. 191–205.

———. "The Deferred Enigma in Juan Benet's *Un viaje de invierno*." *Anales de la Literatura Española Contemporánea* 10.1–3 (1985): 41–59.

Nelson, Esther W. "Narrative Perspective in *Volverás a Región*." In *Critical Approaches to the Writings of Juan Benet*, ed. Manteiga, Herzberger, Compitello. 27–38.

———. "Narrative Perspective in Volverás a Región." *American Hispanist* (May 1979): 3–6.

Núñez, Antonio. "Encuentro con Juan Benet." In *Juan Benet,* ed. Vernon. 17–23.

Oliart, Alberto. "Viaje a Región." *Revista de Occidente* 80 (November 1969): 224–34.

Orringer, Nelson R. "The Biblical Perspective on Civil War in Benet's *Saúl ante Samuel.*" In *Rewriting the Good Fight,* ed. Brown, Compitello, Howard, and Martin. 57–68.

———. "Epic in a Paralytic State: *Volverás a Región.*" In *Critical Approaches to the Writings of Juan Benet,* ed. Manteiga, Herzberger, and Compitello. 39–50.

———. "Juan Benet a viva voz sobre la filosofía y el ensayo actuales." *Los Ensayistas* 8–9 (March 1980): 59–65.

Ortega, José. "Estudios sobre la obra de Juan Benet." In *Juan Benet,* ed. Vernon. 61–92.

———. *Ensayos de la novela española moderna.* Madrid: José Porrúa Turanzas, 1974.

Orwell, George. *Homage to Catalonia.* New York: Harcourt-Brace, 1952.

Payne, Stanley G. *The Franco Regime 1936–1975.* Madison: U of Wisconsin P, 1987.

———. *Falange: A History of Spanish Fascism.* Stanford: Stanford UP, 1967.

Pearson, Keith Ansell. *Philosophy and the Adventure of the Virtual: Bergson and the Time of Life.* London: Routledge, 2002.

Pérez, Janet. "The Rhetoric of Ambiguity." In *Critical Approaches to the Writings of Juan Benet,* ed. Manteiga, Herzberger, and Compitello. 18–26.

Pérez Magallón, Jesús. "Tiempo y tiempos en *Volverás a Región,* de Juan Benet." *Hispanic Review* 59.3 (1991): 281–94.

Pope, Randolph D. "Benet, Faulkner, and Bergson's Memory." In *Critical Approaches to the Writings of Juan Benet,* ed. Manteiga, Herzberger, and Compitello. 111–19.

Preston, Paul. "The Urban and Rural *Guerrillas* of the 1940s." In *Spanish Cultural Studies: An Introduction,* ed. Graham and Labanyi. 229–37.

———. *The Triumph of Democracy in Spain.* New York: Methuen, 1986.

———. "The Agrarian War in the South." In *Revolution and War in Spain 1931–1939,* ed. Preston. 159–81.

———. "War of Words: The Spanish Civil War and the Historians." In *Revolution and War in Spain 1931–1939,* ed. Preston. 1–13.

———. *The Coming of the Spanish Civil War: Reform, Reaction and Revolution in the Second Republic.* London: Methuen, 1983.

———, ed. *Revolution and War in Spain 1931–1939.* London: Methuen, 1984.

Putnam, Samuel. *Marvelous Journey: Four Centuries of Brazilian Writing.* New York: Octagon, 1971.

Rapin, Ronald, F. "Juan Benet's *Volverás a Región*: The Amorphous Nightmare." *Neophilologus* 73.4 (1989): 541–47.

"Real Decreto-Ley 10/1976 de 30 de julio." Accessed 20 March 2012. www.boe.es/boe/dias/1976/08/04/pdfs/A15097–15098.pdf.

Rivero, José. "Juan Benet: proyecto y cartografía." *Cuadernos Hispanoamericanos* 651–52 (September–October 2004): 147–54.

Rivkin, Laura. "La búsqueda literaria en *Una meditación*." In *Juan Benet*, ed. Vernon. 108–26.

Rodríguez, Joe. "Reason, Desire and Language: Reading Juan Benet's Trilogy as a Relational Totality." *Bulletin of Spanish Studies* 86.2 (2006): 241–63.

Rodríguez Padrón, Jorge. "Apuntes para una teoría benetiana." *Ínsula* 296–297 (noviembre–diciembre 1979): 3, 5.

Rodríguez Rivero, Manuel. "En el corazón de *En la penumbra*." *Ínsula* 68.559–60 (julio–agosto 1993): 16–17.

Rodríguez Vellando, Javier. "Guía para viajeros a Región (notas sobre la narrativa de Juan Benet)." *Barcarola* 5 (1981): 141–48.

de la Rosa, Julio M. "Encuentro con Región." *Cuadernos Hispanoamericanos* 369 (1981): 587–92.

Ruiz Bautista, Eduardo. *Los señores del libro: propagandistas, censores y bibliotecarios en el primer franquismo*. Gijón: Trea, 2005.

Saénz García, Clemente. "Evocación del ingeniero de caminos D. Manuel Lorenzo Pardo, Fundador del Centro de Estudios Hidrográficos." *Revista de Obras Públicas* 118.3072 (1971): 239–47.

"Sáenz Ridruejo—blog" [Blog of Clemente Sáenz Ridruejo]. Accessed 20 March 2012. saenzridruejo/blogspot.com.

Sáenz Ridruejo, Fernando. "Ingeniería e Historia." *Ingeniería y Territorio* 78 (2007): 38–47.

———. "Los ingenieros de Caminos de la generación del 98." *Los cuadernos de Cauce 2000* 14 (1987).

Salcedo Megales, Damián. "A propósito del contrato social: literatura y reflexión en Juan Benet." *Olvidos de Granada* 13 (1986): 57–58.

Sandarg, Jana. "The Natural and Supernatural in Selected Novels of Juan Benet." *Discurso Literario* 3.1 (1985): 171–81.

Santana, Mario. "Antagonismo y complicidad: parábolas de la comunicación literaria en *Volverás a Región* y *La verdad sobre el caso Savolta*." *Revista Hispánica Moderna* 50.1 (1997): 132–43.

Sanz Villanueva, Santos. *Historia de la literatura española*. Literatura actual. Barcelona: Ariel, 1988.

Sauer, Carl. "The Fourth Dimension of Geography." *Annals of the Association of American Geographers* 64.2 (1974): 189–92.

———. "The Morphology of Landscape." *University of California Publications in Geography* 2 (1925): 19–54.

Schmid, Christian. "Lefebvre's Theory of the Production of Space." In *Space, Difference, Everyday Life: Reading Henri Lefebvre*, ed. K. Goonewardena, S. Kipfer, R. Milgrom, C. Schmid. New York: Routledge, 2008. 27–45.

Sevilla-Guzmán, Eduardo. "The Peasantry and the Franco Régime." In *Spain in Crisis: The Evolution and Decline of the Franco Régime*, ed. Paul Preston. New York: Harper and Row, 1976. 101–24.

Shubert, Adrian. "The Epic Failure: The Asturian Revolution of October 1934." In *Revolution and War in Spain 1931–1939*, ed. Preston. 113–36.

Sobejano, Gonzalo. *Novela española de nuestro tiempo, 1940–74*. Madrid: Mare Nostrum, 2005.

———. "Juan Benet en sus títulos." *Ínsula* 68.559–60 (julio–agosto 1993): 3-5.

———. "*Saúl ante Samuel*, historia de un fratricidio." In *Juan Benet*, ed. Vernon. 158–76.

———. "Dos estilos de comparación: Juan Benet y Luis Goytisolo." In *Juan Benet*, ed. Vernon. 254–81.

———. "Teoría de la novela en la novela española última (Martín-Santos, Benet, Juan y Luis Goytisolo)." In *Romanistik in Geschichte und Gegenwart (Rom GG): Aspekte der Hispania im 19. und 20. Jahrhundert*, ed. Dieter Kremer. Helmut/Buske/Verlag/Hamberg, 1983. Accessed 20 March 2012. www.cervantesvirtual.com/obra-visor/teora-de-la-novela-en-la-novela-espaola-ltima-martnsantos-benet-juan-y-luis-goytisolo-o/html/021677dc-82b2-11df-acc7-002185ce6064_3.html.

Soja, Edward W. *Thirdspace: Journeys to Los Angeles and Other Real-and-Imagined Places*. Oxford: Blackwell, 1996.

Solana, Angeles. "Temporal Shifting in *Herrumbrosas lanzas*." In *Juan Benet: A Critical Reappraisal of his Fiction*, ed. Margenot. 167–87.

Spires, Robert C. "Juan Benet's Poetics of Open Spaces." In *Critical Approaches to the Writings of Juan Benet*, ed. Manteiga, Herzberger, and Compitello. 1–7.

———. *La novela española de posguerra*. Madrid: CUPSA, 1978.

———. "Volverás a Región y la desintegración total." *La novela española de posguerra. Creación artística y experiencia personal*. Madrid: Cupsa Editorial, 1978. 224–46.

Summerhill, Stephen J. "Prohibition and Transgression in *Volverás a Región* and *Una meditación*." In *Critical Approaches to the Writings of Juan Benet*, ed. Manteiga, Herzberger, and Compitello. 51–63.

———. "Prohibition and Transgression in Two Novels of Juan Benet." *American Hispanist* 4.36 (May 1979): 20–24.

Thorns, David. *The Transformation of Cities: Urban Theory and Urban Life*. Houndmills, Basingstoke, Hampshire, UK: Palgrave, 2002.

Tilly, Charles. "Epilogue: Now Where?" In *State/Culture: State-Formation after the Cultural Turn*, ed. George Steinmetz. Ithaca, NY: Cornell UP, 1999. 407–19.

Torres Fierro, Danubio. "Entrevista a Juan Benet," originally from the supplement 'Diorama de la Cultura' from *Excélsior* 1974. Accessed 21 April 2010. www.ddooss.org/artculos/entrevistas/Juan_Benet.htm.

Trapiello, Andrés. *Las armas y las letras: Literatura y Guerra Civil (1936–1939)*. Barcelona: Península, 2002.

Tuan, Yi-Fu. *Space and Place: The Perspective of Experience*. Minneapolis: U of Minnesota P, 1977.

Ugarte, Michael. "Hispanism's Crisis and the Compitello Generation." In *Capital Inscriptions: Essays on Hispanic Literature, Film and Urban Space in Honor of Malcolm Alan Compitello*, ed. Benjamin Fraser. Newark: Juan de la Cuesta, 2012. 65–78.

———. *Literatura española en el exilio: Un estudio comparativo.* Madrid: Siglo XXI, 1999.

Ullman, Joan Connelly. *The Tragic Week: A Study of Anticlericalism in Spain 1875–1912.* Cambridge: Harvard UP, 1968.

Vásquez, Mary S. "The Creative Task: Existential Self-Invention in *Una meditación.*" In *Critical Approaches to the Writings of Juan Benet,* ed. Manteiga, Herzberger, and Compitello. 64–71.

Vernon, Kathleen M., ed. *Juan Benet: El escritor y la crítica.* Madrid: Taurus, 1986.

———. "Amor, fantasía vacío en un cuento de Benet." In *Juan Benet,* ed. Vernon. 220–26.

Vicent, Manuel. "Prólogo: Benet en la corta distancia." In Juan Benet, *Cuentos Completos.* Madrid: Alfaguara, 1998. 11–16.

Vilar, Pierre. *Historia de España.* Barcelona: Crítica, 2002.

———. *Spain: A Brief History.* Trans. Brian Tate. Oxford, UK: Pergamon P, 1977.

Villanueva, Darío. "Las narraciones de Juan Benet." *Novela española actual.* Ed. Andrés Amorós. Madrid: Fundación Juan March/Ediciones Cátedra, 1977. 133–72.

———. "La novela de Juan Benet." *Camp de l'Arpa* 8 (noviembre 1973): 9–16.

Walkowiak, Marzena. "The Creative Metaphor of *Una meditación.*" In *Juan Benet: A Critical Reappraisal of His Fiction,* ed. Margenot. 189–200.

———. *A Study of the Narrative Structure of Una meditación.* Lewiston, NY: Edwin Mellen P, 1992.

———. "La ambigüedad del argumento en la novela moderna: la repetición de *Una meditación* de Juan Benet." *Revista Canadiense de Estudios Hispánicos* 26.1 (1991): 143–50.

Wasmuth, Axel. "Polifonía y armonía de los espacios en *Herrumbrosas lanzas* de Juan Benet." In *Espacios y discursos en la novela española: del realismo a la actualidad,* ed. Wolfgang Matzat. Madrid: Iberoamericana/Vervuert, 2007. 239–59.

Wood, Guy H. "Una aproximación cartográfica a *Herrumbrosas lanzas.*" *España Contemporánea* 6.2 (1993): 7–18.

Yerro Villanueva, Tomás. *Aspectos técnicos y estructurales de la novela española actual.* Pamplona: Ediciones Universidad de Navarra, 1977.

Yglesias, Jose. *The Franco Years.* New York: Bobbs-Merrill Co., 1977.

Index